Fund-Raising
Cost Effectiveness

A Self-Assessment Workbook

The NSFRE/Wiley Fund Development Series

The NSFRE Fund-Raising Dictionary by The National Society of Fund Raising Executives

Fund-Raising Cost Effectiveness: A Self-Assessment Workbook by James M. Greenfield

Fund-Raising Cost Effectiveness
A Self-Assessment Workbook

JAMES M. GREENFIELD

JOHN WILEY & SONS, INC.
New York   Chichester   Brisbane   Toronto   Singapore

This text is printed on acid-free paper.

REQUIREMENTS:
An IBM® PC family computer or compatible computer
with 256K minimum memory, a 3.5" high-density floppy drive,
PC DOS, MS DOS, or DR DOS Version 2.0 or later, and a printer.

Library of Congress Cataloging-in-Publication Data:

Greenfield, James M., 1936–
    Fund-raising cost effectiveness : a self-assessment workbook /
James M. Greenfield.
       p.   cm. — (Nonprofit law, finance, and management series)
    Includes bibliographical references and index.
    ISBN 0-471-10916-9 (cloth/Disk : alk. paper)
    1. Fund raising—Cost effectiveness.   I. Title. II. Series.
HG177.G75   1996
658.15'224—dc20   95-42250

Printed in the United States of America

10 9 8 7 6 5 4 3 2 1

To those who have shared their enthusiasm for this topic and those who have helped to define processes that evaluate and measure fund-raising performance; your good efforts over many years have encouraged me to prepare this workbook.

Tom Broce

Art Collier

Jim Connell

Nick Costa

Charley DiGange

Warren Heeman

Bruce Hopkins

Harvey Jacobson

Dick Larkin

Bill Levis

Wes Lindahl

Dennis Murray

Anne New

David Ormstedt

Vance Petersen

Jack Schwartz

Steve Smallwood

Rick Steinberg

Steve Wertheimer

The NSFRE/Wiley Fund Development Series

The NSFRE/Wiley Fund Development Series is intended to provide fund development professionals (and others interested in the not-for-profit sector) with top-quality publications that help advance philanthropy as voluntary action for the public good. Our goal is to provide practical, timely guidance and information on fund raising, charitable giving, and related subjects. NSFRE and Wiley each bring to this innovative collaboration unique and important resources that result in a whole greater than the sum of its parts.

The National Society of Fund Raising Executives

The NSFRE is a professional association of fund-raising executives which advances philanthropy through its more than 16,000 members in 138 chapters throughout the United States, Canada, and Mexico. Through its advocacy, research, education, and certification programs, the Society fosters development and growth of fund-raising professionals, works to advance philanthropy and volunteerism, and promotes high ethical standards in the fund-raising profession.

1995–1996 NSFRE Publishing Advisory Council

About the Author

Jim Greenfield is a veteran fund-raising professional with 34 years experience as a development officer at three universities and five hospitals on both the east and west coasts and in between.

He has served NSFRE as a chapter officer and national board member. He remains active in support of NSFRE as a member of the Journal Advisory Council and the Task Force on Fund-Raising Costs. He was reelected to the NSFRE Foundation Board in 1996 and serves on the Major Gifts committee.

Jim is a frequent speaker at NSFRE conferences, First and Survey Courses, and author of three books and several articles on fund-raising practice. He was selected as the 1994 fund-raising professional of the year by NSFRE's Orange County Chapter, and also was honored by AHP with its Harold J. (Si) Seymour Outstanding Fund-Raising Professional Award in 1993.

Contents

PART 1

PREPARATION FOR SOLICITATION ACTIVITY

PART 2

ANNUAL GIVING SOLICITATION PROGRAMS

CONTENTS

SOLICITATION PROGRAMS FOR GIFTS OF SIZE

SUMMARY PERFORMANCE ANALYSIS TECHNIQUES

Preface

This workbook is about evaluating the cost of fund-raising. The fund-raising profession lacks industrywide guidelines and standards on cost-effective performance measurement. The Philanthropic Advisory Service of the Council of Better Business Bureaus and the National Charities Information Bureau promulgate bottom-line yardsticks of 35 and 40 percent respectively. No federal laws or regulations govern this area. There have been state regulations in the past that proscribed an administrative percentage, but these have been struck down by the U.S. Supreme Court on free-speech protection grounds.

Evaluating overall fund-raising performance using cost of fund-raising ratio analysis is complicated by the fact that nonprofit organizations are not the same in how they conduct fund-raising, nor do fund-raising programs perform the same for every organization. Notwithstanding the absence of guidelines and comparison difficulties, questions are increasing about fund-raising performance. Unfortunately, many are stimulated by media reports of fraud, con artists, scandals, or other abuse. Some of these reports are based on excessive costs, others on illicit and deceptive practices. Still others expose the misuse of funds raised, which is separate from fund-raising but a black eye for philanthropy just the same.

No voluntary national data-collection and analysis program is in place to establish guidelines and standards based on the actual experiences of the more than one million nonprofit organizations in the United States actively soliciting gifts. Part of the difficulty in conducting such studies stems from the absence of professional accounting guidelines on how to allocate fund-raising costs. The Financial Accounting Standards Board (FASB) and the American Institute of Certified Public Accountants (AICPA) have long studied this deficiency and have published criteria for only one area of practice, joint cost allocations for direct mail solicitations. These criteria have created more confusion than clarity, and AICPA is now attempting to revise this guideline. Without uniform guidelines for allocating expenses for each method of solicitation activity, there is little hope for any progress to define and publish reasonable cost standards.

One national data-collection agency receives financial information that includes fund-raising expenses—the Internal Revenue Service. IRS Form 990 requires a detailed disclosure of fund-raising costs in its statement of financial expenses (Part II, lines 22–44, column D). Nonprofit organizations, which lack clear guidelines on how to account for these expenses, are further burdened to separate program expenses as well as management and general operating costs from fund-raising expense. Lacking any other common report, the IRS Form 990 has become by default the only national data source available to study nonprofit organizations' direct experience with fund-raising costs.

Questions about fund-raising performance will continue. Professional fund-raising executives remain unclear about how to document and report their results. Comparing results with other nonprofit organizations is extremely problematic given the disparity in reporting guidelines. Some groups of nonprofit organizations, notably the Council for Advancement and Support of Education (CASE) and United Way of America, have developed independent guidelines and uniform report forms to summarize the collective performance of their members.

Total contributions received and total expenses are valuable data, but there also must be demographic details on the size of the organization, number of fund-raising staff, summary budget figures, and more, to develop a valid analysis model. Also necessary is direct measurement of *each* of the several methods of solicitation activity and their individual performance. Lastly, the costs for each solicitation activity must be further segregated by its direct, indirect, and overhead expenses. Only with all these details can the true and total costs required to produce each and every contribution be known.

The evaluation process presented in this workbook first reports the total amount of money raised and segregates the sources into groups such as board members, prior donors, corporations, and foundations. The second figure is total expenses to perform these solicitation activities, which is subtracted from contributions received to realize the third figure, net proceeds available for charitable purpose. These are reasonably easy figures to gather, but there is much more to performance measurement than a simple "bottom-line" analysis of the ratio of total costs to total dollars raised. In fact, such simple direct comparisons are often deceptive and can be misleading.

As an example, a nonprofit organization reports $500,000 in total contributions received last year at a fund-raising cost of $100,000, a bottom-line cost of fund-raising of 20 percent and a 400 percent return of net income, certainly a strong performance. Included in the $500,000 was a bequest worth $250,000. No effort and no expense were incurred to solicit this gift during the year; the donor decided 10 years ago to include this legacy in her will. Actual gifts raised from the $100,000 fund-raising budget were $250,000, which is a cost of fund-raising of 40 percent and a 150 percent return. Quite a different story, especially when the board of directors, pleased to hear the report of $500,000, believes it should recommend (and can anticipate) a $550,000 goal for next year based on another $100,000 budget. Were this goal to be approved by the board, it would create an unrealistic expectation. This organization should not assume $450,000 in net revenue for its operating budget. Likewise, the staff should make every effort to educate the board and management that the prior year's results were misinterpreted and misunderstood, or they may be looking for new jobs.

Boards of directors, nonprofit managers, donors, volunteers, legislators, regulators, and the media will continue to press for performance details. There is an urgent need to provide fund-raising results in a manner and style that will be complete enough to establish credibility and that can be measured against reliable standards. To understand the true cost of fund-raising requires a study of the operating details of *each* method of solicitation because *each* has a separate level of effectiveness and efficiency and should be measured against its own performance criteria.

Evaluations likewise should be conducted on the performance of the overall organization, its mission and vision, its long-range and strategic plan, its programs and services, its goals and objectives, its budget and expenses, and its money management and use of all available funds. Evaluations should be objective in their review of concrete outcomes, and subjective when interpreting the data for follow-up action. The results should illustrate effectiveness and efficiency measured against a set of goals defined in advance.

One caution about evaluating fund-raising efficiency: It should not be confused with fund-raising effectiveness. Fund-raising programs also must continue to be engaged in research, cultivation, communications, gift processing, donor relations, and other expense areas to fulfill the obligation for continuous friend-raising and relationship-building, not just solicitation alone.

Evaluations must be able to analyze results, assess strengths and weaknesses, and audit all systems related to overall performance. Measuring results at regular intervals provides the advantage to make decisions to modify plans, to guard against errors, and to improve results. Performance studies illustrate productivity, profitability, and progress according to plans. Fund-raising results ought to be fully accountable for positive returns based on the application of principles of professional practice.

This workbook is designed to provide the methods and tools to accomplish public accountability. It provides descriptions of the traditional fund-raising activities used in annual giving (Chapters 3–10) and in major giving (Chapters 11–16); it uses a uniform assessment model, the nine-point performance index, throughout for consistent performance measurement and comparative analysis purposes.

This workbook is organized in four parts: Preparation for Solicitation Activity, Annual Giving Solicitation Programs, Solicitation Program for Gifts of Size, and Summary Performance Analysis Techniques. Part I begins with a review of the critical requirements for successful fund-raising for every nonprofit organization: mission, vision, long-range and strategic plans, an internal audit, goals and objectives. These are the ingredients needed to prepare the annual business plan. With these elements in place, the annual budget for each solicitation activity can be prepared as an investment calculated to provide a positive return. The nine-point performance index is described here.

Part II presents an approach to measuring the performance of all the traditional annual giving programs. Each fund-raising method is measured qualitatively as well as quantitatively. Similarly, Part III evaluates major giving solicitation activities. Part IV describes how the overall fund development program is brought together for summary performance measurement. Forecasting techniques are introduced, as are methods to set specific standards for future performance. The workbook concludes by discussing the value of public reporting of these results and reciting the issues representing future challenges.

The exhibits provided with each chapter illustrate a scorecard that board members, managers, volunteers, donors, and staff can use to measure performance. The results of each fund-raising method will be critiqued against the nine-point performance index for comparative analysis. This uniform measurement tool facilitates understanding and appreciation of each fund-raising activity along with the multiple interdependent characteristics of these methods.

Successful fund development programs must stand out in an environment of public accountability where donors and volunteers will benefit from sharing in the results and their evaluation. Open and full disclosure contributes to integrity and ethical conduct and leads to wide acceptance of the basic tenets of professional practice by all involved.

The bottom line is that it will cost money to raise money. Fund-raising cost-effectiveness is a workable and reliable method to measure the relationship between budget invested and net return. Performance evaluation helps to monitor progress, to manager budgets, and to forecast future results with reliability. All these reports should be shared with board members and managers, volunteers and donors, and the general public, to reinforce their confidence and trust in each nonprofit organization and its fund-raising practices. These same detailed measurements and evaluations should be used to monitor progress, demonstrating a commitment to integrity and professional practice to all concerned. Doing this work is necessary and recommended; disclosing the results is laudable and brave. Take courage pills; the results will be praiseworthy and more than worth the effort.

JAMES M. GREENFIELD

Newport Beach, California
November 1995

Acknowledgments

Fund-raising cost-effectiveness is a subject that has plagued nonprofit organizations and professional fund-raising executives for years. It is a difficult topic, not because the mathematics are hard but because it has not been easy to transfer measurement techniques routine in the business world into credible and workable tools that fit nonprofit financial operations, especially fund-raising practice.

My introduction to this frustration began in the late 1960s at the California Institute of Technology (CalTech) with the challenging task of converting donor records to a mainframe computer and designing ways to get the information back in some kind of report format. In the years since, I have continued to experiment with report forms to display fund-raising results including the costs required to secure them. In 1974, at the invitation of Steve Smallwood and Bill Levis (we were all working at Children's Hospital in Boston at the time), we designed a report form for a direct mail program that would give us data on the size of each list used, number and percentage of replies received, average gift size, and a gain-loss report on renewal.

That effort led Steve and Bill to develop the first National Society of Fund Raising Executives fund-raising cost study, where I met many of the people to whom this workbook is dedicated. The project was to attempt to collect information on fund-raising results by each solicitation method. We made a good effort, designed a model report form (the now famous "FR-1") that any nonprofit organization could use to report fund-raising results, and tested it on a selection of NSFRE members. Only a few of them returned completed forms because nonprofit organizations did not have consistent accounting guidelines on how to allocate fund-raising costs and thus did not keep their records in a manner that would allow any uniformity of data in completing the FR-1 report. The project was closed down in 1979.

Despite its failure, the project stimulated a lot of other good work that has contributed to continuing progress. A few of these improvements deserve special acknowledgment. Warren Heeman led the effort at the Council for Advancement and Support of Education (CASE) to develop their model report form (first published in 1982; a second edition was released in 1990), which is now used by every college, university, and private school, with the results reported annually by the Council for Financial Aid to Education (CFAE). In the mid 1980s, Jack Schwartz, Bill Levis, and a team of experts worked with the National Association of Attorneys General (NAAG) and the National Association of State Charity Officials (NASCO), on a model law for state regulation of fund-raising which was approved by both but never used consistently by the states. Bruce Hopkins, David Ormstedt, and others continue to work with the Internal Revenue Service to modify the 990 report to provide more consistent income and expense data, although many organizations still cannot complete it with accuracy. Everyone listed on the Dedication page has either written a book, contributed articles, published research papers, or been willing to speak up and speak out to keep attention on this subject alive.

This workbook reflects the work of all these professionals. They believe, as I do, that performance should be measured and that the results should be made public, not always a popular point of view. Accountability is a big, scary word. It is my hope that this workbook will add to their continuing efforts and encourage others to take their courage pills and apply these formula wherever they can.

I am most grateful to Tom McLaughlin and Carleen Rhodes for their extra help in the preparation of this text; they read several chapters and offered constructive comments as well as encouragement. The Wiley team, great to work with again, is led by Marla Bobowick, Acquisitions Editor and chief architect for Wiley's highly successful Nonprofit Law, Finance, and Management Series, whose personal attention to this project has been most beneficial and who remains a good friend despite her insistence on starting over (twice!) and still sticking to that awful deadline last August. I am also grateful to Cathy Dillon, development editor, and Charlotte Saikia, copy editor, for their consummate skill, to my good friend, John Holland of Holland Design, who ably illustrated the nine-point performance index exhibits, and to Nancy Marcus Land and Pam Blackmon at

Publications Development Company, for converting all our efforts into the easy-to-use workbook now in your hands.

Finally, writing books takes time away from the rest of your life. For exceptional patience, tolerance, and unfailing love, thank you again, Karen, for without your understanding and support, I could not do this work.

J.M.G

List of Exhibits

Definitions of Fund-Raising Cost-Effectiveness Terms

Accountability The quality or state of being accountable, answerable, liable, or responsible.

Analysis Separation into constituents or component parts for individual study.

Appraisal An expert or official valuation.

Audit Examination of records or accounts to check their accuracy.

Capacity A measure of ability; the maximum possible output or amount of production.

Effectiveness Production of the intended or expected effect.

Efficacy Power or capacity to produce a desired effect; ability to achieve results.

Efficiency Competence for producing a desired result or maximum effect with minimum effort or expense; extent or degree to which this quality is exercised.

Evaluation Placement of a value on; appraisal, estimation, examination, judgment.

Forecast To estimate or calculate performance or results in advance.

Measurement Quantification of ability; dimensions, capacity, quality, or standard of comparison.

Monitor To oversee; keep a check on. To observe and record. To scrutinize or check systematically with a view to collecting certain specified categories of data.

Perform To do or carry out to conclusion; to execute or complete.

Potential Possible but not yet realized; capable of being or becoming. Latent or inherent ability for excellence.

Productivity Ability or power to produce; output of the means of production. Yielding favorable or useful results; constructive activity.

Profitability An advantageous gain or return; the quality of being lucrative, useful, beneficial.

Results A consequence or effect; conclusion, outcome, product.

Success Favorable or prosperous termination of attempts or endeavors. Achieved end or result; attainment or accomplishment.

Introduction: Questions and Answers about Fund-Raising Costs

1. Why is fund-raising cost effectiveness important?

Controlling fund-raising costs and managing cost effectiveness are important because the public expects that most of the money they give to nonprofit organizations will be spent on charitable programs and services, not on fund raising. There is a limited awareness of how fund raising is performed and what constitute reasonable levels of expense. Costs will vary greatly from organization to organization because of the size, history, geography, leadership, access to wealth, and financial stability of the organization as well as by the type of solicitation and its relationship to other solicitation also in active use by the organization.

There is the common misperception that low fund-raising costs mean that an organization is well managed and therefore efficient. When initiating new solicitation methods, start-up costs are likely to be high in order to establish a cadre of donors and volunteers, whether or not the nonprofit organization is a newer or older entity. In any case, any solicitation method should be able to demonstrate that is can function in a cost-effective manner after three years. If careful analysis of its results during this period suggests it does not have a potential to be profitable, it should be revised or discontinued.

2. Are there any national standards or guidelines for fund-raising costs?

At present there are no national standards, nor has any national research study established fund-raising cost guidelines for all nonprofit organizations to use. However, two watchdog agencies have promulgated standards in philanthropy to evaluate the activities and practices of national charitable organizations and to promote informed giving. The Philanthropic Advisory Service of the Council of Better Business Bureaus advocates an expense ratio of 35 percent fund-raising costs to 65 percent cost for programs and services. The National Charities Information Bureau advocates a 40 percent fund-raising cost to 60 percent program and service ratio as its guideline. These figures apply only to overall bottom-line cost–benefit ratios, not to ratios for individual solicitation methods.

Studies performed on a few of the individual solicitation methods have concluded that each performs at different levels of effectiveness and efficiency. For example, it is well established that the cost to acquire a new donor is greater than the cost to renew that donor's gift. Similarly, major gift programs (corporate and foundation grantseeking) will average larger gifts for each solicitation than is the normal gift size for routine annual giving methods (benefit events, gift clubs, and so on), but few major gift programs can expect to succeed without a broad-based, efficient annual giving program in operation for a minimum of three or more years.

3. What is a reasonable cost for fund-raising activities?

Professional fund-raising executives suggest that a mature fund development program should be able to achieve a bottom-line cost–benefit ratio of $0.20 to $0.30 to raise $1.00 after three years of operation. A mature fund development program is one that actively uses one or more methods of annual giving, major giving, and planned giving solicitation activities. An annual giving program (the most common form of fund raising), which uses direct mail, benefit events, donor clubs, and the like, can be expected to perform at the $0.35 to $0.40 level in three years or less (see Chapter 10), while major gift programs will average $0.10 to $0.20 or better.

The separate methods of annual giving solicitation also perform at quite different levels of cost-effectiveness when compared with one another. The use of mail to acquire a first-time donor may cost as much as $1.25 to $1.50 for each $1.00 raised, while renewing that donor's gift by mail is likely to perform at a cost between $0.20 to $0.30 each time.

Benefit events (in all their multiple variations) should be used only if they can deliver a reasonable amount of net proceeds for charitable purposes; the ratio of $0.50 to raise $1.00 is recommended. While this estimate is based solely on direct costs, it is still difficult for many nonprofit organizations to achieve this level of cost-effectiveness for each of their benefits in less than three years.

4. Should not all nonprofit organizations have the same fund-raising cost guidelines and standards?

Because nonprofit organizations exist for a variety of purposes, serve a vast array of public needs, and exist in communities of all sizes, it is not reasonable to expect each to possess the same ability to conduct fund raising with identical efficiency and effectiveness any more than they possess the ability to provide their programs and services in an identical fashion. Thus, even when using the same solicitation methods, neither their fund-raising costs nor gift results should be considered as comparable.

Nonprofit organizations are free to choose how and when they will perform public solicitations. Some rely more heavily on local community support while others request funds from the entire state, region, or country. Some rely on a full-time staff of experienced fund raisers (usually called fund development or advancement officers) for solicitation while others organize volunteers to conduct the majority of their solicitations. Some place most of their emphasis on one or two solicitation methods (mail and telephone) while others offer a broad variety of solicitation activities that include annual giving, major giving, and planned giving techniques.

Nonprofit organizations with years of experience, trained leaders and volunteers, a large number of faithful donors, and access to wealth will achieve greater results at lower costs that those without such favorable resources. However, the true test for fund-raising success will depend more upon the charitable mission and vision of the nonprofit organization itself, its well-defined present and future plans, the relevance and quality of its programs and services as they meet and fulfill community needs, and its ability to manage its operations and financial affairs. These are the ingredients that spell success; fund raising is only the means to invite the public's participation.

Finally, experience has shown that fund raising does not perform the same for every organization, even when the organization itself is well managed and has a positive image and reputation. Solicitation activities also must be well-defined, well-led, and well-managed in order to succeed. The common adage, "money is not given; it has to be raised," still holds. All these factors make it unlikely that every organization can generate similar levels of gift results with similar amounts of fund-raising expenses.

5. How profitable should a fund-raising program be after 3 years?

Fund-raising programs should be profitable every time they are used. If they are not, they should be discontinued unless their efficiency and effectiveness can be improved. Generally, the extent of their profitability should be a cost-benefit ratio of $0.20 to $0.30 to raise $1.00 after three years provided a broad range of solicitation methods are in use. (See Question #3.)

6. Are there any accounting guidelines on calculating fund-raising costs?

No. Separating direct costs for solicitation activity from all other management and administrative functions is the first problem. Expenses are incurred by separate departments who also communicate with the public (marketing, publications, public relations, volunteers, community relations, and so on) to ask for their involvement and to encourage them to use their services. These departments have a major influence on the public image and reputation of a nonprofit organization. The willingness of the public to give is rooted in their level of confidence and trust in the organization, its image and reputation, its plans and performance. Fund-raising activities utilize all the same communications channels (mail, brochures, newsletters, radio, TV, video, paid advertisements in newspapers and magazines) as these other departments, but for a different purpose—to ask for contributions.

The American Institute of Certified Public Accountants (AICPA) has issued guidelines to address only allocating the joint costs of fund raising for organizations using direct mail solicitation (SOP 87-10). A discussion draft to update this 1987 guideline was circulated during 1994 and 1995 and received a large number of negative comments regarding the methodology proposed to calculate the costs of all other external communication for organizations separate and exclusive from the cost of fund raising. There is also the question of how to calculate the cost of each solicitation method in use at the same time plus how their expenses are to be estimated and reported. Even as this workbook goes to press, it is unclear whether or not this accounting guideline will be reissued with new instructions to clarify the subject and whether or not other accounting guidance on this complex subject will be provided anytime soon.

7. Wasn't the issue of fund-raising cost settled by the U.S. Supreme Court?

During the 1980s, the U.S. Supreme Court handed down three decisions prohibiting individual states from regulating solicitation activity by restricting fund-raising costs to a percentage of operating or administrative costs. While the federal government does not regulate the conduct of solicitation, 45 states currently have solicitation laws that govern annual registration and reporting by nonprofit organizations. The U.S. Supreme Court decisions do *not* limit the states in the amount of registration information they require nor the amount of financial details asked for in their annual reports. Further, there is as yet no uniform report form accepted for use by all the states.

8. Should the cost of fund raising be disclosed at the point of solicitation?

There is always value in informing the public about fund-raising costs. Disclosure about nonprofit financial affairs including fund-raising costs will help to improve the public's confidence and trust in solicitation activities. However, some people may not understand what the figures mean. They may recall what they've heard or read about the cost of other fund-raising programs (United Way reports of their expenses in the $0.15 to $0.20 per $1.00 raised ratio, or less—see Question #9) and assume incorrectly that this is the standard to be applied to every other nonprofit organization.

Some states require that an application with details about estimated fund-raising costs be submitted in advance of solicitation, perhaps to aid nonprofit organizations in their own understanding of this issue. Some of these and other states (plus one city—Los Angeles) may also require that these details about estimated fund-raising expense be disclosed in their materials at the point of solicitation, to better inform the public of the ratio.

There is a serious potential for misunderstanding about what fund-raising cost figures mean. If a young nonprofit organization is just beginning a new solicitation activity, it is reasonable to expect it to have higher costs than the same solicitation activity at an established organization. The public may not know this history nor appreciate that higher costs are quite normal and reasonable in a start-up situation.

Reporting fund-raising costs at the point of solicitation also requires some explanation. The public also needs to understand the different cost–benefit ratios associated with whichever solicitation activity is used, but, unfortunately, this explanation is likely to cause more confusion than clarity. This complicated situation is not ameliorated by the use of total costs measured against total gift revenue or bottom-line figures alone, because these numbers can be misleading and easily misinterpreted or misunderstood. A large bequest in one year will suggest a better level of cost-effectiveness has been achieved, but will fail to reveal the actual relationship between funds spent to raise all the other gifts and their comparative performance.

The Internal Revenue Service requires invitations to charity benefit events to disclose the difference between the ticket price and the charitable contribution value allowed as a deduction from income tax. (The remainder is not deductible because it represents the material value of the food and drink consumed by the donor at the event.) While this example cannot explain how the public might react to increased disclosure about overall fund-raising costs, it does suggest that this new disclosure regulation, in force since 1986, might be tracked to learn whether it has had any negative effect upon ticket sales and consequently upon net proceeds for charity.

9. What should nonprofit organizations tell the public about their fund-raising costs?

Begin by reporting that "it costs money to raise money." Every nonprofit organization has to invest some of its operating budget in fund raising in order to solicit and receive contributions. In many cases, the source of this budget is unrestricted contributions received from previous and ongoing solicitations.

The public may have heard or read about the fund-raising costs of other nonprofit organizations. Several United Ways across America report their fund-raising cost figures in their annual campaign literature—they usually spend less than $0.15 or $0.20 to raise $1.00. These numbers are exceptionally low for annual giving program performance for other nonprofit organizations but remember that United Ways conduct their campaigns within two to three months each fall, rely heavily on businesses and corporations and employee contributions using payroll deduction, and synchronize their appeals with a national media campaign including prime-time ads during National Football League games. Other organizations, including those agencies designated as the United Way beneficiaries of this annual campaign, cannot compare their bottom line solicitation costs fairly with United Way because they use a variety of other solicitation activities. To attempt a fair comparison, they would have to be able to conduct a national campaign directed at national and local businesses and corporations and their employees, with television support; they cannot.

What nonprofit organizations can and should do is prepare detailed reports on the costs and results of each of their own solicitation methods. (Several examples of these reports measuring the performance for each area of solicitation activity are provided in this workbook for this express purpose.) By measuring their own performance each year and comparing it to their past efforts and their results, the relationship between amount of effort expended (time and talent plus costs) and results achieved (number of donors, repeat gifts in the same year, and dollars) will be quite evident.

Analysis of these summary performance data using the nine-point performance index introduced in this workbook will point to opportunities for increased productivity as well as profitability. These results are the success stories to share with everyone; publish these statistics in your newsletters, magazines, and annual reports. Open and full disclosure helps to build image and reputation plus respect and to develop confidence and trust in the performance of efficient and effective solicitation activities.

10. Can fund-raising costs be forecast with reliability?

Yes. However, in order to do so, you first must collect the data required to understand actual performance for each solicitation method used (total expenses and actual gift results). Then, following the analysis techniques suggested in this workbook, define performance trends, identify likely areas of improvement for both effectiveness and efficiency, and design a program to achieve any unrealized potential remaining. This workbook presents strategies for capturing the data required for performance analysis and also suggests a process to develop reliable forecasts of future fund-raising results (see Chapter 18).

For example, it may be relatively simple to increase the gift amounts received in an existing solicitation activity without changing anything other than the requested amount; just ask the same donor group for a larger amount of money. This technique, called "upgrading," accomplishes a dual objective. First, a percentage of an established donor group (between 10 and 15 percent) are likely to increase their gift size simply because they were asked. Second, it ensures gift preservation; the remainder are more likely to give again and at the same level as before.

11. Why do different fund-raising methods have different costs?

How the mix of solicitation methods (among them mail, telephone, events, grantseeking, planned giving) is applied to audiences available governs the level of efficiency as well as the effectiveness of every fund-raising activity. Next, the cost of solicitation varies in terms of how much effort is required to carry out the solicitation methods used. Communities are not the same in their history, their respect for education and health, their dependence on social and welfare services, their desire for arts and culture, their respect for and response to fund-raising activities, and more. The sources of funds within each community are the same for every nonprofit organization—individuals, corporations, and foundations. Only a few communities in America are the residences of large numbers of wealthy people, national corporate headquarters, or major national foundations. As a consequence, any effort to solicit gifts (choice of fund-raising methods and costs) begins with access to these three financial resources, to which are added the list of intangibles—image and reputation of the nonprofit organization, acceptance of local fund-raising style, prominent leadership and trained volunteers, and much more.

Not every nonprofit organization has an equal ability to operate a broad range of solicitation methods within its community. Some organizations may have only enough budget to support one or two fund-raising staff members, possibly only part-time, which limits how many methods can be put to use in any month or year. Adding staff and increasing the budget can be decided on performance and results that will suggest where improvements may lie (net returns, increased efficiency and cost-effectiveness, and so on). Efficiency should improve over time as an organization increases its ability and competence to manage several solicitation methods at the same time while remaining flexible in reacting to changing external conditions (for example, natural disasters, economic downturns, or political change) that can affect the best of efforts.

12. Is there any relationship between the cost of fund raising and the quality of programs and services provided to the public?

Successful fund-raising programs provide a variety of benefits to nonprofit organizations, including improved programs and community services. To begin, volunteerism and contributions represent public participation in local organizations serving community needs. Many donors give to selected nonprofit organizations because they may be frequent or occasional clients of their services, and they want them to be first rate and available. Charities often cite the margin of excellence to donors to convey the important difference their contributions enable.

Fund raising provides other benefits as well. Contributions are extra dollars that permit nonprofit organizations to use their other funds for these same purposes or apply them to other beneficial programs. Contributions often represent new funds for new programs, expended services to benefit greater numbers of people, or improved quality of facilities and technology available. Contributions restricted for capital purposes (facilities and equipment) increase assets and depreciation allowances and even improve financial ratings for borrowing money when needed. Contributions restricted to endowment provide perpetual revenue in the form of interest and investment earnings and increased financial stability. These examples illustrate that extra resources delivered from successful solicitation activities provide far more than opportunities for improved quality in programs and services for community benefit.

13. What's the relationship between fund-raising cost effectiveness and fund-raising efficiency?

Effectiveness is doing the right things; efficiency is doing them well. A mature fund-raising program should be able to demonstrate both in describing its fund-raising performance in detail, adding such revealing data as productivity and profitability data.

Effectiveness and efficiency are the products of a variety of opportunities. First, volunteers who participate in solicitation are not only less expensive than hired staff solicitors, but they are often more successful as solicitors. Donors are more likely to trust a friend or neighbor who is taking the time to bring them information about a community need and their organization's plan to meet that need than they are to trust a stranger who is hired to solicit their money.

Second, consider memberships. An annual membership club requires a gift for dues of $100. By adding categories of membership at higher levels ($250, $500, $1,000), including a life membership of $2,500 to perpetuate their annual dues as an endowment gift, the club increases its total gift revenue from the same membership body and at minimal added expense.

Third, by soliciting sponsorship and underwriting gifts above regular ticket prices for a major benefit event, gross revenue is increased while production costs remain the same, increasing net proceeds dramatically. This same result is achieved by soliciting in-kind gifts of materials to be used for the event (flowers, beverages, decorations, printing, and so on), thereby reducing the amount of direct costs and increasing net profits again.

Together, these examples illustrate how attention to fund-raising costs can contribute to improved effectiveness as well as efficiency. How to achieve better results takes extra thought, planning, and effort but must be based on good data. This workbook offers to provide these tools in the hopes that more nonprofit organizations will be able to benefit from their use and demonstrate their proficiency, their productivity, and their profitability. The fund development program is a profit center, not another cost center. And, as a profit center, it probably achieves the highest rate of return on the budget invested in it than any other department in the organization. If it can prove this level of efficiency as well as effectiveness, the organization should be asking how much more can be raised with what increase in budget.

PART 1

Preparations for Solicitation Activity

Public confidence is critical to the success of every nonprofit organization. Those who believe in and support the mission of a nonprofit organization must be able to trust its public stewards, the board of directors, and management. Therefore, nonprofit organizations must be willing to submit to a public evaluation of their conduct and achievements, eager to demonstrate how their outcomes have been beneficial to others and forthcoming in disclosing how they managed their resources to accomplish these goals and objectives.

Identifying the best way to do this has been a stumbling block. How should performance be judged and who are the judges? Against which standards can public benefits be measured? The answers revert back to the business model, because profit and loss are universally accepted. Investors do not evaluate Exxon or General Motors by counting the number of people who use their cars for vacations and holidays, but by studying their financial performance as shown in the profits they share with stockholders.

Board members and management, volunteers, and donors can be expected to form judgments about the performance of nonprofit organizations by concentrating on their financial performance. Success is evident if the organization remained within budget, was able to secure necessary revenues, managed its money carefully, and observed generally accepted accounting principles. Much harder to measure are operational results, such as efficiency of the organization's staff-to-client ratio, quality of programs and services, appropriate use of restricted gifts, and ethical and legal behavior.

Fund-raising is an action program, necessarily aggressive in seeking support. A budget, staff, space, and support system must be provided to find and develop friends, build relationships, and conduct solicitations, all of which take time and effort, money and patience, and professional leadership and direction. How can the board and management, volunteers, and donors identify how much time and effort, how many employees, how much budget, will be needed to be able to raise the money needed? What are the indicators to evaluate this performance and measure these results? In answering these questions, the organization must always keep the public's concerns in mind.

Business criteria are most effective for measuring decisions of how much budget is required and what level of investment must be made to achieve efficiency and effectiveness in solicitation activities. These criteria can be applied to determine the proper relationship between the budget spent on fund-raising and the results returned for this investment. Perhaps more important and quite germane to this workbook, what is the relationship between fund-raising costs and a donor's decision to make a gift? The view held by many is that disclosure of fund-raising cost does influence this all-important decision.

The challenge to nonprofit organizations and their fund development staff is to be able to provide the evidence donors want. This is neither a revelation nor a new problem, but it persists and the need for answers has grown over time. There are no national standards that donors and organizations alike can use to evaluate fund-raising results. Further, there are no accounting guidelines on how to prepare the figures, to separate direct costs from indirect and overhead expenses.

This workbook presents measurements that will help to evaluate all the data collected about fund-raising activities. The process begins with creating a written annual business plan for the nonprofit organization. Once the business plan is in place, a realistic budget can be prepared for each fund-raising activity to follow. Then solicitation can begin. Fund-raising may be more like a business than any other area of nonprofit management. Throughout this workbook, following good business practices will be useful in the evaluation of each solicitation activity and the measurement of its results.

1

Preparing the Annual Business Plan and the Budget

Preparations for solicitation activity must begin with establishing ways to measure all results for their effectiveness, efficiency, productivity, and profitability. Your organization first sets its priorities based on its mission, vision, and values expressed as its current purposes, goals, and objectives. But to invite public support, it must be able to explain itself in terms of meeting community needs. Therefore, you should develop an annual plan. The steps that precede the annual plan are development of a mission statement, a vision and values statement, a strategic plan, and a communications and marketing plan.

The fund development process requires a constant commitment to the acquisition of new donors, renewal of prior donors, and upgrading of as many current donors as possible to higher levels of performance. This combination of ongoing efforts requires the commitment of a continuous budget investment to produce reliable levels of contributions income. Annual budget decisions can be based on measurement of prior performance—the direct results of investing dollars in solicitation activities.

Budget preparation should reflect two major ares, institutional master plans and revenue sources. Budgets are a commitment to achieve specific plans scheduled to occur in the coming year. These plans are based on established goals and objectives to represent annual operational priorities, capital and equipment needs, new program directions, and more. To produce the required revenue, these priorities become the goals for the fund-raising program and its budget. Integrating your organization's annual and long-range plans with scheduled solicitation activities allows fund development planners to anticipate priority needs and to manage annual budgets to deliver funding for current and future program plans on schedule, year after year.

The details of financial operations associated with preparation, approval, and review of annual operating budgets will fulfill a nonprofit organization's stewardship and accountability duty to the public.

Mission and Vision

The first draft of a mission statement usually appears in the application for tax-exempt status. After legal status is granted and operations begin, the mission statement may change as the organization learns more about its own purposes and abilities. A mission statement is, of necessity, an evolving document that must preserve the original purposes for which the organization was founded while keeping pace with changes in society affecting that mission. The board of directors is the authority responsible for defining and protecting the mission, reviewing it periodically, and changing the description (but not its intent) when necessary. The qualities of a good mission statement are precise: It must be clear, concise, and forward thinking; provide a guide to action; define whom the organization serves; be expressed in broad, nonquantifiable terms; provide inspiration; reflect a broad consensus; and be easily understood by people outside the organization.[1] A mission statement expresses direction and purpose out of which goals and objectives can be defined.

The difference between a mission statement and a statement of vision and values is the leadership factor. Mission statements are concise expressions of purpose; a vision and values statement is a human expression to provide a reason for action, an emotional, philosophical, or special interest that inspires people beyond financial and programmatic goals. Vision and values reflect a concern for others that can be measured in outcomes achieved by organizations and people working together. Vision and values are overarching goals that serve as standards, even ideals, to be attained. They explain why a course of action is taken and what outcomes are desired because of their ability to influence human behavior. Vision and values express personal and life purposes and can be translated into aspirations that motivate others.

Master Plans, Long-Range Plans, and Strategic Plans

A nonprofit organization can develop a 20-year master plan, which is the basis for a 5-year long-range plan, which serves as a guide for strategic plans as a series of 1-year goals and objectives. All three will express the same view of the future and a common direction to be taken to realize that future.

These detailed plans contain the exact list of projects to move the current organization into higher qualities of achievement, to add new programs, and to expand the levels of service currently offered. They define each and every project on a master timetable, assigning each its position of priority corresponding to when it will be needed, and estimating all the costs required. A master list of essential facilities and equipment to support each of these programs and services, along with a financial master plan that defines the amounts of revenue required, including philanthropic support, rounds out the story. The benefits and uses of these three plans are subject to periodic evaluation and change (see Exhibit 1.1), but to fund-raising leaders, volunteers, donors, and staff, the plans are a giant shopping list!

Communications and Marketing

A nonprofit organization's objectives for marketing and communications are substantial: To establish an image, identify the desired audience and general constituency, reach out to clients needing its programs and services, elicit a positive response to its messages, and stimulate the public to act. Your marketing plan identifies:

1. The details of the story you want to tell the public about how your organization is meeting community needs.
2. The way you will get this story to the public.

Nonprofit organizations must inform and educate their selected target markets or audiences to stimulate them to reply. They must likewise report the results of their programs and services, especially how they have served their clients and the public, and have made valued contributions to the general welfare of the community. An informed audience

Exhibit 1.1

Benefits and Uses of Master, Long-Range, and Strategic Plans*

	SCORE				
	low				high
Think strategically	1	2	3	4	5
Clarify future directions	1	2	3	4	5
Make today's decisions in light of their future consequences	1	2	3	4	5
Meet mandates facing the organization and further fulfillment of the organization's mission	1	2	3	4	5
Develop a coherent and defensible basis for decision making	1	2	3	4	5
Exercise maximum discretion in the areas under organizational control	1	2	3	4	5
Address major issues and solve major organizational problems	1	2	3	4	5
Deal effectively and rapidly with changing circumstances	1	2	3	4	5
Build teamwork and expertise	1	2	3	4	5
Improve organizational credibility and enhance organizational legitimacy	1	2	3	4	5

Median Score

*John M. Bryson, "Strategic Planning and Action Planning for Nonprofit Organizations," in *The Jossey-Bass Handbook of Nonprofit Leadership and Management*, Robert D. Herman & Associates, eds. San Francisco: Jossey-Bass, 1994, p. 155.

must precede any request for their participation or these invitations will fall on deaf ears.

To compete for public attention and to stimulate the public to act, nonprofit organizations must use the same channels as everyone else. Successful communications result from studying the marketplace and surveying public opinions to target those who need to hear the organization's messages using one or more media options singly or in multimedia combinations for added effectiveness. You can use Exhibit 1.2 to evaluate your organization's use of the media.

Exhibit 1.2

Measurement of Media Options and Multimedia Mix for Communications

	SCORE Access/Use		SCORE Multimedia	
	low	high	low	high
Direct Mail				
First class	1 2 3 4 5		1 2 3 4 5	
Third class	1 2 3 4 5		1 2 3 4 5	
Telephone/Telemarketing				
Volunteer callers	1 2 3 4 5		1 2 3 4 5	
Professional callers	1 2 3 4 5		1 2 3 4 5	
Radio				
Advertising	1 2 3 4 5		1 2 3 4 5	
Public Service Announcements (PSAs)	1 2 3 4 5		1 2 3 4 5	
News coverage	1 2 3 4 5		1 2 3 4 5	
Magazines				
Advertising	1 2 3 4 5		1 2 3 4 5	
Feature articles	1 2 3 4 5		1 2 3 4 5	
Newspapers				
Advertising	1 2 3 4 5		1 2 3 4 5	
Feature articles	1 2 3 4 5		1 2 3 4 5	
News coverage	1 2 3 4 5		1 2 3 4 5	
Television	1 2 3 4 5		1 2 3 4 5	
Advertising	1 2 3 4 5		1 2 3 4 5	
Feature presentations	1 2 3 4 5		1 2 3 4 5	
Tapes/records	1 2 3 4 5		1 2 3 4 5	
Videotapes	1 2 3 4 5		1 2 3 4 5	
Computer disk/CDs	1 2 3 4 5		1 2 3 4 5	
Modem/Internet/World Wide Web	1 2 3 4 5		1 2 3 4 5	

Median Scores

Communications about solicitation activities represent an additional message medium to market and promote programs and services, inform and educate the same target markets, and stimulate requests for service as well as to ask for financial support. People want to know what their time and money are being used for before they decide to give these valuable commodities away. Marketing, communications, and solicitation activities perform most effectively and efficiently in a coordinated and cooperative effort that, like a mathematical formula,

Exhibit **1.3**

Measurement of Coordination of Marketing, Communications, and Fund Development Activities

	SCORE				
	low				high
Marketing Objectives					
Establish an image	1	2	3	4	5
Create clients for programs	1	2	3	4	5
Elicit a positive response	1	2	3	4	5
Stimulate the public to act	1	2	3	4	5
Communications Objectives					
Inform and educate	1	2	3	4	5
Tell a story, and repeat it often	1	2	3	4	5
Report results, accomplishments, outcomes	1	2	3	4	5
Build confidence and trust	1	2	3	4	5
Build community consensus	1	2	3	4	5
Fund Development Objectives					
Friend raising and relationship building	1	2	3	4	5
Develop a willingness to volunteer	1	2	3	4	5
Develop a willingness to give	1	2	3	4	5
Develop gifts to meet priority needs	1	2	3	4	5
Provide continuous contact with donors through donor relations activities	1	2	3	4	5

Median Score

will produce desired results for each participant. You can use Exhibit 1.3 to evaluate your organization's coordination of these activities.

Once the mission and vision are established, you can develop details about the different pieces and parts of the strategic plan and then institute an overall marketing and communications plan.

The Internal Audit[2]

A completed shopping list is not a fund-raising program. The hard work that produced this roster of tempting priorities likewise has to be matched with an equally detailed and solid fund-raising strategic plan. Several options are available to create such a plan beginning with a thorough review of every area of activity already in operation. Here are some leading questions to get the thinking started for an internal audit process:

1. How to get the staff to be more productive?
2. How to use a limited budget more effectively?
3. How to secure the added equipment and budget needed?
4. How to increase the pool of prospects?
5. How to stimulate prospects to begin giving?
6. How to excite current donors to give again?
7. How to identify, recruit, and train more volunteers?
8. How to organize staff and volunteers to work together better?
9. How to get the board of directors more involved in fund-raising?
10. How to raise more money?

These answers will be helpful, but this short-form evaluation is too limited and fails to probe the areas affecting effectiveness, efficiency, productivity, and profitability. You also need to perform an objective analysis that reflects facts and figures from prior results and a subjective analysis that evaluates both internal and external criteria and relates them to the immediate goals. Both reviews are necessary to capture a true picture of present capabilities, strengths and weaknesses, future potential, and the improvements necessary to meet all the funding requirements.

Current staff and volunteers might attempt a comprehensive internal audit provided anyone has prior experience with this process and has knowledge about fund-raising operations. The recommended alternative is to hire a professional fund-raising consulting firm with wide experience in conducting fund development audits for a variety of nonprofit organizations.

This level of comprehensive audit should be performed every five years or so, and it is most strongly recommended as the first step in preparation for a major capital campaign. Exhibit 1.4 provides a list of audit areas. There are four parts to the audit process: data gathering and examination, interviews and site visits, analysis and report writing, and final report presentation with action plans.

Data gathering is the homework assignment to inventory every fund-raising resource. The fund development office is asked to gather specific information and sample materials, including:

1. All gift results from the previous three to five years.
2. The roles played by the board of directors, management and professional staff, and employees.

Exhibit 1.4

Information Categories for Internal Audit Purposes

1. Mission and vision statement, master or long-range or strategic plan.
2. Gift reports for prior three to five years reflecting number of donors, dollars received, fund-raising budgets, gift analysis, and performance measurements.
3. Prospect and donor research capability, rating and evaluation process, and cultivation plan and strategic preparation and monitoring.
4. Computer equipment and software support, network access, standard and special request report capability, e-mail, and modem data access.
5. Planning process for annual goal-setting, business plan, budgeting, and performance evaluation procedures.
6. Departmental organization, reporting relationships, job descriptions for staff and volunteers, department meetings, and training programs.
7. Donor recognition components, policy and procedure, gift clubs, recognition systems, and continuing donor relations activities.
8. Marketing and communications plans, coordination with other departments, promotion and publicity, printed publications and brochures.
9. Volunteer recruitment, orientation and training, assignment, performance evaluation, leadership development, recognition and reward.
10. Board and management involvement, development committee operations, participation in activities, and personal giving history.

---

3. The structure and operating systems that support fund-raising, such as the board's development committee and its working committees and support groups.
4. Details on the records system.
5. Information about gift processing and data processing procedures and controls.
6. Prospect and donor research.
7. The donor relations program.
8. Communications materials (including sample case statements).
9. Volunteer involvement.
10. Budget.
11. Staffing.
12. Space.
13. Job descriptions.
14. Operating policies and procedures.

Finally, fund development staff and senior volunteers will be asked to complete a questionnaire and provide their views and opinions to rate the performance of current programs, operating systems, leadership, and support staff. All this information is delivered to the fund-raising consulting firm for review and evaluation before it begins on-site inspections and interviews.

Site visits are conducted for two or three days to interview board members, volunteers, and staff participants. If the development audit is conducted in preparation for a major gifts program, special project, or capital campaign, this examination will assess the state of readiness for that effort and offer recommendations for these more complex solicitation activities.

The firm evaluates all the information and prepares a summary report of its findings and recommendations. The report will be specific, even candid, about strengths and weaknesses and will suggest steps to retain and expand areas of competence and accomplishment alongside desired improvements.

If the internal audit was performed to begin preparations for a special project or capital campaign, the report will be expanded into a strategic plan and provide complete details on recommended goal(s), campaign leadership, structure and timetable, and estimated giving levels from available and potential sources. The report further will identify all the documents needed along with a publicity and promotion program, a total budget including staffing and support systems, and the balance of recommendations on how to begin and complete the campaign successfully. The audit's final recommendations will set priorities for action steps, which should begin immediately after the report is accepted.

The Annual Business Plan

Armed with the results of the internal audit and challenged to define the optimal program to provide all the funds to finance the organization's future plans, the fund development department can prepare its multiyear strategic plan for solicitation activity, beginning with the annual business plan. A business plan provides direction, a basis for performance comparisons, commitment to its goals, and performance evaluation on results. The best time to prepare the annual business plan is right before the annual budget so all plans and their financing can be reviewed and approved at the same time.

If it is not possible to devote time to preparing an annual business plan, a forecast of results may be used instead. In the absence of an annual plan, the following guidelines can be used to explain about investing budget dollars in fund-raising performance:

1. Set aside negative attitudes toward fund-raising.
2. Match fund-raising costs with related revenue.
3. Recover fund-raising investments from related gifts.
4. Invest by appropriate categories of fund-raising.
5. Give investors decision-useful information.
6. Keep fund-raising cost percentages reasonable.
7. Do *not* try to lower bottom-line cost percentages.
8. Test new fund-raising efforts.
9. Learn from every fund-raising investment.[3]

When preparation of the annual business plan is possible, it need not result in more than two to three pages for each method of solicitation, beginning with the individual goals and objectives of the staff member responsible for each fund-raising activity. Every solicitation plan should include:

1. The text of the activity's unique mission statement.
2. Identified target markets.
3. Volunteer support.
4. An organization chart.
5. Promotional plans.
6. Measurable goals and objectives.
7. Evaluation criteria.
8. Report forms.
9. A budget request.

Clerical and support staff should also prepare their business plan, using the same format. Everyone's plans can be shared in a half-day or full-day planning retreat held off-site to debate priorities and build consensus and teamwork around the consolidated business plan for fund-raising. The final product that develops from this planning session is reviewed by fund-raising volunteer leaders and perhaps a few key donors for their consensus and commitment, and then by the board of directors and management for final approval of the overall business plan and the budget required to carry it out.

A progress review should be conducted after six months to measure results and, if necessary, adjust goals and plans to fit reality. At year-end, the planning process can begin again, this time with a review of results and the advantage of experience gained from the previous year's operations as a guide for the next business plan.

The annual business plan includes support staff and systems to reflect the degree that coordination, cooperation, and communication are essential to realize success with both individual and departmentwide fund-raising goals. The plan further depends on everyone's performance to achieve the nonprofit organization's overall goals. There can be disadvantages if the planning model is not well understood or respected (see Exhibit 1.5), but preparing and following an annual business plan will contribute to the annual growth of the fund development program. At the least, it will document how results were produced each year. A completed annual business plan is superb preparation for developing a budget.

Program-by-Program Budget Preparation

A program-by-program budget preparation method is recommended. This requires that fund development staff begin with a review of each solicitation activity currently in use and prepare a separate budget to support its continuation. Each solicitation program will have direct costs as well as indirect and overhead expenses. Not all solicitation programs produce their gifts within the 12-month fiscal year. There are further budget areas that are not used in direct solicitation, but are necessary to support it. These expenses include prospect research, gift processing, equipment maintenance, accounting fees, and the like. To prepare a complete budget for each solicitation activity, begin by collecting the results in three separate reports:

1. *Sources of gifts.* List each source to capture its performance as a separate group. The list reflects each audience identified as a prospect or new donor group that was solicited in the prior year (see Exhibit 1.6). The key information at the top of the exhibit (number of donors, gift income, and average gift size) remains the same for these three reports.

2. *Purposes or uses of gift income.* Nonprofit organizations ask for support for their most urgent needs; as a result, many gifts are received for specific purposes and cannot be used for any other project or

Exhibit 1.5

Advantages and Disadvantages of an Annual Planning Model*

Advantages	Disadvantages
1. Is comprehensive	1. Creates a paper mill
2. Is adaptable	2. Fosters bureaucratization
3. Brings precision and clarity to setting goals and objectives	3. Leads to the creation of too many goals
4. Helps assure a realistic match between targets and potential	4. Leads to inappropriate behavior
5. Provides the basis for establishing priorities	5. Produces an unrealistic assessment
6. Encourages focus on results, not efforts	6. Fails to set priorities
7. Clarifies and pinpoints responsibility	7. Overemphasizes objectives
8. Forces clarification of roles	8. Fails to produce sufficiently detailed action plans
9. Provides the basis of a control system	9. Fails to create feedback mechanisms
10. Reduces "continual absorption"	10. Omits reviews
11. Enhances communication	11. Fails to create reward mechanisms
12. Heightens motivation	12. Fails to adequately involve top management
13. Identifies training needs and advancement potential among staff and volunteers	13. Fails to allow for education
14. Produces a professional-quality, written planning document	14. Ignores the need to change behavior
15. Creates greater respect for fund-raising and nonprofit management in general	15. Fails to allow sufficient time for planning
	16. Consumes too much time
	17. Is poorly integrated with other management systems

*Dennis J. Murray, *The Guaranteed Fund-Raising System: A Systems Approach to Planning and Controlling Fund Raising* (1st ed.). Poughkeepsie, NY: American Institute of Management, 1987, pp. 54–58.

Exhibit **1.6**

Gift Report on Sources of Gifts Received

Sources of Gifts	Number of Gifts	Gift Income	Average Gift Size
Trustees/Directors	15	$25,500	$1,700
Professional staff	21	3,025	144
Employees	65	3,675	57
New donors (acquisition)	285	8,030	28
Prior donors (renewal)	282	18,010	64
Corporations	17	8,500	500
Foundations	12	38,800	3,233
Associations/societies	6	2,850	475
Bequests received	3	31,500	10,500
Unsolicited gifts	42	2,950	70
Other gifts recieved	12	21,500	1,792
Grand Total	760	$164,340	$216

priority. Restrictions control where funds are deposited and how they may be used. The list of purposes or restrictions also represents the broad categories of support an organization will accept (see Exhibit 1.7). The terms used in these categories reflect new accounting standards published by the Financial Accounting Standards Board (FASB) and corresponding guidelines issued by the American Institute of Certified Public Accountants (AICPA), effective for fiscal years beginning after December 31, 1994.

3. *Solicitation activities and results.* The results of each solicitation activity must be tracked and reported. These data are important for performance measurement, such as average gift size. Solicitation activities perform differently from one another as this report makes apparent (see Exhibit 1.8).

Monthly preparation and distribution of these three gift reports is recommended as regular statements of results, progress, and performance. Monitoring the number of donors participating is essential; money follows people. If the numbers are increasing, the organization and its priority projects have met with approval; if the number declines, it is important to understand whether changing

Exhibit 1.7

Gift Report on Purposes or Uses of Gifts Received

Purposes or Uses of Gifts Received	Number of Gifts	Gift Income	Average Gift Size
Unrestricted Funds	225	$34,519	$153
Temporarily Restricted Funds			
Capital/equipment purposes	295	$26,950	$91
Programs/services purposes	138	18,500	134
Education/training purposes	14	22,500	1,607
Research/study purposes	15	26,450	1,763
Staff/employee purposes	58	3,016	52
Other restricted purposes	12	905	75
Subtotal	757	$132,840	$175
Permanently Restricted Funds			
Unrestricted endowment	2	$6,500	$3,250
Restricted endowment	1	25,000	25,000
Subtotal	3	$31,500	$10,500
Grand Total	760	$164,340	$216

economic conditions, increased competition, natural disasters, and other situations outside the organization's control explain the decline.

Reviewing all three reports will pinpoint where increases and decreases are occurring. Gift income data explains what sources and which programs are most productive in terms of total gift receipts. Average gift size is an early and steady performance measurement and helps with understanding how well chosen each source was for its potential to give and how well matched it was to the solicitation method used to solicit the support received.

Continuing to monitor each solicitation activity and to report its results will help board members, managers, donors, and volunteers understand and appreciate the relationships between sources, priority projects, and solicitation methods along with the interdependence involved in fund-raising techniques. Gift income varies from source to source and purpose to purpose each year, just as individual solicitation activities will vary in their results. Collecting and reporting results using these three gift reports begins performance measurement and

Exhibit 1.8

Gift Report of Solicitation Activities and Results (by Program)

Solicitation Activities	Number of Gifts	Gift Income	Average Gift Size
A. Annual Giving Programs			
Direct mail (acquisition)	285	$8,030	$28
Direct mail (renewal)	282	18,010	64
Membership dues	0	0	0
Donor clubs	0	0	0
Support groups	0	0	0
Telephone gifts	0	0	0
Benefit events	2	12,850	6,425
Volunteer-led solicitations	65	3,675	57
Unsolicited gifts	42	2,950	70
Other gifts received	16	21,500	1,344
Subtotal	692	$67,015	$97
B. Major Giving Programs			
Corporations	17	$8,500	$500
Foundations	12	28,800	2,400
Individuals	36	28,525	792
Special projects	0	0	0
Capital campaigns	0	0	0
Bequests received	3	31,500	10,500
Subtotal	68	$97,325	$1,431
Grand total	760	$164,340	$216

guides the budgeting process that controls where funds will be spent to achieve future results.

With these basic reports in place, added measurements can be taken of each solicitation activity, such as percent participation, donor retention rates, average cost per gift, and net income realized. These data add valuable insights to performance beyond counting gift revenue received and will help to estimate future budgets and their revenue results based on the following interpretations:

1. Percent participation shows how well prospects and donors liked what was presented to them.

2. Donor retention rates show the extent of their commitment to the nonprofit organization and will help to forecast what these same donors might be expected to give the next time they are asked.

3. Average cost per gift reflects the effort required to secure each contribution. Monitoring this figure as the solicitation activity is repeated is a clue to its effectiveness as well as its efficiency.

4. Net income shows the productivity and profitability of each solicitation activity in use. These are the dollars available to the organization for its programs and services.

Accuracy in budget preparation will be increased with program-by-program budgeting and results reporting. The next report can be prepared one year later and will compare income received with actual expenses incurred for each solicitation activity (see Exhibit 1.9). The results are quite valuable in preparing the next budget. They also yield an important new measurement, cost per dollar raised reflecting the level of efficiency and profitability of each solicitation activity.

Budget Worksheet

The fund-raising budget must translate its activities into categories of expense that fit the organization's chart of accounts. A chart of accounts is a uniform list of expense categories to which all expenses are assigned (telephone, travel, printing, etc.). There is no single or uniform chart of accounts used by all nonprofit organizations, and there is no uniform budget worksheet that converts the expense categories for solicitation activities into a standard chart of accounts; a bit of work is required to convert fund-raising cost areas into whatever labels the organization chooses for its budget and accounting functions.

Following the recommendation that *each* area of solicitation activity define the separate expenses it requires, these individual budget worksheets must then be combined to fit the organization's chart of accounts to become the consolidated fund development budget request. Some separation also must be made between direct fund-raising expenses and the necessary costs of management and supporting activities (indirect and overhead expenses). The consolidated budget for fund development

Exhibit 1.9

Gift Report of Solicitation Activities with Gift Income Measured against Approved Budget and Actual Expenses (by Program)

Activities	Gift Income	Approved Budget	Actual Expenses	Cost per $ Raised
A. Annual Giving Programs				
Direct mail (acquisition)	$8,030	$10,500	$9,855	$1.23
Direct mail (renewal)	18,010	3,750	3,890	0.22
Membership dues	0	0	0	0
Donor clubs	0	0	0	0
Support groups	0	0	0	0
Telephone gifts	0	0	0	0
Benefit events	2,850	1,800	1,350	0.47
Volunteer-led solicitations	3,675	500	485	0.13
Unsolicited gifts	2,950	0	0	0
Other gifts received	21,500	0	0	0
Subtotal	$57,015	$16,550	$15,580	$0.27
B. Major Giving Programs				
Corporations	$8,500	$20,215	$18,250	$2.15
Foundations	38,800	34,525	33,555	0.86
Individuals	28,525	3,210	3,250	0.11
Special projects	0	0	0	0
Capital campaigns	0	0	0	0
Bequests received	31,500	500	550	0.02
Subtotal	$107,325	$58,450	$55,605	$0.52
Grand total	$164,340	$75,000	$71,185	$0.43

is added into the overall operating budget request for management and board approval.

The budget of a nonprofit organization also must include estimates of both revenue and expense. Fund development staff may be asked to estimate both as well (or assigned income goals), which will reveal the direct relationship between cost of fund-raising and net income produced to support the organization's programs and services. There is no standard for this comparison; each organization must establish its own balance of necessary costs to level of contributions income. The best guide will be good data on prior experience with solicitation activities.

At the end of the operating year, total figures can compare the efficiency and effectiveness of each solicitation activity (see Exhibit 1.9) and can also serve as a budget-planning document for the following year. Published annual reports and audited financial statements will disclose revenue from all sources along with expense details. These figures are of interest to funding sources outside the organization as well as to the board of directors and management staff responsible for financial management. Each nonprofit organization also must submit a tax return to both the state and federal government. Most states accept the federal return (IRS Form 990), which includes a variety of financial details including a summary of expenses separated into three groups: program services, management and general, and fund-raising costs (see Exhibit 1.10). This report provides interested parties with details about categories of expense. This form also can serve as a budget worksheet in the event any other is not available.

Exhibit 1.10

Sample Budget Worksheet Based on IRS Form 990

Part II Statement of Functional Expenses (IRS Form 990, p.2)

	(a) Total	(b) Program Services	(c) Management and General	(d) Fundraising
22 Grants and allocations	$0	$0	$0	$0
23 Specific assistance to individuals	0	0	0	0
24 Benefits paid to or for members	0	0	0	0
25 Compensation of officers, directors	0	0	0	0
26 Other salaries and wages	828,305	575,855	214,895	37,555
27 Pension plan contributions	18,565	12,650	5,915	0
28 Other employee benefits	2,610	1,305	1,305	0
29 Payroll taxes	6,750	4,905	1,845	0
30 Professional fund-raising fees	0	0	0	0
31 Accounting fees	6,950	0	6,950	0
32 Legal fees	3,500	0	3,000	500
33 Supplies	28,555	18,305	9,550	700
34 Telephone	5,695	3,555	1,575	565
35 Postage and shipping	28,610	10,115	11,240	7,255
36 Occupancy	0	0	0	0
37 Equipment rental and maintenance	9,557	4,551	3,750	1,256
38 Printing and publications	28,750	9,885	12,665	6,200
39 Travel	12,560	1,800	3,200	7,560
40 Conferences, conventions, and meetings	8,500	4,550	2,795	1,155
41 Interest	8,500	0	8,500	0
42 Depreciation, depletion, etc.	16,750	16,750	0	0
43 Other expenses				
a Lawsuit settlement	7,567	5,505	2,062	0
b _____				
c _____				
44 Total Functional Expenses	$1,021,724	$669,731	$289,247	$62,746

The following four general principles provide further guidance on budget preparation:

First, each category should be well defined. In other words, the definitions of the funds expended and the gifts raised by the unit must be clear and precise as possible.

Second, the resources allocated and the corresponding funds generated by the well-defined category should be traceable in the accounting system.

Third, the categories should be commonly applicable from institution to institution and not unique to a particular organization.

Fourth, categories should be selected so that there is a difference between the ways they react to development efforts.[4]

Indirect Costs and Overhead Expenses

A budget must also contain the indirect costs and overhead expenses for routine operating areas that support direct solicitation activities. What are these expenses and how are they to be identified and included in the budget? How are they to be allocated fairly across the spectrum of expenses required for each area of solicitation activity? Indirect costs and overhead expenses are a difficult problem for the fund development budget because they must be shared among all solicitation activities. Indirect and overhead costs that directly influence solicitation activities and their net results also include:

Time and money spent with volunteers to prepare them to conduct the programs they lead as well as to identify, recruit, train, and evaluate their results.

Time and money spent on prospect and donor research, on meetings and their planning, on gift processing and donor records, and on donor recognition.

Time and money spent on administrative work such as budget preparation and accounting, gift reports, personnel supervision, and personal and professional training of staff and volunteers.

Time and money spent on office equipment and its maintenance, light and heat, rent and lease costs, travel and meals for staff, and entertainment of prospects and donors as well as volunteers.

Time and money spent on community relations, friend-raising, overall visibility, and accessibility.

Time or money lost because of a lack of revenue, excessive demands on development staff for other management assignments, or vacations, holidays, and sick time.[5]

Additional suggestions on how to estimate these expense areas are offered in the following instruction:

One method of allocating indirect cost is the simplified method. It is applicable when every responsibility center or program contributes roughly the same to the overhead costs or according to one simple index. The overhead or indirect costs is divided up evenly.

For accounting and contracting purposes, overhead or indirect costs are usually stated as a percentage of direct labor costs or a percentage of total direct costs (labor, materials, and other costs directly and exclusively caused by an activity). These percentages are referred to as overhead rates.

A second method, known as the multiple allocation method, is applicable when there are different pools of indirect costs (depreciation, personnel and administration, utility) and the responsibility centers are unequal in their contribution to each cost pool. Thus, the allocation of overhead should be based on some basis that reflects accurately the different contributions to each pool. Using this method, the organization could allocate one set of indirect costs based on direct labor, another set based on direct materials, and still a third or more sets based on other indices (for example, time of use in the case of a computer).

A third type, known as direct allocation, is applicable when the nonprofit divides up its activities into major responsibility centers, such as fund raising and general administration, and requires each to consider its contribution to overhead as part of its own direct costs. This method transforms an indirect to a direct cost by concentrating the activity into an identifiable, manageable, and controllable responsibility center. This is analogous to setting up a fund-raising center, to handle all fund-raising. All fund-raising costs will now become costs of the center, hence one consequence of reorganization is to shift costs between direct and indirect.[6]

There is no uniform method or guideline for allocating indirect and overhead expenses to multiple solicitation activities. Business managers and chief financial officers understand the realities of indirect costs and overhead expenses and have devised methods for including these expenses in their annual operating budgets, perhaps in the same manner as pro rata depreciation expenses shared with every department. The best solution for allocating these expenses is to consult with the business and accounting staff as well as the auditor and follow their instructions. Because organizations are likely to be inconsistent in how they allocate expenses for solicitation activities, there will continue to be limitations on performance comparisons between nonprofit organizations.

Evaluations of Budget Preparation and Performance

A budget prepared with complete information contributes important details to use when measuring the results of the organization's entire operating year and its many programs and services provided for public benefit. This measurement begins with a basic question: "Did we finish the year in the red or the black?" Much more analysis than a simple "bottom-line" evaluation is required, of course, but this evaluation is not easily accomplished.

Each solicitation activity performs at different levels of efficiency and effectiveness. Some activities (direct mail, membership, benefit events) enjoy larger numbers of donors, receive modest average gifts, and require more budget. Others (volunteer-led solicitations, foundations, planned giving programs) enjoy large contributions from fewer donors and cost less to operate. *Each* solicitation activity needs to be evaluated independently, and the evaluation should give consideration to the uniqueness of each solicitation method used. Some solicitation activities will be more efficient and more profitable than others. Those that appear to be less efficient (raise less money) or more expensive (require more budget) should not be judged as failures because their results do not compare as well; they may be most effective in finding and retaining large numbers of donors who will become reliable major contributors for the future.

Direct measurements of the results of solicitation activities can be made using businesslike methods, many of which are not applicable to the charitable programs and services provided by the nonprofit organization. Begin with data in Exhibit 1.9, where the calculation of cost per dollar raised for each area of solicitation activity is reported. The direct relationship between budget spent and results achieved reveals details about the efficiency and effectiveness, productivity, and profitability of each solicitation activity. A three-year summary of these results will provide added insight into performance (see Exhibit 1.11) leading to realizable levels of forecasting for future revenues. Solicitation activities that perform above expectations can be reviewed to determine whether more resources (time and budget) will produce more net revenue at lower costs. Similarly, activities performing below expectations can be studied to determine whether their shortfall was due to inadequate attention and limited resources, or whether they are unlikely to perform any better with added funds.

Exhibit **1.11**

Summary Budget Request with Estimated Expenses and Revenue

	Previous Year	Last Year	Current Fiscal Year	Coming Fiscal Year
Budget				
Labor costs	$66,009	$74,164	$80,165	$90,259
Nonlabor costs	43,594	50,026	44,210	50,000
Total Budget	$109,603	$124,190	$124,375	$140,259
Gift Revenue				
Gross revenue	$342,738	$563,384	$630,114	$655,000
Minus expenses (budget)	109,603	124,190	124,375	140,259
Net revenue	$233,135	$439,194	$505,739	$514,741
Cost of fund-raising	32%	22%	20%	21%
Return	213%	354%	407%	367%

Because the budget for solicitation activities is prepared as a "profit center," details about revenue to be received should be included with the budget to illustrate the relationship between required expenses and expected revenue. Submitting a combined revenue and expense budget is an opportunity to inform the board of directors and management who review this request about the performance of the fund development program. For many, this once-a-year exercise is the only period when prior performance and proposed activities are given serious attention. The summary budget should include projected results along with estimated costs so that the investment principle can be demonstrated, especially with figures reporting cost of fund-raising and return to be realized (see Exhibit 1.11).

The regular use of gift reports such as Exhibits 1.7, 1.8, and 1.9 during the operating year will continue to display the relationship between budgets expended and results achieved. In addition, many nonprofit organizations report their current financial activities alongside a summary of the same data from one year ago to monitor progress and focus attention on areas that appear to deviate from expectations. These results are valuable to share with volunteers and donors, who are quite interested in the outcomes of their solicitation efforts and how their gifts were used to meet the priorities of the organization.

2

Developing a Nine-Point Performance Index

Comparative analysis between nonprofit organizations, even those using the same fund-raising methods, is never fair. No two nonprofit organizations are identical in how they provide programs and services, including how they conduct and track costs for their fund-raising programs. Organizations do not solicit at the same time and in the same way any more than they reach the same donors and prospects, have the same volunteers and leaders, possess the same history with prior donors, operate with the same budget and staff configurations, and so on. Consequently, their results always will differ. What is similar and worth studying is how each solicitation activity performs measured against its own results from prior years. This comparison leads to an accurate understanding and appreciation of how existing solicitation activities are working to achieve their potential, what improvements can be made based on previous results and changing conditions, and what expectations can be made for higher levels of productivity and profitability with reliability.

Fund-raising practice does not have a uniform standard of measurement, although many solicitation methods use similar ingredients (lists, volunteers, events, requests by mail). A nine-point performance index can be used to evaluate the unique performance of each fund-raising method based on its results. Measuring each solicitation activity with the same index provides a uniform grid for comparative analysis. Each of these nine elements is, in itself, an indicator of performance success. Together they provide more than adequate detail to allow nonprofit organizations to interpret their results and estimate future income with reliability based on how well each solicitation method has proven its mix of ingredients for success. The nine elements of the performance index are presented in two sections. Group A provides the three data elements—number of participants, income received, and expenses—that are required to complete the six performance measurements in Group B.

GROUP A: BASIC INFORMATION FOR MEASUREMENTS

(1) *Participants*

Each solicitation method is designed to stimulate a number of responses. Decisions on how many prospects to ask to make a gift are tied to how many responses are likely to be received, which helps the solicitors determine whether the group(s) solicited were the best ones to ask. The number of participants provide evidence of the degree of acceptance of the appeal's message. Tracking the number of participants from each group solicited helps to decide whom to ask again. Because success depends on stimulating numerous replies, what rate of response is required for success? This answer will be different for each fund-raising method used and can range from 1 percent to 25 percent or higher.

(2) *Income Received*

In addition to stimulating responses, each solicitation also is expected to produce revenue. How much income depends on several factors. Most annual giving solicitations offer donors a range of gift sizes (e.g., $10, $25, $50, $100, Other: $_____). The objective is to tell those being asked for money how much is being requested, or what level of gifts are considered appropriate responses. The amount of income received is directly linked to these suggestions. Gifts above $100 can be requested when prospect research or other information suggests a pool of candidates capable of giving more than $100 is available. Results also can be influenced by the urgency and relevance of the appeal message (giving to the American Red Cross is greatest after a disaster), who does the asking, timing, follow-up, and more.

To avoid making faulty assumptions, you should not rely on the performance ratio of number of gifts to number of prospects solicited until after two or more solicitations of the same group are complete. The actual results establish the willingness and generosity of each likely donor *at that point in time*. For example, if the request is an invitation to attend a black-tie dinner dance priced at $100 a couple, the number of reservations received will be linked to the invitation list and ticket price, *plus* the quality of the location, its reputation for food and service, quality of the entertainment, prior experience from attending events produced by this organization, effective volunteers who sell tickets, and more.

(3) *Expense*

The budget or cost required to conduct a fund-raising activity should be estimated in advance. Budget dictates how much effort will be put into every solicitation. When reasonable expense levels are allocated for each solicitation activity, reasonable rates of return can be expected. However, the cost-to-return ratio will not be the same for each solicitation method used. This lack of uniformity is not due to any failure among the separate solicitation activities; rather, it is a function of the type of solicitation used and the external environment in which the organization must solicit, its image and reputation, prior fund-raising history, volunteer leadership, urgency and relevance of the project, prospect understanding of public benefits to result, and much more.

GROUP B: BASIC PERFORMANCE MEASUREMENTS

(4) *Percent Participation*

The number of replies received is a percentage of all who were invited to participate. Percent participation first indicates acceptance of the message. As an example, 1,156 replies from 80,575 prospects after two mailings is a 1.43 percent response rate, while one renewal letter to these same 1,156 donors the next year results in 602 new gifts and represents a 52 percent response rate.

Sample calculation:

	Acquisition Mailing	Renewal Mailing
Divide number of responses received by the number of solicitations made	$\frac{1,156}{80,575} = 1.43\%$	$\frac{602}{1,156} = 52\%$

This result may suggest all acquisitions mailings are a waste of time and money, but a 1.43 percent response rate is considered above average for a first-time donor acquisition effort. By comparison, the letter sent to all 1,156 donors a year later that produced a 52 percent response would be considered only average level of participation.

(5) *Average Gift Size*

How much each donor contributes is a valuable indicator of financial success. Gift size is important to donors; they give what they can afford at the time. Size is also an indicator of whether the solicitation method, prospect list, and amount requested were well matched, as well as how worthwhile donors believed the project to be, either for themselves or for others in the community. In the preceding direct mail example, the 1.43 percent response rate is considered successful. But, if the average gift was $5, the solicitation would have failed to raise enough money to pay for the cost of mailing the request. Similarly, if prior donors who made an average gift of $100 the prior year were to give only $52 this year, this mailing also would fail by losing half the donors and half the money raised previously.

Sample calculation:

	Acquisition Mailing	Renewal Mailing
Divide total contributions received by number of donors	$\frac{\$5,758}{1,156} = \$5.00$	$\frac{\$31,304}{602} = \$52$

(6) *Net Income*

Net income is sometimes neglected in reports of fund-raising success because focusing attention on gross revenue makes results look as successful as possible. True success is net income the nonprofit organization can use for its programs and services *after* deducting the costs of solicitation.

Sample calculation:

	Acquisition Mailing	Renewal Mailing
Subtract total contributions received from full solicitation costs	$\frac{\$35,758}{\$32,641} = \$3,117$	$\frac{\$31,304}{\$1,625} = \$29,679$

Focus on net income reveals profitability as well as the efficiency of the prospect list chosen and solicitation method used. Renewal mailings are more profitable because those who are asked are already donors; acquisition mailings have to be sent to a large number of nondonors because, at the 1 percent normal response rate, not many donors will be acquired unless the mailing goes to thousands of prospects. Also, renewal solicitations with prior donors should be expected to cost less because a lot fewer people have to be asked. It should become a matter of concern to the organization when renewal percent participation falls below 50 percent and when average gift size drops.

(7) *Average Cost per Gift*

How much does each gift cost to solicit? What is the reasonable guideline for expense? Average cost per gift helps to confirm the relationship between net income and cost to produce it. Using mail program results again, an average gift of $30.93 was realized at a cost of $28.24 per gift from acquisition, while renewal gifts were produced at an average cost per gift of $2.69 to realize $52.

Sample calculation:

	Acquisition Mailing	Renewal Mailing
Total fund-raising costs divided by number of donors	$\dfrac{\$32,641}{1,156} = \$28.24$	$\dfrac{\$1,625}{602} = \$2.69$

When compared together, 1,156 new donors were realized first at a much higher cost per donor and, after expenses, net profits of only $3,117 were available compared with renewal's net return of $29,679. All four measurable criteria (number of donors, average gift size, net income, and average cost per gift) are quite revealing in evaluating whether this mail solicitation effort was successful. Combining acquisition with renewal results each year is the final program performance measurement for the overall direct mail program.

(8) *Cost of Fund-Raising*

The cost-effectiveness of each fund-raising method is a bottom-line measurement of overall profitability and productivity. Acquiring new donors is more expensive than renewing prior donors, but new donors must be found in order to have candidates to renew later. In addition, not all donors renew each time they are asked, further reducing the pool of best prospects. If regular investments are not made in acquisition, the donor pool will shrink more rapidly and net proceeds will drop quickly.

For a comparison, what is the reasonable cost that a for-profit business will spend to acquire a new customer? Depending on the product for sale and other factors (marketplace, competition, advertising and promotion, etc.), the answer is often as much as $4 to $5 to raise $1, because the executive knows that profits are the result of customers buying their product many times again.

In the nonprofit world, the guideline for reasonable cost to acquire new donors by mail is $1.25 to $1.50 for each $1 raised. Is this not more efficient than the for-profit world? Board members and management staff who challenge these expense levels need to be encouraged to compare the investment standard in the business world with the performance of the nonprofit world when using the same method (acquiring customers by mail). Also, it is worth emphasizing the equal expectation of higher profits from investing time and attention to building relationships with prior donors and asking them to give again and again in the future.

Sample calculation:

	Acquisition Mailing	Renewal Mailing
Fund-raising expenses divided by total contributions received;	$\frac{\$32,641}{\$35,758} = 0.9128$	$\frac{\$1,625}{\$31,304} = 0.5191$
multiply by 100 for a percentage	$\times 100 \quad = 91.28\%$	$\times 100 \quad = 5.191\%$
(Expressed as cost to raise one dollar)	($0.91)	($0.052)

(9) Return

Budget dollars spent in solicitation activity always should be able to demonstrate success in positive terms. Results ought to be expressed as the direct relationship between the investment made and its result (another term would be "profit," not necessarily a comfortable word for nonprofit executives). Actual performance will vary from year to year among solicitation methods, but each should be able to improve on previous results and, over time, provide reliable levels of efficiency and profitability.

The larger the number of active donors available for renewal, the greater the net return they will provide. Continued success for annual giving depends not only on the choice of solicitation method but also on whether community needs are perceived as urgent and relevant as well as whether energetic, well-trained volunteers use efficient and well managed fund-raising solicitation methods.

To return to the direct mail examples, even a "cold call," first-time acquisition effort, as previously shown, produced a 1.43 percent response rate and an average gift of $30.93. This performance was achieved at an average cost per gift of $28.24 to produce a net "profit" of $3,117. The cost to raise $1 was $0.91 and this fund-raising program achieved a 9.55 percent rate of return within two to three months. By comparison, renewal data achieved a remarkable return rate of 1,826 percent; where can you achieve this level of performance in the for-profit world?

Sample calculation:

	Acquisition Mailing	Renewal Mailing
Net income received divided by fund-raising expenses,	$\dfrac{\$3,117}{\$32,641} = 0.095$	$\dfrac{\$29,679}{\$1,625} = 18.26$
and multiplied by 100	$\times\,100 \quad = 9.55\%$	$\times\,100 \quad = 1,826\%$

Exhibit 2.1

Nine-Point Performance Index

Basic Data

1. Participants = Number of donors responding with gifts
2. Income = Gross contributions
3. Expense = Fund-raising costs

Performance Measurements

4. Percent Participation = Divide participants by total solicitations made
5. Average Gift Size = Divide income received by participants
6. Net Income = Subtract expenses from income received
7. Average Cost per Gift = Divide expenses by participants
8. Cost of Fund-Raising = Divide expenses by income received; multiply by 100 for percentage
9. Return = Divide net income by expenses; multiply by 100 for percentage

Annual Giving Solicitation Programs

Assessing fund-raising performance begins with an evaluation of annual giving programs. Annual giving is the foundation of every fund development program. Nonprofit organizations depend on this base of continuing and new contributors for some portion of their annual operating revenue, from limited support to significant support of overall operations. Understanding all the factors that lead to successful fund-raising permits better decisions on where to invest budget dollars to increase results in both dollars and numbers of reliable (and increasingly generous) donors.

Each chapter in Part 2 offers consistent measurement criteria for the various fund-raising methods available, presenting each in the following order:

1. *Purposes* The essential features and design objectives of each fund-raising activity will be defined, along with a description of its role within the overall fund development program.

2. *Preparation* The steps required to plan each solicitation activity will be provided, including a review of prior performance, anticipated results, documents and volunteers needed, timetable, and more.

3. *Budget* A review of anticipated fund-raising expense areas, including direct, indirect, and overhead cost areas based on prior experiences, goals set, and estimated results, will be detailed.

4. *Execution* The steps involved in completing the solicitation activity from start to finish, including interim progress reports, gift processing, and donor recognition opportunities, will be outlined.

5. *Analysis* Several measurement tools will be provided to assess the effectiveness and efficiency of each solicitation activity and to demonstrate its productivity and profitability and the interdependence of the several methods and techniques used.

6. *Action Plans* The objective of analysis is to understand the results of actions taken, identify problems along with improvements, and take steps to continue to invest in solicitation activities with greater assurance of reliable results in the future. How to develop and update action plans will be provided.

7. *Related Benefits* Methods for assessing other benefits than fund-raising results will be suggested. Examples relating to marketing the public benefit programs and services offered by the organization, media relations, image building, community relations, major gift cultivation, public education, donor relations, leadership development, and more, are added by-products of an annual giving solicitation program.

In addition, assessment of results for each method will be measured with a nine-point performance index. The intent of this index is to establish a uniform tool to be applied throughout this workbook for consistent performance measurement. The nine-point performance index will illustrate efficiency and effectiveness and will be used to explain the differences between each solicitation method presented in this workbook. The nine-point index also is useful for interpretation by the fund-raising manager for decisions on next steps to take.

Each method of solicitation possesses separate performance characteristics. It is essential to understand the merits and limitations of each, their relationship to one another, and their individual levels of effectiveness and efficiency.

Further, nonprofit organizations are not the same in how they conduct fund-raising, and fund-raising activities do not perform the same for every organization. The nine-point performance index will apply a uniform method to measure each solicitation program for its ability to produce results with effectiveness and efficiency as well as to understand their separate strengths and weaknesses, potential, and capacity to produce the desired results.

3

Direct Mail: Acquisition and Renewal

Nearly every nonprofit organization uses the mail for solicitation purposes as well as for a variety of routine communications with donors, volunteers, and others in their constituency. Direct mail solicitation is not the most expensive or least efficient form of fund-raising today. (Benefit events hold that distinction.) Nonprofit organizations spend their money on volume mailings because they are beneficial for multiple purposes, not for raising money alone. Direct mail solicitation can be successful as well as profitable, but a certain expertise is required to achieve some level of successful performance.

To appreciate the results that direct mail solicitation can provide, study each mailing's replies and interpret them to your board members, management, and volunteers. In their minds, lots of money is invested here and the returns (at 1 percent with a $20 average gift) do not look like a success. However, they will see the value of direct mail solicitation if you analyze the combined results of acquisition, renewal, and upgrading. It is important to analyze these results together because profits occur in combination after two to three years of continued investment. Once well established, direct mail solicitation will remain one of the most effective means to acquire the largest number of first-time donors and to retain and expand their support.

Direct mail solicitation requires a series of solicitations, beginning with acquisition of new, first-time respondents from qualified prospect and suspect mail lists, and including follow-up mailings for renewal and upgrading of previous donors' gifts. Success ought to be measured by several criteria in addition to the amount of money raised. To manage direct mail solicitation successfully requires a series of solicitations, beginning with acquisition of new, first-time respondents and including follow-up mailings for renewal and upgrading of previous donors' gifts. The goal is not only to raise money through solicitations but also to find people who will share their disposable cash with others and who will continue to support the cause or organization for several years. This latter objective is called constituency building. Acquisition and renewal together compose a comprehensive direct mail solicitation program. The nonprofit organization that continues to invest in carefully designed mail communications can expect profitable results from a large number of supportive friends and donors within three years of launching a direct mail program. They will also be able to write often to these friends and donors without their letters being thrown away unopened.

Purposes

The purposes of direct mail fund-raising are to convert prospects and suspects into new donors, stimulate their first gifts, renew and upgrade their gift levels over time, increase the number of gifts they make each year, and encourage them to become personally involved in the other fund-raising activities and programs offered by the nonprofit organization. To acquire a first gift is to begin a relationship between donor and organization. The renewal process maintains and expand the relationship for mutual benefit, and mail communication is the most effective method of maintaining direct communication with a great many donors.

There is much more to mail solicitation than just writing letters and shipping them to thousands of people. What is said to prior donors must be different from what is said to people who have yet to join the cause and make their first gift, although the same vehicle, a letter package, still delivers the message. People who have made gifts expect the organization to remember who they are, how much they gave last time, what project they supported, and what benefits and privileges they were offered. The organization that makes the effort to customize or, better yet, personalize its continuing communications with donors will be rewarded with a better response. Separate your prospects from your donors and use different letter texts designed to address each type of reader. The balance of contents in the envelope may contain the same support materials (brochure, reply envelope, etc.). Prospects first must be selected from everyone who can be asked to give. The groups chosen are crucial to success.

Selecting the invitation list is *the* most important decision in direct mail solicitation. Monitor each group for their response to each invitation, using percent participation and average gift size to evaluate their answers as well as to estimate their future potential from additional mailings. The purpose of these letters is to stimulate a first gift so that you can begin to build a relationship between new donors and the organization. Progress in the relationship will be measured easily by their continued replies.

Preparation

Every mail solicitation program should begin with testing. A reasonable test will require a sample mailing to 5,000 people from each list you intend to use and is conducted to learn how they are likely to respond. Testing helps to refine the list into segments, usually ZIP code or even smaller zones, that appear to be most responsive. Testing also extends to the message, package contents, options on the response form, even the reply envelope, all designed to learn what combinations will work to get the best results. All these choices are cost factors, too. To prevent needless errors and to increase net results, observe the seven rule of testing:[1]

1. All tests should have as their goal a measurable increased percentage of return and/or average gift.
2. To be accurate, test only one thing at a time. (This rule excludes lists, which you are *always* testing.)
3. Mail test packages within the same week.
4. Mail test packages at the same postal rate, unless it is postage you are testing.
5. Mail test packages to the same lists and split your list for testing on an nth (or random sample) select.
6. Any test conducted using fewer than five lists of 2,500 names each is rarely valid. Ten lists of 5,000 names each is preferable.
7. After test results are in, test the same thing once again.

Measure test results against three criteria: (a) a minimum response rate of 1 percent (with at least 25 responses from each list tested), (b) an average gift size of $20 or more, and (c) a direct cost of $1.25 to $1.50 per dollar raised. Add measurement of the following criteria to help decide how to proceed with a full mailing to any list that passes these tests:

1. How many replies were received from each mail list tested?
2. What percentage of these respondents sent money?
3. How many mail pieces were returned as undeliverable (verifies the accuracy of each list)?
4. How many people wrote back with a message (with or without money) and what were their comments?
5. How many people asked that *no* further mail be sent?
6. What was the amount of gross revenue received?
7. What were the total direct costs for the test mailing?
8. What were the total indirect and overhead costs?
9. What was the true net revenue produced?

What testing proves is which lists and package combinations can be expected to respond best with the largest number of donors who will give the most money. Testing also reveals an estimate of the cost-benefit ratio required to achieve a minimum 1 percent rate of return or better with an average gift of $20 or more, the desired performance level to justify this budget investment. Testing can be conducted at any time of year to learn when those written may prefer to reply more often. October, November, and December are considered the best months for solicitation but nearly everyone is active at that time. The cost of testing 5,000 names is minimal compared with wasting the mail budget on large lists that will not reply.

Testing provides the data you need to make an informed decision based on actual facts and demonstrated results. Tests can compare two separate appeal letters to learn which will spark the highest number of replies. If one package achieves a higher average gift but from fewer donors, you can decide whether your primary goal is to increase the number of donors or raise the largest amount of money. In general, you should use the package that stimulated the largest number of respondents for acquisition and the one that brought in the larger gifts for renewal requests. More revenue will flow from having more donors to renew and upgrade each year. However, cash needs of your organization may dictate concentration only on those who will give more money in the short term.

Budget

The budget must include adequate dollars for renewal mailings not only because these results are more profitable but also because it is a continuing investment designed to encourage and expand each donor's relationship with the nonprofit organization. Donors represent the primary source of reliable income from previously invested budget dollars. The rest of the mail budget should be invested in finding new donors to replenish those who move away or lose interest. Typical expenses for a direct mail acquisition are shown in Exhibit 3.1.

How much money should be spent on direct mail solicitation? That answer is found in the context of a mature fund development program (three years or more of continuous operation) that uses acquisition and renewal solicitations only as one of several annual giving methods. Mail costs should not exceed 15 to 20 percent of the annual giving budget after three years. For the organization that is just starting a fund-raising program and has no other annual giving methods in operation, the budget for acquisition is where friend-raising and solicitation begins. In my

Exhibit 3.1

Sample Budget Worksheet for Direct Mail Letter Contents

Cost Elements	Cost per Unit
Lists	$0.035
Outer envelope	0.080
Reply envelope	0.050
Insert	0.080
Letter/Response form	0.060
Data processing	0.080
Mail preparation	0.020
Postage	0.090
Total	$0.495 per unit

experience, it will take a minimum of three years for the direct mail program (acquisition, renewal, and upgrading working together) to become efficient and effective and to provide reliable amounts of net proceeds. Three years allows for successive acquisition mailings followed by renewal mailings of all new donors. After three years, donor renewals should be performing at a cost between $0.20 to $0.30 per $1.00 raised, while acquisition can cost as much as $1.25 to $1.50 per $1.00 raised, yielding a net profit in combination.

Execution

A sequence of mailings should be planned over several months so that a minimum of two to three mail solicitations will be sent to each list after testing to realize the gift potential each list may possess. Each full mailing is yet another test of each list chosen as well as the appeal message, package, timing, and more. Monitor all these results continuously to maximize available budget dollars and adjust accordingly.

For example, for a first-time donor acquisition mailing, monitor the response rate and average gift size—by donor age, if known—and trim the list of nonrespondents before the next mailing. My experience in soliciting prior hospital patients is that 45- to 55-year-old prospects reply less often and with less money than those above 55 years; those below 45 years are the least responsive to mail solicitation of any age group tested. Those 55 to 65 reply with the most money; more people above 65 will reply more often but with lower average gifts.

When the response from any segment of a list or group is less than one-half of 1 percent, stop mailing to that segment. Similarly, when the average gift falls below $20, stop mailing to that list. Enough money must come back from the mail program to cover expenses. Keep mailing to those parts of the list where performance exceeds these minimums until they, too, fall below these performance levels. Then move on and begin acquisition mailings to newly tested lists.

Prior donors perform differently. They require the use of separate guidelines based on:

1. The length of time they have been a donor.
2. Their prior giving levels (numbers of gifts and amounts).
3. The extent of their personal involvement in other organization activities.

Expectations are that at least half (50%) the donor file should renew at the same gift level, while 12 to 15 percent will increase their annual gift (upgrade) if asked to do so. Upgrade requests are the best way to retain prior gift levels, an important fact that recommends including upgrading as a regular part of *all* renewal mailings. Keep mailing to the nonresponding prior donor list with regularity but not endlessly. Their lack of response and smaller gifts will tell you when they have had enough.

Finally, the chief benefit of direct mail solicitation is its immediate response. Some replies will arrive within days; peak response is within 14 to 21 days. Be prepared with thank-you letters matched to gift size. Be ready also to evaluate the replies quickly so that you can adjust the lists used, revise the message, add or delete inserts, or make other adjustments for the next mailing. Two or more mailings to the same list are recommended so long as the replies are within guidelines and the time between mailings is not more than eight weeks.

Analysis

You should analyze the combined results of acquisition, renewal, and upgrading because profits occur in combination after two to three years. What is most important about the results of a mail program is what the organization does with its newfound friends and donors. The keys to efficiency and profitability are in the follow-up, not the acquisition. Donor relations is an active program to be managed to use mail communications as the means to stimulate personal interaction between donors and nonprofit organizations. To realize the maximum potential from a mail solicitation program, time and attention also must be given to cultivating the donors acquired by mail to higher levels of involvement with the organization.

Summary Interpretation

Exhibits 3.2 and 3.3 apply the nine-point performance index to a fictitious, two-year old direct mail program. Testing was done on eight lists for a total of 30,000 names before the full "roll-out" mailing was sent to 300,000 prospects on four of the eight lists, with the following results:

(1) Testing demonstrated a 1.43 percent response rate, with average gifts of $30.93 at a cost of fund-raising of 91 percent. These four lists with their letter text and contents proved the potential for better than average results and a full mailing to these lists was justified. Test results from the other four lists were below 1 percent in responses with average gifts below $20 and costs approaching $2 to raise $1 or more. With limited budget for mailings, choose only the best performing lists.

(2) The full mailing achieved a 0.92 percent response rate and average gift of $32 for a net profit of $17,911 after expenses of $99,000. The cost of fund-raising was 85 percent, suggesting renewal mailings also should produce net profits. While this level of performance is higher than normal, certain segments of the mail lists did not perform as well as others and will need further analysis after the next mailing.

(3) The first renewal mailing to the original donors achieved a 60.77 percent response rate. The cost to solicit 4,809 donors was modest because the list was small. The average gift increased slightly to $33.99, which helped the average cost per gift ($2.00) and cost of fund-raising (6%). These donors were quite generous, and careful attention must be given to them from this point forward to realize their long-term potential to benefit this organization with their support.

(4) The combined results illustrate a 1.20 percent rate of return from all three mailings with average gift of $32.31 (see Exhibit 3.3). Net proceeds were $50,265, certainly a solid beginning for a direct mail solicitation that is part of an annual giving program. The cost to produce these results was $133,468, not a small sum and possibly more than

Exhibit 3.2

Nine-Point Performance Index Analysis of Direct Mail

	Testing		Full Mailing		Renewal		Totals
Participation	1,156	+	3,653	+	914	=	5,723
Income	$35,758	+	$116,911	+	$31,064	=	$183,733
Expense	$32,641	+	$99,000	+	$1,827	=	$133,468
Percent participation	1.43%	+	0.92%	+	60.77%	=	1.20%
Average gift size	$30.93	+	$32.00	+	$33.99	=	$32.31
Net income	$3,117	+	$17,911	+	$29,237	=	$50,265
Average cost per gift	$28.24	+	$27.10	+	$2.00	=	$23.32
Cost of fund-raising	91%	+	85%	+	6%	=	73%
Return	10%	+	18%	+	1600%	=	39%

Exhibit 3.3

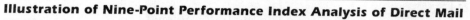

Illustration of Nine-Point Performance Index Analysis of Direct Mail

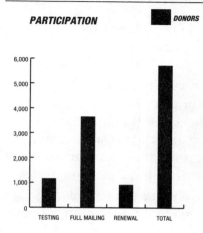

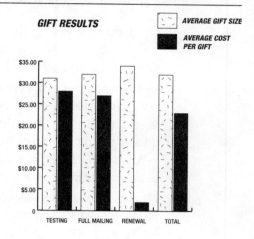

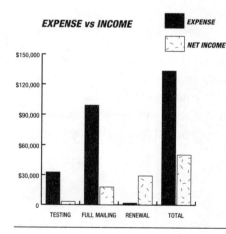

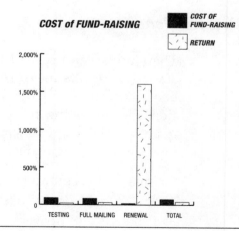

most new nonprofit organizations could afford to spend. The cost of fund-raising was 73 percent with a 39 percent return within two years, certainly profitable enough.

This example illustrates that direct mail solicitation, while it can be effective and profitable, is not the most efficient form of fund-raising available and should not be used exclusive of all others.

Action Plans

The analysis suggests the following actions:

1. Continued mailing to these four prospect lists will yield positive results, but some segments can be expected to perform under expectations and should be dropped.
2. Use some budget money each year to begin testing new lists. Compare their results against prior test performance to decide if added investments are worthwhile. Lists that perform well should be added to the next full mailing and their results compared with current lists again. Once a mail program begins, its own performance sets the guidelines for measuring all the other mailings.
3. Donor renewal was so positive that a donor club program with gift levels above $32 should be considered next, offering options of $50, $100, and $250, to increase net revenue and to begin to identify major gift prospects. The donor club package also should be offered in future acquisition mailings as added potential exists for finding other major gift candidates in these lists.

Related Benefits

There are several related benefits from mail communications. These statistical results measure only replies to direct solicitation. Related benefits, such as enhancing the image and reputation of an organization and educating the public about available services, are hard to quantify. Mail communications can influence perceptions about one or more of the following factors:

1. Image and reputation.
2. Strengths and weaknesses.
3. Products and price.
4. Market share.
5. Competition.

Each mailing is but one message sent and received. A planned sequence of mailings has a much greater ability to penetrate the market and influence the public's knowledge and awareness of the organization, its programs and services, and its sincere invitation by mail for their active participation.[2]

4

Membership Organizations

Direct mail is a successful solicitation technique for finding new donors and, as a result of their continued gifts, building their relationships with your organization. One of the best ways to preserve and expand this relationship is through a membership program. Membership adds a link between donors and organizations, a sense of belonging to a group as opposed to acting alone. Membership offers access to others with compatible interests plus the opportunity to expand on the affiliation through active participation in the organization itself. Direct mail donors are one source of member candidates; others include current and past members, donors to other programs, volunteers, and other sources.

A variety of civic, social, and service clubs exist as membership groups in the United States and throughout the world. Their goal is to bring people of like interests together to address a problem, advocate a cause, offer a service, provide a forum for common purposes, or build friendships and business contacts. Some formal structure is required, and most membership organizations operate with bylaws or articles of association to govern their activities; members are often directly involved in the association's management as officers, members of the board of directors, and committee positions. These associations also require annual dues to provide the revenue needed for operations and member services.

A membership organization also opens several fund-raising opportunities to a nonprofit organization because it strengthens the relationship between member/donor and organization based on a shared commitment to common goals. A membership organization that is officially recognized and sanctioned by a parent nonprofit organization is allowed to use its name and tax-exempt status. A common example is the alumni association of a college or university. In exchange for its relationship with the college, the alumni association pledges its support to the mission and purposes of the college. Many membership organizations also adopt one or two operating areas within the parent's programs and services as a focus for financial support. Membership organizations, through their activities, provide the parent organization with visibility and outreach into the community. They also offer a variety of active volunteer roles for members to contribute to the parent organization. Different membership levels combine gift amounts with extra benefits and privileges available for larger contributions. These rewards are designed to retain the friendship and annual gift support of as many members as possible.

Purposes

A nonprofit organization should manage each of its membership organizations with a written mission, purposes, goals, and objectives, along with a plan for its annual operations. Bylaws or articles of association should define the several classes and levels of membership, as well as election proceedings for officers and their duties, annual meeting requirements, financial operations, and the like. If sponsored by a parent nonprofit organization, the membership organization can use the incorporation standing and tax-exempt status of its parent and need not seek its own to enjoy these same privileges. One added benefit for individual members is that annual dues are deductible contributions. Should any of what the Internal Revenue Service calls material benefits accrue to individual members in exchange for their annual membership dues, the value of these goods and services must be itemized by the nonprofit organization and the nondeductible amount reported to the donors-members for use in preparing annual income tax returns. This calculation can be complicated in assessing whether a subscription to the alumni magazine is a member benefit, or not. Would the college have sent it to them anyway because they want to stay in touch with all alumni? If so, the exchange of a dues payment is not a subscription and the value of the magazine is not reported to the donor-member as a nondeductible amount.

The purposes of a membership organization include:

1. Recruitment of new members and their dues.
2. Renewal of current members to preserve full standing.
3. Offering higher dues or gift levels linked to expanded benefits and privileges (upgrading).
4. Voluntary service with orientation and training.
5. Leadership identification and training.
6. Defined linkages with a specific area or areas of the organization as supplemental giving opportunities.
7. Communications avenues and community relations outreach.
8. Access to interested friends and supporters who can act as advocates.

To achieve all the elements of this considerable list, your organization must provide a qualified staff and adequate budget support. To do less is to limit the support members can provide.

Preparation

Starting a membership organization within the overall fund development program of a nonprofit organization requires advance market analysis to:

- Learn what competition exists.
- Assess public opinion on the worth of such a proposal.
- Measure the effort required to succeed with an adequate number of members.
- Estimate their potential for annual dues support.

Once in operation, a membership program will forever require the conduct of an annual acquisition, renewal, and upgrading campaign.

You should identify the benefits and privileges your organization will offer to members in exchange for their annual dues payment. Considerable creativity is needed to fit these benefits to the mission of the organization. Four examples of such benefit packages are:

1. *Informational benefits,* such as newsletters.
2. *Token benefits,* such as thank-you letters, membership cards, and membership directories.

3. *Prestige benefits*, which attach privileges to higher membership levels that encourage generosity and offer extras not available to other members.

4. *Throwaway benefits*, which might include coupons, affinity credit cards, car rental discounts, group insurance, or travel tour packages.

In addition, volunteer tasks need to be defined, and a volunteer training program should be developed. Both management by professional staff and an adequate budget are essential to the success of any member-volunteer program.

Budget

The costs of operating a membership program can be separated into two parts to include:

1. Direct costs for annual membership recruitment and renewal programs (similar to costs identified for direct mail in Chapter 3, Exhibit 3.1) plus printing and postage for general communications, membership cards, a printed directory of members, invitations to all activities, benefits, and special events, and the like.

2. Membership services, including support for board and committee meetings; newsletters and annual reports; member benefits; conferences and workshops; heat, light, and maintenance; space and equipment; and other routine operating costs typical of a nonprofit organization, its members, and their association.

Membership dues are the chief source of annual revenue; other areas of income include net proceeds from conferences and workshops, merchandise and publications sales, sale of membership lists, and the like. Therefore, member dues levels must be set high enough to cover annual operating costs. And, because annual expenses can be expected to rise over time, dues increases (always unpopular) may be required unless the original levels are set high enough to anticipate future increases and expenses are well managed.

It is more expensive to acquire new members than to renew current members. Greater revenues come from retaining as many current members as possible. Budget dollars invested in services to current members are quickly repaid from high renewal and upgrading results each year. Offering a variety of member levels with expanded benefits and privileges helps to increase net revenue from an established pool of satisfied donors and enlarges the potential commitment from these more generous members for years to come.

Execution

Memberships are annual gifts that must be recruited and renewed each year. Success in the annual membership drive depends on the members acting as recruiters, inviting their family, friends, neighbors, business contacts, and social associates into membership. One strategy is to install an obligation for each member to recruit at least one new member each year. This policy will enhance member renewal as well as help recruitment efforts. Some help is going to be needed with both. A common example is to stage an attractive event to be used as a kickoff party to launch the membership campaign. Another is a victory celebration to conclude the drive, with free admission limited to new members and their sponsors. The form and style of this annual campaign must be reinvented each year. The most successful tactic is to personalize the invitation wherever possible, as follows:

Previous Annual Gift	Improved Request
1. Form letter/Dues bill	1. Personal letter
2. Personal letter	2. Personal letter plus phone call
3. Personal letter plus phone call	3. Phone call to ask for an appointment
4. Appointment	4. Personal tour

Analysis

Performance characteristics to be reviewed after each membership campaign might include answers to the following questions:

1. How many prior members renewed? What percentage is that?
2. What was the average membership gift amount?
3. How many members increased or upgraded to a higher membership level?
4. How many new members were recruited?

5. How many new members were added to each membership level?
6. What was the new members' average gift amount?
7. How many prior members failed to renew?
8. What was the amount of their prior annual dues?
9. What were the total costs of the membership drive and the cost of fund-raising comparison with dues revenue received?
10. What changes are needed for the next membership drive?

Summary Interpretation

Exhibits 4.1 and 4.2 illustrate the nine-point performance index for a combined membership recruitment, renewal, and upgrading campaign, with the following results:

(1) New member recruitment realized 125 new members from invitations to 3,000 prospects, a solid 4.17 percent response rate, with an average gift of $103 in reply to $100 as the first level of active membership. Net income was $4,400, showing a cost of fund-raising of 66 percent and a return of 52 percent. The 4.17 percent response rate from the 3,000 candidate list is excellent and should possess additional potential; nonrespondents should soon be invited again to join.

(2) Renewal membership was directed at 650 prior members. The invitation asked them to rejoin and repeat last year's gift, plus to consider

Exhibit 4.1

Nine-Point Performance Index Analysis of a Membership Campaign

	New		Renewal		Upgrading		Totals
Participation	125	+	525	+	68	=	718
Income	$12,900	+	$58,500	+	$20,000	=	$91,400
Expense	$8,500	+	$3,280	+	-n/a-	=	$11,780
Percent participation	4.17%	+	80.77%	+	10.46%	=	16.2%
Average gift size	$103	+	$111	+	$294	=	$127
Net income	$4,400	+	$55,220	+	$20,000	=	$79,620
Average cost per gift	$68.00	+	$6.25	+	-n/a-	=	$16.41
Cost of fund-raising	66%	+	6%	+	-n/a-	=	13%
Return	52%	+	1684%	+	-n/a-	=	676%

Exhibit 4.2

Illustration of Nine-Point Performance Index Analysis of Membership Campaign

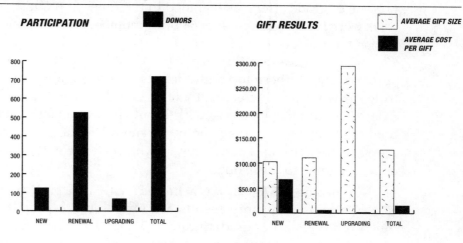

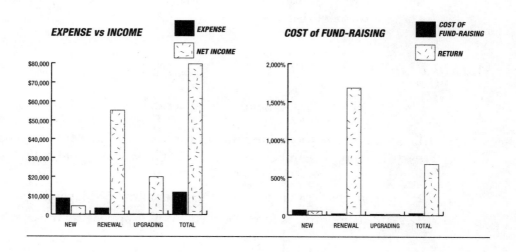

an upgrade to the $250 or more membership level. A total of 525 prior members renewed (80.77%) with average gifts of $111 at an average cost of $6.25 per gift. Net income was $55,220, at a cost of fund-raising of 6 percent and a return of 1,683 percent. This strong performance affirms that other activities staged during the year to maintain members' interest and enthusiasm paid off handsomely. The remaining 125 prior members who did not renew or upgrade at this time are certainly worth asking again and soon.

(3) The upgrade offer was included in the renewal request, so no extra costs were incurred. A total of 68 prior members (10.46%) agreed to increase their gifts—60 at $250, 6 at $500, and 2 at $1,000—for a total of $20,000 and an average gift size of $294. Follow-up should include conversations with these top eight donors to thank them personally and to learn why they increased their gifts at this time. Using feedback from their comments, along with input from a dozen or more of the donors at $250, strengthen the next renewal request by stressing the message, benefits, and privileges, or whatever else in the original offer appealed most to these donors.

(4) Net income of $79,620 was achieved, with an overall average gift of $127. These membership results are impressive, especially the combined renewal and upgrading rate of 91 percent. The bottom-line cost for the entire solicitation was 13 percent, more than adequate proof of the efficiency and effectiveness of this membership program. Enough potential exists in all three areas (acquisition, renewal, and upgrading) to justify committing more budget dollars to support this program in the next fiscal year.

Action Plans

The analysis suggests the following actions:

1. Schedule a second campaign in three to four months to recruit additional new members out of the 3,000 prospect pool, which can be expected to produce good results.

2. Plan another appeal letter to those remaining 57 lapsed donors, too.

3. Wait 10 months before the next annual appeal to those who just renewed.

4. Consider asking current members to be responsible for identifying and recruiting 5 to 10 prospective members, to increase future acquisition results.

5. Ask selected current members about the value of current benefits and privileges, to verify they are well received. Be willing to adjust membership offerings to keep them interesting and fresh when

appealing to members to renew and to prospects to join. Acquiring benefits and privileges is not the objective in membership; gift support to the organization and its mission remain paramount. But attractive, useful, and memorable benefits can and will catch people's attention and encourage them to act favorably.

Related Benefits

A major opportunity is available to ask current members to become active solicitors in support of the membership program. This is their opportunity for personal involvement and participation. Appoint a membership committee to work on each of the three areas—new member recruitment, renewal, and upgrading. This committee can work with staff to prepare the next membership drive, collect new prospect lists, identify those benefits and privileges to highlight in the appeal, and prepare the kickoff and victory celebration activities. Offer a one-hour orientation and training program on personal and telephone solicitation techniques to prepare committee members to talk with prospects and current members about the values of membership and the public benefits their dollars provide to others in the community. After a few positive experiences, committee members will be more comfortable in making their calls, more confident that personal contact produces better results for their organization, and more likely to continue to renew and upgrade their own membership.

5

Donor Clubs

Donor clubs should be one of the most cost-effective and profitable of annual giving activities within the overall fund development program. Donor clubs offer a variety of opportunities for annual contributors to expand their giving to their favorite nonprofit organizations. They also offer nonprofit organizations a variety of opportunities to convey honest gratitude for higher contribution levels. Donor clubs usually ask for larger gifts than might be acceptable as annual dues in a membership organization.

Donor clubs help to identify prospective major gift donors because of the size and frequency of their gifts. Friend-raising and relationship-building are the vital underpinnings of a donor's continuing association with nonprofit organizations. The organization that takes the time and makes the effort to address personal needs will benefit the greatest from its investment in each donor. A donor club program allows an organization to formalize this effort and address the personal needs of several donors by providing a thoughtful program of extra benefits and privileges and by arranging for these special patrons to associate with one another.

Several features in a donor club program lend themselves to performance evaluation. Exhibit 5.1 provides a measurement tool for the board of directors, development committee, and others to assess the progress of each donor club in member satisfaction and value to the sponsoring organization.

Purposes

A major purpose for all donor clubs is the opportunity for nonprofit organizations to display their appreciation for their patrons and

Exhibit 5.1

Areas for Program Assessment of Donor Clubs

		low		SCORE		high
1.	Comparison with prior year results	1	2	3	4	5
2.	Growth in donor universe	1	2	3	4	5
3.	Penetration of new markets	1	2	3	4	5
4.	Quality of renewal effort	1	2	3	4	5
5.	Quality of upgrading effort	1	2	3	4	5
6.	Consistent application of benefits and privileges	1	2	3	4	5
7.	Efforts at personalization	1	2	3	4	5
8.	Identification of major gift prospects	1	2	3	4	5
9.	Identification of planned gift prospects	1	2	3	4	5
10.	Leadership development opportunities	1	2	3	4	5
11.	Regular reports and analysis of results	1	2	3	4	5
12.	Forecasting future income and program performance	1	2	3	4	5

Median Score _____

benefactors and to acknowledge their exceptional generosity in a public way. A wise organization keeps track of cumulative giving totals for each donor. When all gifts are tabulated on a historical basis, they can be linked to a permanent recognition program to honor each donor's total giving achievement. A small organization may prefer to honor all its donors for the size of their annual gifts only, reserving the concept of cumulative recognition plans for the future when the volume of donors and their gift size will be appropriate.

Because donor clubs emphasize the size of annual gifts, they provide nonprofit organizations with above-average gift income at low solicitation costs. They usually do not promote active volunteer roles and responsibilities as duties required of club members; in fact, they may stress the option of noninvolvement as an attractive feature for giving to a donor club. One area where members are asked to assist is in recruiting their friends and neighbors to join them with their own gifts.

Donor clubs represent excellent "farm teams" for their parent nonprofit organization when they may be seeking potential big donors and committed volunteers. The club's long-term payoff is likely to come when a special project or major capital campaign calls for a volume of qualified major gift prospects whose current level of support reflects an established and sincere commitment to the organization's programs and services.

Preparation

Careful thought must be given to the design of each donor club. You can start by answering the following questions:

1. How many clubs should a nonprofit organization offer?
2. What gift levels are appropriate to each constituency?
3. How are the best titles for gift levels chosen for each club?
4. Should all clubs offer similar gift levels and privileges?
5. How many benefits and privileges should be offered?
6. How much money can they provide each year?
7. What level of annual budget will they require?
8. Will each club offer an opportunity for committees and advisory councils to foster volunteerism and leadership development?
9. How will each donor club and its list of benefits fit within the organization's overall donor relations and recognition program?

Each of these questions is not easily answered. The answers should come from consideration of several factors, which also can serve as a checklist for annual performance evaluation:

- Potential for donor interest and continued participation.
- Gift levels that stretch annual giving but remain attainable for annual gift purposes.
- Club name that provides a separate, meaningful, and prestigious identity.
- Volunteer or advisory position that serves to honor donor achievements.
- Names for gift levels that are meaningful.
- Benefits and privileges that are useful.
- Attractive materials to encourage attention and stimulate participation.
- Progressive benefits and privileges to aid commitment and lead to opportunities for expanding donor interest and involvement.
- Increased visible recognition at higher gift levels.
- Opportunities for volunteerism and leadership development.

- Consistency and equality for all donors based on gift size.
- Ability to endure a minimum of 10–20 years of active use.

Once you have designed a gift club and obtained approval for its program of benefits and privileges, you should formalize the full details in a written policy statement. This will help ensure that all members are treated equally, no matter which solicitation activity was used to qualify them for a donor club.

Prepare a brochure to explain each donor club program. The brochure should explain the club's purpose, programs, and special benefits to current and future donors. When a donor club is first established, early donors can also be designated to receive a "charter membership" certificate or other special symbol to recognize their being among the first to qualify. You should plan to provide such visible forms of ongoing recognition as donor walls, plaques, and certificates. There is great merit to setting up donor recognition sites at a nonprofit organization's facilities. The sites should be attractive and permanent and should be located in high traffic areas.

Budget

Donor clubs are inexpensive to operate and highly cost-effective. The number of participants is limited because the requested gift amounts are well above average. The costs to provide the array of benefits and privileges are often routine budget items an organization would provide to its donors whether they were donor club members or not, such as newsletters, annual reports, invitations to annual meetings, and special events. Modest expenses will be required to add names to the donor wall and provide VIP identification cards, annual donor luncheons, plaques, and certificates. Indirect expenses and overhead charges usually consist of management staff time and support services from the fund development office. Overall, the budget required to support a donor club of 500 members or less should not exceed $0.20 to $0.30 for each $1.00 raised (see Exhibit 5.2). With increased numbers of donor club participants, the cost of fund-raising will decline as long as the price of benefits and privileges remain within reason.

The Internal Revenue Service has established criteria regarding the amount that nonprofit organizations can spend on recognition of donors. Called "give-backs," these material benefits should not exceed

Exhibit 5.2

Sample Budget for Donor Club Operations

Cost Elements	Cost per Donor	
Recruitment and Renewal mailings		
Donor records	$0.50	
Gift reports	0.50	
Donor Communications		
Directory	$1.00	
Newsletter	1.00	
Annual report	1.00	
Invitations to other events	1.00	each
Donor Recognition		
Identification card	$10.00	
Certificate of appreciation	15.00	
Plaque and/or paperweight	25.00	
Annual luncheon	40.00	
Donor Relations		
Special reports	$1.00	
Annual site visit	-0-	
Birthday/Anniversary cards	4.00	
Special guest at a benefit event	100.00	
Total (est.)	$200.00	/donor/year

2 percent of the value of the original gift or $66; otherwise, they result in a reduced charitable contribution deduction value to the donor. This IRS rule does not apply to what donors do not personally possess or can use, such as their names on a donor wall. The IRS does consider items such as the food and drink at a donor recognition luncheon and a discount at the gift shop to be "material benefits" received in exchange for a gift, which must be subtracted from the original gift amount.

The relationship between gift size and amount of recognition requires serious attention. You should consider how it can reward donors at smaller gift levels in a manner that will serve to encourage their continued giving. You also will need to reserve higher rewards for those willing to make larger gifts. Gift levels should begin at least at the $100 level and expand with more privileges offered for increased gift amounts. If a donor club program were to begin at $25 with the other levels at $50, $100, $250, and $500, the cost of maintenance at the lower levels would exceed the gift income received and the higher levels would be "paying" more for theirs and each smaller donor's benefits. Fund-raising consultant, instructor, and author Tom Broce reinforces this opinion:

> First let me say that in today's economy few organizations can afford to make solicitations for gifts of less than $100. All gifts below that amount should be solicited by mail. Even telephone solicitations should be for $100 or above. We should not waste valuable manpower on small gifts; moreover, most organizations should set their minimum gift level at $100 (though many prospects may respond with less than $100). This is difficult for many people to accept, but it makes good business sense.[1]

Execution

Once in place, donor clubs should establish an image and quality reputation for their special purpose and accomplishments. If they bear the name of an individual honored as an example of generosity, the organization should feature how the funds raised by the club are used by the nonprofit organization. If the club features personal contact with institutional leaders and professional staff members, concentrate more on the privileged associations. If the club's intent also is to sponsor programs and services within a part of the organization, address how these activities have increased the numbers of people served, the quality of services available, and the outcomes achieved—all due to the extra generosity made possible by donor club participants.

Here are some additional steps an organization can entertain to ensure it achieves full value for its investment in donor clubs; these factors also can serve as criteria for performance evaluation:

- Get to know the individual members.
- Ask for members' thoughts about giving and the programs they prefer to support.
- Ask for members' thoughts about the benefits and privileges offered and what they would like to receive in return for their annual gifts.
- Find out what else they might be willing to do; ways they might like to be involved.
- Introduce them to members of the board, professional staff, management, and volunteers.
- Continue to offer them privileges they can and will use.

- Invite them and their spouses along with special friends they might choose to be guests at an activity, benefit, or special event.
- Show them appreciation in a personal way that is unexpected; send them a birthday or anniversary card, or call them with a report.

The chief advantage of gift clubs is the opportunity to get to know these donors and to learn of their areas of interest within the organization. To the degree these interests hold donors' attention, their annual gifts will likely continue and be expanded when extra needs arise.

Analysis

Performance evaluation of donor clubs must concentrate on donor retention. The criteria you should measure include the following:

- How many prior donors renewed? What percentage is that?
- What was the average gift for all donor club members?
- How many donors increased or upgraded to a higher gift level?
- How many donors responded to each invitational activity?
- How many new donors were recruited and at what gift levels?
- How many prior donors failed to renew or decreased their gift?
- What were total costs for support of each donor club including fulfillment of all benefits and privileges?
- What are donor opinions on current benefits and privileges?
- What are their responses to volunteerism and leadership opportunities?
- What are their responses to advisory council invitations?
- What changes does their performance suggest?
- How will these changes increase retention and participation?

A review of these indicators and analysis of the overall progress of donors is recommended every six months, if possible, and at least once a year at a minimum.

Summary Interpretation

Exhibits 5.3 and 5.4 illustrate the nine-point performance index applied for donor club effectiveness and efficiency. At first glance, the

Exhibit 5.3

Nine-Point Performance Index Analysis of Donor Clubs

	Friends of the Library ($100/yr.)	Friends of Law School ($250/yr.)	Boosters Club ($500/yr.)	Ambassadors ($1000/yr.)
Participation	118	225	485	140
Income	$11,800	$81,250	$255,500	$180,000
Expenses	$2,525	$8,225	$38,500	$24,800
Percent participation	82%	73%	91%	79%
Average gift size	$100.00	$361.11	$526.80	$1,285.71
Net income	$9,275	$73,025	$217,000	$155,200
Average cost per gift	$21.40	$36.56	$79.38	$177.14
Cost of fund-raising	21%	10%	15%	14%
Return	367%	888%	564%	626%

figures are the best yet recorded in this workbook. Remember, these are the results of renewed giving by special donors who are willing to raise their giving levels in order to support their area of special interest and gain access to the benefits and privileges that accompany them. Here are some observations based on these examples:

(1) The expenses required are quite modest compared with direct mail and membership recruitment programs because limited numbers of prior donors are involved. Regular costs for newsletters, annual meeting invitations, and the like are charged to donor clubs correctly; if the clubs were not present, donors at these levels would receive complimentary copies that would be allocated to other cost centers.

(2) Percent participation is quite good across the board and consists of renewals only. Lower renewal rates for the Friends and Ambassadors programs should be monitored closely. If they begin to decline, review the gift amount required, which may be too high for those who are interested. Perhaps too many levels are being offered, dividing these donors too finely. Perhaps the benefits and privileges, although well intentioned, lack honest appeal.

(3) Average gift size reflects the gift levels required for active standing in these donor clubs. Some donors will exceed the minimum required, especially if several gift levels are offered with increased benefits.

Exhibit 5.4

Illustration of Nine-Point Performance Index Analysis of Donor Clubs

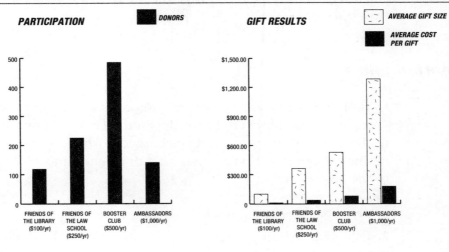

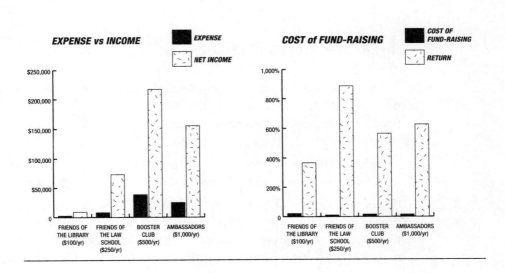

(4) Average cost per gift and cost of fund-raising percentages show that costs are required to support these solicitation activities, but they are well within the guidelines of $0.20 to $0.30 per $1.00 raised.

(5) The return percentage illustrates just how profitable donor clubs are in generating net income. Quantitative data do not report on

donor involvement and satisfaction, which is essential to preserve donor interest and enthusiasm. Separate surveys and focus groups can be conducted to collect this information, a good idea every two to three years.

Action Plans

Initiating a donor club program should be accompanied by appointment of a Committee on Donor Relations. This Committee will report to the board of directors and be charged with direct responsibility to define the organization's donor relations policy and procedure so it is in the position to:

1. Oversee all communications with prior donors.
2. Establish a single policy and procedure for all donor clubs and volunteer recognition.
3. Supervise active programs associated with donor relations, recognition, and reward.

In addition, you should take the following steps:

1. Review all regular reports and measurements of donor club performance with this committee. The board of directors should require that any proposed changes or additions to existing recognition and reward programs always be presented first to this committee.
2. Conduct annual performance reviews of donor club activities. You should identify problems early and take corrective action.
3. Regularly review and revise the benefits and privileges offered to donor club participants before these attractions become stale. During periods of economic recession or internal budget reductions, you may need to offer donors diminished benefits. Or, you may find ways to lower expenses that are not apparent to donors. You may be able to explain this effectively because donors can appreciate that spending money on them can be less important at times than directing more of their money to public programs and services.
4. Preserve the memory of past donors. Current donors will be watching to see how the organization is likely to treat their gifts later on.

A history wall or special area can be set aside for preservation of prior donors' recognition materials. If your organization relocates or renovates its facilities, you can remove plaques and other recognition signs from older areas and relocate them to a replacement site.

Related Benefits

Gift club donors have the potential to become advocates for your organization because of the extent of their commitment and loyalty. Donor clubs serve to keep the organization focused on these best of friends who already have demonstrated their commitment to the organization and its mission, and whose level of generosity represents the primary source of net contributions income to be raised each year. They are also an attractive venue to entice new donors to become valued friends.

6

Support Group Organizations

A support group organization is a unique method of annual solicitation activity that:

1. Identifies and recruits new friends.
2. Offers attractive membership services.
3. Renews and upgrades members' annual gift support.
4. Plans and conducts a variety of activities, benefits, and special benefits on behalf of a sponsoring nonprofit organization.

Support groups combine the attributes of membership associations with the benefits of donor clubs and add meaningful volunteer responsibilities for leadership of a semi-independent organization. As a separate organization, a support group also can undertake responsibility to carry out one or more civic duties for its sponsor nonprofit organization, including legislative and advocacy assignments.

Support groups possess organizational skills to marshal the time, talent, and energy of their members to meet any purpose that can help their sponsor to fulfill its mission. Successful support groups are well-organized, volunteer-led enterprises committed to support their sponsoring nonprofit organization. They rely on their parent for legitimacy, tax-exempt status, support staff, and operating budget. As a major avenue for public participation, awareness, and support, support groups offer special value to nonprofit organizations through the training of volunteers and development of future leaders, their experience with multiple tasks, and their reliable levels of annual gift support.

A support group offers membership dues and member benefits along with an open invitation to participate in a variety of volunteer-led, volunteer-staffed committees whose duties are aligned with the programs and services of a nonprofit organization. The group can adopt one or two of these areas, such as a client program or public service, as their special purpose or cause, or they may choose among several that represent annual priority projects. The greatest benefits they bring to a nonprofit organization are:

1. Their ready availability to take on important assignments.
2. The flexibility to change their fund-raising and public service focus from one project to another as needs arise.
3. Their commitment to advocacy and financial support at all times.

You can sponsor several support groups in addition to one or more membership organizations and donor clubs, all without conflict. To do this, you must clearly understand the purpose of each group. The groups should be managed by professionals who are trained to guide their activities for efficient operations and to achieve each group's maximum potential.

Each support group organization will be charged with multiple goals and objectives that lend themselves to a variety of performance measurements. Each will stress a serious level of volunteer commitment with assigned duties and responsibilities to individual members who agree to carry out specific purposes and will be subject to an evaluation of their results.

Attributes of support groups include the following:

- They have a single purpose or mission.
- They require annual gifts for membership status.
- They ask for a commitment of time.
- They offer enhanced benefits and privileges.
- They feature a semiindependent style.
- They are more volunteer-led than staff-directed.
- They will undertake specific assignments with goals.
- They reach out to the community.
- They offer networking opportunities for members.
- They promote various programs and services.
- They define an image that enhances their sponsor.
- They provide reliable annual financial support.

Support groups offer the following benefits, all of which are easily measured for performance:

- Improved communications, image enhancement, and public awareness.
- Increased marketing opportunities and market penetration.
- Improved community relations and direct public participation.
- Increased media awareness and responsiveness.
- Improved volunteer participation and training.
- Increased avenues for leadership development.
- Improved public relations.
- Increased opportunities for broad public influence.
- Improved cost-effectiveness and efficiency.
- Increased revenue from contributions.

Support groups are sophisticated enterprises and will require more time and attention from management than most other forms of traditional annual giving solicitation activity. Their programs also must be well coordinated with other solicitation activities. Their professional direction, which must keep in mind their favored status of partial independence and semi-autonomous governance, will require measurable amounts of guidance and support from the fund development office.

Purposes

A support group is possibly the best vehicle available to a nonprofit organization for achieving active participation by the community because of the breadth of volunteer opportunities. There is a place for everyone who wishes to join and to participate in helping the group realize its annual goals of friend-raising, relationship-building, fund-raising, and advocacy. A support group organization should be allowed and encouraged to foster its own identity, style, and reputation on behalf of its parent organization. Use of a separate logo, stationery, and other features that emphasize its uniqueness are encouraged as long as these symbols also include direct references to the sponsor.

Each of the group's programs must support the nonprofit organization (e.g., a fund-raising activity, direct public service, advocacy campaign) or the support group (e.g., the awards program, membership campaign, newsletter), or both. The fund development's professional staff must actively provide guidance and technical support. The group will also need clerical and budget support.

Preparation

Forming a new support group organization begins with interviews among volunteers and staff from other nonprofit organizations where similar groups are already in operation. The mission and purpose of each group must be defined with clarity and assessed for potential complements and conflicts with all the other solicitation activities already in place. An analysis also should be conducted externally to:

1. Address the willingness of the community to support a new group with volunteer members who are willing to become active participants.
2. Evaluate its proposed activities, benefits, and special events to sort out those considered valuable, potentially profitable, and not overly repetitious of exiting programs.
3. Establish that a valid need exists for their mission and purpose, even if in competition with others outside the organization.

Internal issues to address in starting a support group organization include:

1. The size and tenure of the board.
2. Officers and election procedures.
3. Setting annual membership dues levels, benefits, and privileges.

The support group's leadership should research the direct and indirect expenses required to support routine annual operations and for such activities as board of directors and committee meetings, membership solicitation and member services, and printed materials and supplies for all activities. The support group's leadership should present this information, along with a three-year business plan, to the nonprofit organization's board and management for thorough review and formal approval.

Each operating area also will provide measurable criteria for an annual performance review and will enable the group to reassess the validity of current practices measured against the original design. A key issue to evaluate is the respect and appreciation given to each group, its volunteer leaders, and its members by the parent nonprofit organization. Leaders and members of support groups should be kept well informed about the plans and progress of their parent organization to help define where and how each support group can assist. You should bring serious projects to their attention so they will be able to contribute.

Preserving and enhancing volunteer participation at all levels is the direct responsibility of the fund development office, whose duties include:

1. A professional staff member assigned responsibility to supervise the daily operations, provide professional guidance and direction, and arrange for clerical support.

2. Maintenance of up-to-date and complete mailing lists of current and past members and event participants.

3. Gift acknowledgment and appropriate posting to each member's permanent giving record.

4. Preparation of gift reports and analysis of results, by group and by each activity, benefit, and special event.

5. Advice and counsel to all volunteers in leadership positions, to assist in their success.

6. Inclusion on invitation lists for the organization's activities and public events.

7. Inclusion on mailing lists for the organization's newsletters, marketing information, and annual reports.

8. Coordination of individual, corporate, and foundation prospect lists with other solicitation activities.

9. Separate volunteer awards for distinguished leadership and service to the group and the nonprofit organization.

10. Inclusion in the organization's honors and recognition program for all who qualify as distinguished volunteers and as generous donors.

Performance evaluation and other forms of results management may not be welcomed by every volunteer, although most would agree with its appropriateness. Give careful thought to how assessments of volunteers are defined and implemented. You might ask a group of volunteer members to assist in identifying the criteria to be used, the activities to be measured, the analysis methods, and how the results will be interpreted and reported.

You need to address annual dues levels for support group membership. There are two approaches. First, establish a level that is respectable, provides adequate income for the effort and cost of recruit-ment and renewal, and is reasonably accessible to most people in the community. A recommended figure is $100 a year for active member-ship, with a first-year initiation fee of $150. Once the fee is adopted, never attempt to change it. Members and nonmembers are more easily persuaded to join and to continue at this modest level knowing that it will not change. As a second approach, consider offering more than one membership and fee category.

Budget

The standard list of expense areas for support group organizations is similar to a membership organization, and the same budget guide is suggested when preparing the annual operating budget. Costs will be concentrated where the mission of the organization is focused. For ex-ample, if the group is an advocacy group, legislative affairs and lobby-ing activities (mailings, meetings, travel, and entertainment) will be the expense categories. If the group is an athletic booster club, break-fast or luncheon meetings with coaches, student aid, and an annual awards banquet might dominate the budget. The cost of professional staff help along with other direct, indirect, and overhead support pro-vided by the nonprofit organization will need to be added as well.

Support groups offer a benefit to your organization's budget. Vol-unteers who bring their time and talent to work assignments may be considered a substitute for paid employees. Volunteers may be just as efficient and effective as employees and may even be more successful. Using volunteers for certain activities rather than paid employees may reduce the cost of providing programs and services and raising funds. Improved cost of fund-raising percentages will result in every pro-gram where volunteers are actively involved, which means more net dollars will be available to nonprofit organizations for programs and services that benefit the public.

Execution

A support group's members must take active responsibility for its op-erations. Professional staff will assist as needed and provide orienta-tion, training, and guidance to all those who volunteer for specific

6

assignments. The role of staff is to encourage the members to do all they can to manage their own organization. This unique partnership is appreciated by volunteers who expect to be in control while being able to call on staff for professional guidance and support when and where needed.

The business of managing a support group is a lot like managing a separate nonprofit organization. Committees need to meet to do the work required, and people have to take responsibility for what they agreed to do. The committee system remains a highly effective way to utilize volunteer time and energy because it directs everyone's efforts toward common goals and limits the tendency to wander away from assigned tasks. Committees also are obliged to report back to those who appoint them, which gives the board of directors and staff regular oversight and supervision of all the group's activities in keeping with their mission and in accordance with their operating rules and procedures. The board of directors also must meet regularly to conduct its business. The support group should have operating rules and procedures to provide guidance for routine operations along with process and procedure to nominate and elect new officers and directors, appoint committees, and remain fiscally sound. These same rules and procedures clarify the relationship between the group and its parent, use of the parent's name and tax-exempt privileges, and financial responsibility for all fiscal affairs.

Critical operating areas should be monitored throughout the year. Exhibit 6.1 represents areas of program performance that should be measured every six months to a year as an easy scorecard of the group's growth and development in keeping with its mission. If the volunteer leadership and board members give each of these items a score of 4 or better, their support group is moving in the right direction and should have a strong future. Any area with a score of 3 or lower should receive immediate attention before it drags other areas down and creates additional problems.

Analysis

Further analysis of performance should concentrate on specific areas, such as membership recruitment, renewal, and upgrading results similar to the various measurements discussed in Chapter 4. Exhibit 6.2 provides a list of 10 criteria for overall performance measurement.

Exhibit 6.1

Areas for Program Assessment of a Support Group Organization

		SCORE				
		low				high
1.	Comparison with prior year results	1	2	3	4	5
2.	Growth in donor universe	1	2	3	4	5
3.	Penetration of new markets	1	2	3	4	5
4.	Quality of effort	1	2	3	4	5
5.	Image and reputation	1	2	3	4	5
6.	Volunteer orientation and training	1	2	3	4	5
7.	Leadership development	1	2	3	4	5
8.	Consistent messages and personalization	1	2	3	4	5
9.	Regular reports and analysis of results of each activity, benefit, and special event	1	2	3	4	5
10.	Matching institutional needs on schedule	1	2	3	4	5
11.	Public advocacy and support	1	2	3	4	5
12.	Forecasting future income and program performance	1	2	3	4	5
	Median Score					

Share this scorecard with the board of directors and committee leadership and ask them to rate each item. A median score of 4 or above is solid evidence of a positive performance, and any area with a score of 3 or below should receive immediate attention. For example, if the orientation and training program for volunteers and leaders does not receive high marks overall, recent volunteers may be inadequately prepared to take their place in guiding and directing the group. If the number of members attending activities, benefits, and special events is declining, some added efforts will be required to learn why they are no longer interested.

Exhibit 6.3 adds a program measurement focused on members and public performance. Emphasis must be given to reviewing goals and objectives along with adequate planning for future activities. Again, a median score of 4 or better is desirable, and any element scoring below a 4 should receive immediate attention. For example, if one of the problem areas is staff support, office systems, or budget, you should bring this deficiency to the attention of the nonprofit organization's management and explain that support groups rely on the fund development office for their day-to-day operations. If too few major gift prospects or new leadership candidates are being defined and developed from the support

Exhibit 6.2

Criteria for Overall Performance Measurement for a Support Group Organization

				SCORE			
		low				high	
1.	Number of new members recruited	1	2	3	4	5	
2.	Number of prior members retained	1	2	3	4	5	
3.	Public attendance at each sponsored activity, benefit, and special event	1	2	3	4	5	
4.	Number of volunteers who participate on committees	1	2	3	4	5	
5.	Number of members who attend activities, benefits, and special events	1	2	3	4	5	
6.	Orientation and training programs for volunteers and leaders	1	2	3	4	5	
7.	Long-range plans matched to organizational priorities	1	2	3	4	5	
8.	Performance evaluation carried out for all programs (membership and activities)	1	2	3	4	5	
9.	Attention to budgets and operating net proceeds for all programs (membership and activities)	1	2	3	4	5	
10.	Total net revenue delivered each year from all programs (membership and activities)	1	2	3	4	5	
	Median Score						

groups' membership and activities programs, additional attention should be given to these areas because they are so critical to the future of the group itself as well as to its parent organization.

Summary Interpretation

The nine-point performance index provides an assessment based on hard data that can be compared between three sample support groups (see Exhibit 6.4 and 6.5), as well as with the performance of other annual giving programs presented in this workbook. A good guideline is a balance between membership numbers, public participation in activities, and net income achieved. Here are some comments based on data in the nine-point performance summary:

(1) Support Group A has the highest cost of fund-raising at 48 percent. Its average gift size ($190.20) is the lowest of the three examples, its average cost per gift ($91.94) the highest, and its return (107%) the lowest. It is also the smallest (255 members) and has the lowest membership retention rate (66%). Group A is the newest group among the three, with potential to grow. To date, it is the least successful in developing committed members, volunteers, and sponsors for its activities, benefits, and special events, which is understandable. The other groups and the nonprofit organization's staff can help Group A concentrate on improving these areas.

(2) Support Group B has the highest average gift size ($355.21), has the lowest cost of fund-raising at 23 percent to raise a dollar, and has the best return at 338 percent. The average cost per gift, $81.06, is not the best of the three, suggesting that sheer membership size at 1,085 demands extra attention and expense. The average gift size is a sign of maturity and succeeds in upgrading members to higher participation levels. It also suggests a strong level of sponsorship and underwriting for its activities, benefits, and special events, no doubt due to attention to corporate cultivation and donor relations, a lesson for Groups A and C to emulate.

Exhibit 6.3

Annual Program Measurements for Support Group Organizations

	SCORE				
	low				high
1. Response from each solicitation activity	1	2	3	4	5
2. Analysis of how much each audience might give	1	2	3	4	5
3. Identification of major gift prospects	1	2	3	4	5
4. Identification of leadership candidates	1	2	3	4	5
5. Problem areas (case, timing, image, leadership, staff, systems, budget, etc.)	1	2	3	4	5
6. Overall goals for each membership category	1	2	3	4	5
7. Overall goals for each activity, benefit, and benefit event held	1	2	3	4	5
8. Three-year timetable and program plan for each area of annual operations	1	2	3	4	5
9. Review of support materials and operating systems to assist support group management	1	2	3	4	5
10. Analysis of time and money spent (staff and budget measured against gift results)	1	2	3	4	5
Median Score					

Exhibit 6.4

Nine-Point Performance Index Analysis of Support Group Organizations

	Support Group A	Support Group B	Support Group C	Total
Participation	255	1,085	455	1,795
Income	$48,500	$385,400	$97,850	$531,750
Expenses	$23,445	$87,950	$27,650	$139,045
Percent participation	66%	73%	79%	73%
Average gift size	$190.20	$355.21	$215.05	$296.24
Net income	$25,055	$297,450	$70,200	$392,705
Average cost per gift	$91.94	$81.06	$60.77	$77.46
Cost of fund-raising	48%	23%	28%	26%
Return	107%	338%	254%	282%

(3) Support Group C has the best membership retention record at 79 percent. The average gift size of $215.05 indicates some success with a major gift activity, which also is reflected in the $60.77 average cost per gift, lowest of these three examples. The group's cost of fund-raising at 28% is nearly as low as that of Group B, which has more than twice as many members. This performance suggests Group C is coming to maturity. Increased attention to membership recruitment, renewal, and upgrading should be its primary focus for the next several years.

(4) Overall, these three groups provide an excellent return for their parent nonprofit organization. They have 1,795 active donors whose average gifts were nearly $300. They were cost-effective in delivering nearly $400,000 in net proceeds at a cost of fund-raising of 26 percent and a return of 282 percent. Continuing investment in these three organizations, with emphasis on the improvements these data suggest, should continue to show gains in all categories.

Action Plans

The following areas will benefit from constant attention to support group organizations and the role they play within annual giving and the overall fund development program:

Exhibit 6.5

Illustration of Nine-Point Performance Index Analysis of Support Group Organizations

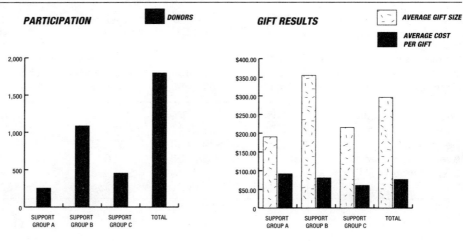

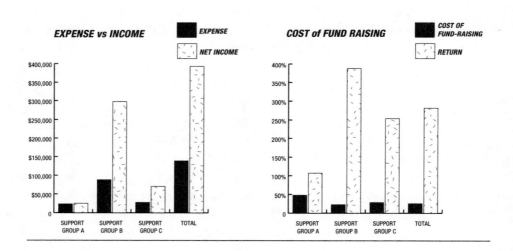

(1) Membership recruitment must remain a focus for each organization, no matter its size or retention rate. Membership dues are the most cost-efficient dollars to raise when compared with managing activities, benefits, and special events. Membership is also where friend-raising and relationship-building occur, which is vital to the support group and to its sponsoring nonprofit organization. Members represent active public participants, a reflection of public confidence and trust. The number of members also represents some achievement in expanding the organization's community relations program that it otherwise could not have achieved.

(2) Support groups are an excellent means to recruit and train volunteers for public solicitation. Volunteers also are an excellent resource to identify and cultivate major gift donors and prospects. Leadership, that most important of volunteer traits, is vital for every nonprofit organization to identify and develop for its future. Individuals who have the ability to lead others and who are willing to give hours of their personal time to work for a nonprofit organization are of incalculable value. Equally, individuals along with corporations and foundations who step forward with annual gifts at the higher membership levels and who agree to contribute larger sums to be sponsors and underwriters for selected activities, benefits, and special events offered by support groups are demonstrating to the general public their confidence in the organization and their trust in its good use of their funds for the benefit of others. Each donor deserves the extra benefits and privileges their gift entitles them to receive along with the extra recognition and reward the organization can bestow to show its appreciation for their example to others and for their extra generosity.

Related Benefits

Among the benefits that can flow from a mature support group are:

1. Trained volunteers for other work, including added solicitation activities.
2. Experienced, proven leaders who are well informed and capable of new assignments.
3. Extra media attention and coverage of activities, benefits, and special events not otherwise attainable to a nonprofit organization.
4. Broad community relations opportunities.
5. Access to new markets.
6. Access to business and professional leaders as members and volunteers.
7. Image and reputation enhancement for the nonprofit organization.

8. Major gift prospect identification, cultivation, and involvement.

9. Planned giving prospecting and marketing opportunities.

10. Enhanced donor recognition and donor relations opportunities.

11. Advocacy group to assist with civic and legislative affairs.

12. Proven, capable organization that can accept a multiyear goal possibly twice its average gifts when needed in a major capital campaign.

7

Telephone Solicitation

The telephone is a splendid instrument for friend-raising, relationship-building, and solicitation activity. Its chief advantage is personal contact, possibly the only opportunity many donors may have to talk with someone from a nonprofit organization. Careful planning is necessary to identify those donors and prospects who will welcome phone calls. Cold calls to nondonor prospects are expensive and inefficient. The best results are from the combination of a letter-call-letter sequence, with prior donors first receiving a letter reporting that a call is coming, followed by the telephone call to ask for their gift decision, then a pledge confirmation letter to follow the next day, ending with a thank-you letter to acknowledge the donor's gift after its receipt.

Unlike most of the other annual giving solicitation activities, telephone solicitation incorporates all the critical factors for success: audience selection, alert notice, personal contact, direct ask, confirmation, and thank-you. Telephone solicitation is recommended highly for renewal and upgrading of direct mail donors, for membership associations, donor clubs, and support group organizations. Another use is to talk with current donors about expanding their giving or upgrading from one program to another, such as from direct mail respondent to a more active affiliation through a membership association or donor club. Finally, telephone contact is an excellent strategy to recapture lapsed donors.

Telephone solicitation has expense levels that are better than direct mail renewal rates ($0.25 to raise $1.00). The letter-call-letter combination gets better results than direct mail in terms of more donors and higher average gifts.

Public opinion about telephone solicitation is increasingly a sensitive matter and an important factor for a nonprofit organization to consider in planning a telephone solicitation program. However, there are many positive opportunities for the use of telephone solicitation with prior donors. Having a conversation with a group of prior donors of $100 or more is a highly advantageous form of donor relations; it is personal, encourages an exchange of questions and answers, can discuss specific gift amounts plus donor benefits, offers follow-up opportunities, and is a natural social exchange between people.

Purposes

The telephone can be used for the following purposes, in descending order of effectiveness:

1. Donor relations calls, to maintain close contact with valued donors.
2. Thank-you calls, to thank a donor for a large gift that has just arrived.
3. Recognition calls, to thank someone for volunteering, announce an award, or invite to a donor-only gathering.
4. Service calls, to offer planned giving and estate planning counsel.
5. Information calls, to alert donors to a major gift opportunity.
6. Upgrade calls, to ask for a larger gift than last time.
7. Renewal calls, to request another, perhaps larger gift.
8. Recruiting calls, to invite someone to volunteer time and talent.
9. Support group calls, to stimulate and retain interest, encourage active participation, and retain membership standing.
10. Donor club calls, to retain interest, stimulate renewal, and explain the added benefits and privileges for a larger gift.
11. Membership calls, to invite, renew, and upgrade annual memberships.
12. Follow-up ticket sales calls on mail invitations to encourage attendance at activities, benefits, and special events.
13. Lapsed donor calls, to recapture prior donors.
14. Cold calls, to acquire a first-time donor.

Choosing the right donors to call for an annual giving program that is well matched to their current interests is an art. Segmenting donors by interest area, gift size, frequency, and geography has become reasonably easy today thanks to computer software systems for donor records. For example, direct mail donors who gave between $50 and $75 can be invited to consider $100 for their renewal gift or be invited into a membership organization or donor club where privileges begin at $100.

There are donors whose giving history and public activity will suggest a call inviting them to volunteer to serve on a committee. This invitation can begin with a letter and be followed by a telephone call.

Some of the other good purposes for telephone use by nonprofit organizations include research surveys, calls to action for legislative initiatives, and direct marketing of programs and services offered to the public.

Preparation

Among the questions you might consider in planning a telephone-based campaign are:

1. What is the perception that will be created and retained by people who receive this telephone solicitation?

2. Will it matter whether the organization can offer any of its programs or services to the people called (combine direct marketing with solicitation)?

3. Can telephone solicitation succeed if the name of the organization is not well known to those who will be called?

You should evaluate other annual giving programs to determine how effective their use of telephone solicitation techniques might be compared with current methods of donor renewal and upgrading. Some effort to learn the experience of other nonprofit organizations who have actively used telephone solicitation in the same community will be invaluable.

Ask 10 to 12 volunteer callers to conduct a test of perhaps 100 to 200 prior donors in one or two evenings. If these results are positive, conduct another test with a second group of volunteers, and compare their results. You should also determine how many volunteers will be available, how large the donor pool is, and whether facilities are available for an expanded phonathon.

A telephone solicitation program will require the same amount of preparation as a volunteer-led personal solicitation effort (see Chapter 9), but less work than a direct mail program, membership association, donor club, or support group organization. A formal phonathon requires a lot of preparation to support the callers. The first decision is who will do the calling—volunteers or a professional telemarketing firm. Volunteer callers may cost less, but a professional firm may raise more money. Exhibit 7.1 lists strengths and weaknesses of volunteer callers and professional callers.

If you choose to use a professional firm to make the calls, your organization must not relinquish its direct supervision. You should:

1. Determine how the firm will conduct this solicitation in your organization's name.
2. Clarify the duties and responsibilities of both parties.
3. Specify how and where all gifts will be delivered.
4. Specify how expenses will be approved prior to payment.
5. Arrange how all gift processing, reporting, and pledge-collection procedures are to be followed.

These details should be summarized in the formal contract for service, which will also define whatever compensation method and payment schedule is agreed upon. Several states have laws that specify the contents of a telephone solicitation contract, including compensation arrangements. A copy of the contract signed by both parties also will need to be filed with state authorities before solicitation begins, to be followed by a full financial report after the solicitation campaign is concluded.

When you use volunteer callers, ask them to make their own gifts before the telephone program begins. Also prepare volunteers with a comprehensive orientation and training program. A professional telemarketer knows how to do this and can provide the orientation and training required. Divide volunteers into teams with captains to supervise each group of callers. A little competition between teams can be healthy and adds to the fun. However, use caution because this technique can also lead to overly aggressive behavior and to fudging results.

Because a volunteer's time is limited, orientation and training sessions are often held right before telephone solicitation begins (see Exhibit 7.2 for a sample agenda). It is important to reserve time to review

Exhibit 7.1

Comparison Criteria between Volunteers and Professional Firms to Conduct a Telephone Solicitation Campaign*

Volunteer Callers	Professional Callers
Strengths	*Strengths*
High contact rate (usually 70%–80%)	High contact rate (usually 70%–80%)
Highly interactive and personal	Highly interactive and personal
Ability to contact large numbers of constituents	Ability to contact large numbers of constituents
Response higher than direct mail	Trained and experienced caller ensuring quality
Ability to absorb many indirect costs	High-cost efficiency promoted by technology, techniques, and experienced staff
Direct supervision of calling by staff	High accountability including prompt, detailed reporting
Utilizes and involves volunteers, staff	Low requirement of institutional staff and management
	Return on investment higher than direct mail
	Use of a precall letter reducing phone costs and negative responses and increasing results
	Demonstrated techniques/results
	Experienced senior staff, unique design and application
Weaknesses	*Weaknesses*
Requires careful list selection and data information	Requires careful list selection and data information
Higher investment cost than direct mail	Higher investment costs than direct mail
High demand on professional staff and management	Relatively new approach
High costs in preparation, recruitment, and training	Limited comparable competition
High turnover in part-time callers	Perceptions and experience with other telemarketing firms
Usually requires investment in equipment and facilities	Less commitment to your cause
Telephone charges usually at market rate	No development of volunteers
Results vary widely	
Volunteer attrition likely if calling is on-site	

*Adapted from "Advanced Fund Raising Endeavors," by Mark W. Bates in *Getting Started: A Guide to Fund Raising Fundaments,* The National Society of Fund Raising Executives, Chicago Chapter, 1988, pp. 59–60.

Exhibit 7.2

Agenda for Orientation and Training Session for Volunteer Callers in Telephone Solicitation

1. Welcome and Introductions	Chair, Telephone Solicitation Campaign
2. Overview of the nonprofit organization	President/CEO or Executive Director
3. Other Annual Giving solicitation activities in progress and their results	Chair, Annual Giving
4. The project to be funded and the "case" for its support	Staff director or program manager
5. Telephone Campaign operating details and caller-program plans	Chair, Telephone Solicitation Campaign
6. Telephone solicitation script and "role-playing" exercises	Vice Chair and/or Team Captains
7. The donor history card and the caller contact report form	Vice Chair and/or Team Captains
8. Telephone etiquette and tips for callers	Chair, Telephone Solicitation Campaign
9. Discussion: Questions/Answers	Chair, Telephone Solicitation Campaign
10. Adjournment to begin calls	

the sample script and ask two or three couples to conduct "role-playing" exercises to illustrate the calling experience. Volunteer callers will need to be trained to listen, as well.

Final details will cover likely responses from an immediate "yes" or "no" to answering machines, outright refusals, requests for more information, perhaps even criticism of the intrusion. The information on the donor history card gives the caller an introduction to the individuals called. Instruct volunteers to complete the call report sheet after each call is made, no matter what reply they receive. Details on the call report will be included in the response letter with the pledge form to be mailed the next day.

If telephone solicitation will be used to support a membership program, donor club, or support group organization, focus volunteer training on the membership gift levels, benefits and privileges accorded to each, and opportunities for volunteerism. Calling prior donors to these programs at the beginning of the membership drive or donor renewal cycle is preferable to using the telephone for cleanup after mailing efforts have been exhausted. The recommended approach to donors is to combine letters and phone calls. This method will make two or three direct contacts, and each can announce the other will follow. Typically, a letter precedes the phone call to inform the donor of the approximate day and time to expect a call (within 10 days of the letter's receipt, or less, if possible). The letter can report facts and other details not easily described over the telephone, such as a summary of past activities, roster of member services, donor premiums and privileges, and the full schedule of activities, benefits, and special events to be offered. The follow-up telephone call can concentrate on eliciting opinions and reactions from the donor and discussing the importance of giving, prior generosity of the donor, and the good works the money has helped to achieve.

The public relations and marketing departments may also use the telephone for public opinion surveys and market research studies. Work with other departments to arrange for such calls to be made at other times than when telephone solicitation is being conducted.

Budget

Three budget options await the planners of a telephone solicitation. If volunteers are the callers, costs may be similar to those of Budget A in Exhibit 7.3. If a professional telemarketing firm is hired to make the calls, costs may be similar to those in Budget B. If you hire a firm to provide advice and counsel to staff and volunteers who will make the calls, you can develop a budget based on Budget C. Several of the routine expense items will be the same in all budgets. Of course, you will have to get estimates that fit your program and prices in your area.

Budgets should estimate income to be received along with the costs to raise it. The results of a telephone solicitation can be predicted with accuracy only if they are based on past experience. Using the telephone to renew prior mail donors, both current and lapsed, will produce one result. Using the telephone to renew membership, donor club gift, or support group participants will produce other results. Therefore, you should base predictions on similar programs.

Exhibit 7.3

Estimated Budgets for Telephone Solicitation (3,000 Calls)

	Budget A Volunteers	Budget B Professional Firm	Budget C Combined Volunteers and Professionals
Estimated Expenses			
Computer-generated donor selection	$500	$500	$500
Printing donor record cards	400	400	400
Volunteer/staff training meetings (food and beverages)	800	800	800
Telephone equipment fee	-0-	1,000	-0-
Telephone charges			
Local calls (2,500)	300	250	300
Long distance (500)	600	500	600
Printing letters and envelopes	600	600	600
Printing pledge forms	100	100	100
Mail assembly and postage	420	420	420
Gift processing and acknowledgment	200	-0-	200
Donor recognition	300	-0-	300
Miscellaneous supplies	200	200	200
Contingency fund	250	200	200
Firm marketing/advertising	-0-	2,000	2,000
Firm travel expenses	-0-	2,000	2,000
Firm professional fees or salaries for employees	-0-	8,000	4,000
Subtotals	$4,670	$16,970	$12,620
Estimated Income (Pledges Paid)	$25,000	$50,000	$35,000
Net income	$20,330	$33,030	$22,380
Cost of fund-raising	19%	34%	36%
Return	435%	195%	177%

Execution

Use of telephone solicitation should be coordinated closely with other annual giving solicitations to cause the least amount of confusion among prior donors and volunteers. If a letter-call-letter solicitation will be used, close coordination with the mail drop date is critical so follow-up calls will be made within 10 days of the letter's arrival. A longer delay lessens the advantage of the linkage between the two. If the calls will be made to members to renew their membership, the solicitation must be made ahead of the deadline for printing the next membership directory so the caller can use this fact as a motive. Each program will have special features to be used by callers that will help to determine the best times to conduct a telephone solicitation. If calls will be made to donor club members, they might be made shortly before benefits and privileges expire. If the calls will be made to volunteers who participate in support group activities, the calendar of coming events will serve as a reminder of their special access to these privileged occasions.

Ask volunteers to arrive 30 minutes before calling begins. A buffet-style meal should be available. Before calling begins, gather the callers as a group and review techniques. Also remind them to be sure that they have made their own gifts. Some donors, when called, ask volunteers if they have made such gifts themselves and may even want to know the amount of the contribution.

Once calling begins, plan to take a 10- to 15-minute break after the first 30 to 45 minutes. Use this time to ask for feedback from callers and to answer their questions. Ask them to report their results for the tally sheets. Volunteers are likely to take more time with each call as they begin, especially if they know the people they are calling. Dialogue is acceptable as long as they also stay on task and talk about the organization, its current priority, importance of each donor's gift, and the other parts of their assignment.

Many volunteer-led telephone solicitation programs take place in the evening, usually Mondays through Thursdays. The alternative is to call during the business day, which will work only if volunteers are well trained and can spare the time, and if donors' work telephone numbers are known. Calling on weekends is possible, but the public may be less tolerant of weekend calls.

Provide callers with donor records that contain basic details needed by the caller, the mailing address, amount of the last gift, other gifts received in the past year, any known special interests, and comments from prior callers.

Instruct volunteers to review each of their donor records before they begin their calls. Use large posters or tally sheets to keep everyone informed of progress during the evening, by teams, by goal, and other details. Establish a deadline when all calling will end. Some states have laws to restrict calling only during daylight hours or between 8:00 A.M. and 9:00 P.M.

Callers will encounter a lot of answering machines, and telemarketing professionals are divided on whether callers should leave a message or hang up and try later. Because so many people have answering machines today, the combined letter-call-letter strategy ensures that a solicitation is made and reinforced.

If a professional firm is employed to conduct the telephone solicitation, the fund development staff is responsible for maintaining close contact with all aspects of the effort. You should request written daily reports from the firm so you can monitor progress and, if necessary, adjust the script, regroup donors selected for calls, and adjust other details based on analysis of early returns.

Analysis

Telephone performance can be measured the same as every other solicitation activity, with the addition of a few other evaluations due to its special nature:

1. Compare telephone results with other annual giving performance to see which was more successful and to demonstrate the level at which the telephone's effectiveness in renewing and upgrading prior donors has been realized.
2. Conduct exit interviews with volunteers to monitor public reaction.
3. If you used a letter-call-letter sequence, compare results with letter-only or phone-only solicitations and with any previous multimedia experiences.
4. Study the results from prior donors and lapsed donors in particular because their renewal is where telephone solicitation often works best. Exhibit 7.4 offers measurements of telephone performance for several annual giving programs.

Pledge collection will have a strong impact on cost-effectiveness. Pledge collection will be related to the list of people called and will be far better for prior donors than for nondonors.

Summary Interpretation

Critical performance factors include the number of donors who participate, their average gift size, upgrading experience, and cost of

Exhibit 7.4

Annual Giving Donor Renewal Using Direct Mail Compared with Telephone Solicitation

	Direct Mail	Membership Organization	Donor Club	Support Group	Total
A. Prior Donors Solicited by Mail					
Number mailed	3,000	300	300	300	3,900
Mail replies	1,575	211	224	222	2,232
Percentage	52.5%	70.3%	74.7%	74%	57.2%
Income received	$59,850	$21,100	$34,720	$22,200	$133,362
Average gift	$ 38.00	$ 100	$ 155	$ 100	$ 59.75
B. Prior Donors Solicited by Telephone					
Number called	3,000	300	300	300	3,900
Calls made	2,250	250	265	254	3,019
Contact percentage	75%	83.3%	88.3%	84.7%	77.1%
Gifts pledged	2,005	225	231	233	2,694
Income pledged	$76,190	$22,500	$35,805	$23,300	$157,795
Average gift pledged	$ 38.00	$ 100	$ 155	$ 100	$ 58.57
Pledge percentage	89.1%	90%	87.2%	91.7%	89.2%
Income received/ gifts paid	$57,038	$18,900	$29,915	$19,700	$136,468
Number paid	1,504	185	201	198	2,209
Average paid gift	$ 37.92	$102.16	$148.83	$ 99.49	$ 61.78
Percentage paid	75%	82%	87%	85%	82%

fund-raising. The nine-step performance index for a volunteer caller program (see Exhibits 7.5 and 7.6) can be interpreted as follows:

(1) Telephone solicitation of 2,005 direct mail donors resulted in net income of $57,038 at a cost of $16,970 based on a 75 percent renewal rate among prior mail participants. Telephone calls to the remaining 25 percent of prior donors, now lapsed, should also be planned so that they are not forgotten. Average gift size at $37.92 suggests that more attention should be given to upgrading opportunities in the next mail message.

Exhibit 7.5

Nine-Point Performance Index Analysis of Telephone Solicitation

	Direct Mail Donors	Membership Donors	Donor Club Donors	Support Group Donors
Participation	2,005	225	231	233
Income	$57,038	$18,900	$29,915	$19,700
Expenses	$16,970	$4,750	$4,750	$4,750
Percentage participation	75%	82%	87%	85%
Average gift size	$37.92	$102.16	$148.83	$99.49
Net income	$40,068	$14,150	$25,165	$14,950
Average cost per gift	$8.46	$21.11	$20.56	$20.39
Cost of fund-raising	30%	25%	16%	24%
Return	236%	298%	530%	315%

(2) Telephone solicitation of the 225 individuals belonging to the membership association was effective with 82 percent renewal at an average gift above the $100 minimum dues level. Plan a second solicitation of nonrenewing donors along with all previous members who have lapsed in the past two to three years.

(3) The renewal rate among donor club members by telephone achieved the highest percentage of all four uses (87%), suggesting strong donor loyalty. The higher average gift size of $148.83 reflects the multiple giving levels offered (membership and support group participants are asked for $100 annual dues). Consider a separate plan for direct mail donors giving $50 and above, to invite them to consider upgrading to the membership, donor club, or support group programs.

(4) Support group participants remained strong, which is to be expected as a result of their higher level of personal involvement as active volunteers. Support groups can entertain more than one membership level, as discussed in Chapter 6, to increase annual income. However, their greater potential lies in their member volunteers, who can conduct high-quality activities, benefits, or special events that produce more net revenue than their annual dues.

All four programs illustrated in Exhibit 7.4 reflect success. Their cost of fund-raising and return percentages certainly demonstrate high value for time and budget expended.

A final area of analysis for telephone solicitation is multiyear performance. You must invest in a second and third year to realize the

Exhibit 7.6

Illustration of Nine-Point Performance Index Analysis of Telephone Solicitation

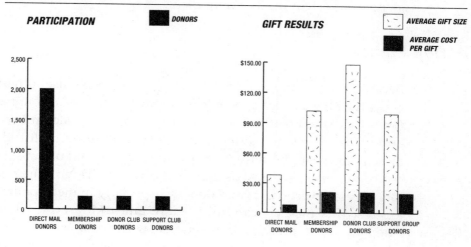

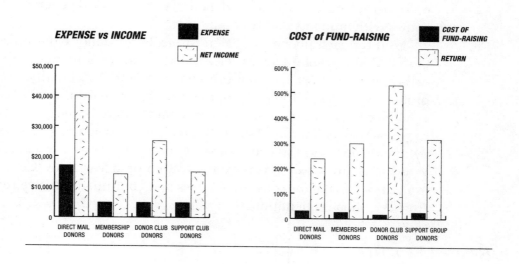

maximum performance this solicitation strategy offers and also to compare these results with all other annual giving solicitations. In addition, you must review the results of other telephone uses by departments other than fund development.

Action Plans

Because telephone lines are available for anyone's use, others will be using the phone to reach people who may happen to be donors. Any volume of calls, no matter the caller, can become a concern because they are intrusive. Telemarketing is used primarily for a multitude of commercial purposes because it works. Advertising and direct sales use exceeds nonprofit use (just as is true of direct mail) with the result being lots of calls to prospects and donors, especially in metropolitan areas.

Test this method carefully before embarking on a telemarketing campaign. Nonprofit organizations with established constituents (church members, college alumni, theater season ticket holders) are likely to find more acceptance than health and human service organizations, advocacy groups, and the like. It is possible that rural areas are more accepting of calls at odd hours than urban dwellers; test 100 names with numbers and find out.

Monitor each phone campaign carefully for donor clues on acceptance. Monitor volunteer callers and their success just as carefully; calling is hard work and not everyone is adept at it. Finally, monitor professional callers too and ask them for their analysis of the results. What is being said by volunteers and paid callers is one thing; how it comes across is another. Watch the mail for comments as well as for money. When success continues, increase telephone use cautiously. When it declines, examine the data to attempt to learn why. Continued evaluations make for constant success and continued positive returns from telephone solicitation.

Related Benefits

The dialogue between caller and donor can provide valuable information. For example, the caller may find out why a donor decided to stop giving. As long as callers are sensitive to donors' feelings about receiving calls at home, a telephone program can help with friend-raising and relationship-building.

8

Activities, Benefits, and Special Events

The key ingredient for success in staging activities, benefits, and special events is volunteers. The primary benefit for a nonprofit organization is public participation from volunteers who stage the affair and from all who attend. People talk about the event and those who contributed, and this can benefit the organization's image. Successful fund-raising events also add net revenue to help meet the annual operating budget needs of their sponsoring nonprofit organizations. They also draw attention to the organization, help to promote its priority of needs, reinforce its dependence on public support to meet these needs, and advocate the community benefits its mission and purpose are dedicated to achieve.

Activities, benefits, and special events are capable of important profits, but not all perform at the same level of efficiency and cost-effectiveness. Each must be assessed for its own levels of efficiency and profitability, with goals set for its next production that work toward identified areas of improvement, containment of expenses, and an increase in number of participants.

Purposes

Planning any activity, benefit, or special event must begin with a clear definition of what specific goals the function will be designed to accomplish and the criteria to measure the outcomes (see Exhibit 8.1). You should:

1. Use these criteria to define the intent of the activity you are proposing.

2. Present the criteria to those whose responsibility it is to authorize the activity.

3. Use the criteria to explain the activity's purpose to the volunteers and donors who will be invited to participate.

4. Match the criteria with the goals of other departments in your organization.

Each activity, benefit, or special event holds potential to deliver a variety of important outcomes for their sponsor as well as all the participants. Public occasions can be a way of reaching out to others to ask for help, of building consensus around a cause, or of effecting change. Not every activity, benefit, or special event is held for fund-

Exhibit 8.1

Criteria to Measure the Opportunity and Potential of a New Activity, Benefit, or Special Event

	SCORE				
	low				high
1. Increase the organization's visibility	1	2	3	4	5
2. Improve public image and reputation	1	2	3	4	5
3. Increase media coverage	1	2	3	4	5
4. Increase volunteer participation	1	2	3	4	5
5. Add volunteer awards and recognition	1	2	3	4	5
6. Increase community participation	1	2	3	4	5
7. Develop trained leaders for the future	1	2	3	4	5
8. Expand market penetration	1	2	3	4	5
9. Test market responsiveness	1	2	3	4	5
10. Increase cash as net proceeds	1	2	3	4	5
11. Expand donor relationships	1	2	3	4	5
12. Add donor honors and recognition	1	2	3	4	5
13. Increase corporate contacts and participation	1	2	3	4	5
14. Showcase the organization's leadership	1	2	3	4	5
15. Focus attention on current programs and services	1	2	3	4	5
16. Focus attention on priority needs	1	2	3	4	5
17. Increase public awareness	1	2	3	4	5
18. Promote the mission and purposes	1	2	3	4	5
19. Build public consensus for the mission	1	2	3	4	5
20. Recruit new donors, volunteers, and advocates	1	2	3	4	5
21. Cultivate major gift prospects	1	2	3	4	5
22. Create an opportunity to have fun	1	2	3	4	5

Median Score

raising purposes. Some help carry out a variety of other priorities for nonprofit organizations. The general purpose remains to raise friends and build relationships between the community and their nonprofit organizations.

Preparation

Careful planning is essential to select the kind of activity, benefit, or special event that will inspire public support, attract help from volunteers, occur at a time that facilitates attendance, and run with near flawless perfection.

A benefit or special event becomes much more challenging when fund-raising is the chief mission because of the financial obligation to produce the greatest profit. These events are business ventures and require commercial decisions not common to nonprofit organizations, such as:

1. Arranging rental space in hotels and convention centers.
2. Filing permits for use of alcoholic beverages.
3. Negotiating liability insurance contracts.
4. Hiring professional entertainers.

They are also a major marketing and sales project that must apply astute fiscal management to:

1. Sell admission tickets.
2. Solicit sponsors and underwriters for gifts in exchange for products of value to these donors.
3. Recruit in-kind gifts and donated services.
4. Seek contributions of a variety of materials and services to be used as prizes and auction items.

You can ask volunteers and donors to bring their regular business and sales skills to these commercial transactions.

Preparations also must include a careful review of federal and state laws, local ordinances, and other requirements. You may need various permits. Outdoor benefits may require traffic control, police security,

Exhibit 8.2

Performance Measurement Criteria for Benefit Events

	SCORE		
	This Year	**Last Year**	

	low high	low high	
1. Was the budget prepared in advance and approved?	1 2 3 4 5	1 2 3 4 5	
2. Was recruitment of sponsors and underwriter gifts successful?	1 2 3 4 5	1 2 3 4 5	
3. What percentage of total revenue did sponsors and underwriters represent?	1 2 3 4 5	1 2 3 4 5	
4. Were sponsors and underwriters satisfied with the visibility their gifts promised?	1 2 3 4 5	1 2 3 4 5	
5. Were the invitations mailed on schedule?	1 2 3 4 5	1 2 3 4 5	
6. Was the percentage of those invited who purchased tickets and attended above 10 percent?	1 2 3 4 5	1 2 3 4 5	
7. Did all acknowledgment letters specify the income tax deduction value allowed?	1 2 3 4 5	1 2 3 4 5	
8. How many guests attended and were they sent invitations to join the sponsor's club?	1 2 3 4 5	1 2 3 4 5	
9. Were all bills for services paid quickly?	1 2 3 4 5	1 2 3 4 5	
10. Were there any unexpected costs?	1 2 3 4 5	1 2 3 4 5	
11. Did total net proceeds achieve the goal?	1 2 3 4 5	1 2 3 4 5	
12. Was a postevent critique conducted?	1 2 3 4 5	1 2 3 4 5	
Median Scores	_____	_____	

Exhibit 8.3

Nonfinancial Criteria for Benefit Event Performance Measurement

	SCORE		
	This Year	**Last Year**	

	low high	low high	
1. Were the support arrangements well prepared and conducted on time?	1 2 3 4 5	1 2 3 4 5	
2. Were accommodations for guests suitable and did they perform satisfactorily?	1 2 3 4 5	1 2 3 4 5	
3. Were accommodations for speakers suitable?	1 2 3 4 5	1 2 3 4 5	
4. Did the planning committee include enough volunteers for all the tasks required?	1 2 3 4 5	1 2 3 4 5	
5. Did employees cooperate with the extra demands on their time and services?	1 2 3 4 5	1 2 3 4 5	
6. Were media objectives attained and was the coverage evaluated?	1 2 3 4 5	1 2 3 4 5	
7. Were the speakers filmed and their comments recorded for future use?	1 2 3 4 5	1 2 3 4 5	
8. Did the committee complete all its assigned tasks within the approved budget?	1 2 3 4 5	1 2 3 4 5	
9. Did the committee conduct its own critique?	1 2 3 4 5	1 2 3 4 5	
10. Was the critique report submitted to the board of directors?	1 2 3 4 5	1 2 3 4 5	
Median Scores	_____	_____	

site inspection and approval by the fire marshal, and on-site paramedics. You should prepare a complete checklist of requirements.

The board of directors should establish operating guidelines for every event they sponsor or allow to be held in their name. They should also monitor the event's progress and evaluate its performance to ensure a success. You should identify performance criteria for each fund-raising benefit (see Exhibit 8.2). Several areas of performance measurement other than fiscal results should be included in the evaluation (see Exhibit 8.3).

Budget

Management of activities, benefits, and special events begins with preparing a budget worksheet estimating every area of projected revenue and expenses (see Exhibit 8.4). The budget worksheet assists you in fiscal management of each public function and serves as a ready-made outline for performance measurement. If the function is a fund-raising program, the performance standard should require *at least* 50 percent of gross revenue as net income after direct costs. New, first-time events may require a minimum of three years to achieve this reasonable cost guideline, and your budget proposal for such an event should include plans for achieving this minimum. If a fund-raising budget cannot demonstrate the ability to meet this level of success after three years, the organization's management and board of directors should decide whether to discard it and plan a different benefit that can achieve the 50 percent performance level. A budget keeps everyone's attention on the "bottom line" as a primary objective, an important feature when inviting individuals, corporations, and foundations to invest in the event as an efficient fund-raising activity for the sponsoring nonprofit organization.

A budget is a statement of financial objectives to be met and exceeded where possible (see Exhibit 8.5). It is also a guide to the multiple details that require attention during the planning period, throughout the actual production, and for the cleanup afterward.

A greater selection of revenue sources are open to activities, benefits, and special events than any other annual giving solicitation program. These include possible income in the following forms:

1. *Direct Contributions.* Ticket sales, cash receipts, and gifts made in lieu of actual attendance.

Exhibit 8.4

Budget Worksheet for an Activity, Benefit, or Special Event

	Estimated Budget	Actual Budget
A. Projected Cash Receipts (Revenue)		
Ticket sales	$	$
Sponsor gifts		
Underwriter gifts		
Auction receipts		
Raffle receipts		
Other revenue		
Contributions		
Donated materials (in-kind gifts)		
Subtotal	$	$
B. Projected Cash Expenses (Costs)		
Cash expenditures (itemized list)		
Printing	$	$
Postage		
Facility use fees		
Food and beverages		
Decorations		
Flowers		
Favors		
Entertainment		
Miscellaneous costs		
Auction/Raffle prizes purchased		
Temporary staff hired		
Consultant fees		
Contingency fund		
Subtotal	$	$
	======	======
C. Projected Net Proceeds (A minus B)	$	$
D. Percent Proceeds (Cost of fund-raising)	%	%

Exhibit 8.5

Sample Budget Worksheet for an Activity, Benefit, or Special Event

	Approved Budget	Actual Expenses
A. Projected Cash Receipts (Revenue)		
Ticket sales (400 at $100/couple)	$40,000	$42,000
Sponsor gifts ($250, $500)	6,750	7,500
Underwriter gifts ($1,000, $2,500)	10,000	8,000
Auction receipts	4,000	4,350
Raffle receipts	1,500	1,250
Contributors	1,000	500
Donated materials (gifts-in-kind)	(3,500)	(2,250)
Subtotal	$63,250	$63,600
B. Projected Cash Expenses (Costs)		
Cash expenditures (itemized list)		
Printing	$7,650	$7,880
Postage	450	365
Facility use fees	1,000	1,000
Food and beverages	9,500	10,555
Decorations	2,500	1,800
Flowers	1,000	<800>
Favors	1,000	<1,000>
Entertainment	3,500	3,500
Miscellaneous costs	1,000	350
Auction/Raffle prizes purchased	1,000	<450>
Temporary staff hired	-0-	600
Consultant fees	-0-	-0-
Subtotal	$28,600	$26,050
C. Projected Net Proceeds (A minus B)	$34,650	$37,550
D. Percent Proceeds (Cost of fund-raising)	55%	59%

2. *Sponsors and Underwriters.* Large gifts matched with visibility (title sponsor, benefactor and patron level underwriter, table sponsors).

3. *Auction and Raffle Income.* Cash receipts from winning auction bids and raffle ticket sales.

4. *Special Events.* Extra activities added to the regular program with extra cash donations required to participate.

5. *Donations.* The direct "purchase" of an item on the expense budget.

6. *In-Kind Gifts.* A "gift" from a vendor or merchant of supplies that would otherwise need to be purchased (flowers, printing, beverages, etc.).

7. *"Something Extra."* A gift stimulated by the invitation, often made in lieu of attendance, or an extra amount given above the base ticket price; a pure gift. If you ask, you will receive.

8. *Other Revenue.* Other income stimulated by an activity, benefit, or special event to another annual giving activity (a guest attends and later makes a gift in reply to another solicitation).

Several areas of expense are directly related to activities, benefits, and special events. The three broad areas of expense that represent the total costs of sponsoring public functions are:

1. *Direct Costs.* Budget items such as printing and postage, food and beverages, rental space and equipment, promotion, printing, decorations, and recognition gifts

2. *Indirect Costs.* Salaries for employees, benefits, supplies, telephone charges, meetings, local travel, gift processing, donor records and files, staff training and education, consultants, and temporary staff

3. *Overhead Costs.* Electricity, heat, office rent, equipment leases, computers, copy and fax machines, maintenance fees, depreciation, and accounting and legal fees

Execution

Any activity that is not well-managed and well-executed raises questions about its ability to achieve success; it also brings attention to the value and worth of the success of others being offered.

Activities, benefits, and special events held for fund-raising purposes are quite demanding of staff in the fund development office. Volunteers are essential to the production of events; staff cannot do it alone. Volunteers gravitate to public functions, not because they are easier to produce (they are not) or receive greater media attention, but because they dread the direct confrontation that other solicitation activity appears to require. Somehow, in their mind, asking their friends to write a check to their nonprofit organization by sponsoring a table, underwriting the flowers, or buying tickets to attend is different from asking their friends to write a check to support their nonprofit organization directly.

Evaluating the execution of activities, benefits, and special events held for fund-raising purposes can begin with the following six areas of performance measurements:

1. Progress in volunteer recruitment and training.
2. Progress in leadership development.
3. Success in prospect and donor identification.
4. Financial performance measured against the approved budget.
5. Net proceeds of at least 50 percent of gross revenue.
6. Postevent critique and written summary for the board of directors.

A postevent critique is important and should be performed for every public function. Detailed analysis should include a review of every preparation step along with notes from all the on-site occurrences, mistakes, delays, glitches, and so on that can be addressed the next time. Volunteers and attendees may offer ideas for improvement that also need to be evaluated and passed along to the next committee. Volunteers and participants should believe that the board of directors and management are as interested in the committee's own assessment of their function as they are in the performance of every activity they sponsor. The critique report should review the goals and objectives agreed on when the event and its budget were approved. It should evaluate all entries in the revenue and expense report, media coverage, public reaction, and suggested improvements. The compliment that volunteers expect is a "well-done" or a "thank-you," but their highest gratification comes from an invitation to do it again.

Gathering opinions is essential too. Begin with placing addressed postage-paid evaluation cards on seats, or distribute them immediately after with a note thanking the guests for their attendance. If nothing else, everyone will appreciate the opportunity to comment. Any postcards returned with comments are a bonus.

Analysis

Activities, benefits, and special events can prove their value in many quantitative and qualitative ways. These are public functions; each has the ability to cement positive relationships with people, both volunteers and donors. Each can stimulate others to begin their support to a nonprofit organization. If you track the results of these events over several years, you will be able to identify which approaches yield effectiveness, efficiency, and profitability. They also have a unique ability to deliver positive information to select audiences, achieve visibility not otherwise attainable, and engender commitment and loyalty from the public. Undeniably, activities, benefits, and special events offer the broadest opportunities for personal involvement and participation by volunteers.

Conducting performance measurement for public events can be as easy as counting the number of people attending. Evaluating how many (and who) were there is evidence of the public's confidence that the organization conducts satisfactory functions.

Summary Interpretation

The data provided in the nine-step performance index is valuable on its own merits and can be used to compare the results of several functions with one another, as long as you remember that each is quite different from the other. Exhibits 8.6 and 8.7 provide three samples of a special event (annual meeting of a membership organization), a new benefit event (fishing tournament in a beach resort community), and a

Exhibit 8.6

Nine-Point Performance Index Analysis of Activities, Benefits, and Special Events (Single-Year Results)

	Annual Meeting	Fishing Tournament	Black-Tie Dinner Dance	Total
Participation	545	182	450	1,177
Income	$32,500	$90,176	$159,336	$282,012
Expenses	$29,850	$26,008	$92,651	$148,509
Percent participation	21%	82%	19%	41%
Average gift size	$59.63	$495.47	$354.08	$239.60
Net income	$2,650	$64,168	$66,685	$133,503
Average cost per gift	$54.77	$142.90	$205.89	$126.18
Cost of fund-raising	92%	29%	58%	53%
Return	9%	247%	72%	90%

Exhibit 8.7

Illustration of Nine-Point Performance Index Analysis of Activities, Benefits, and Special Events

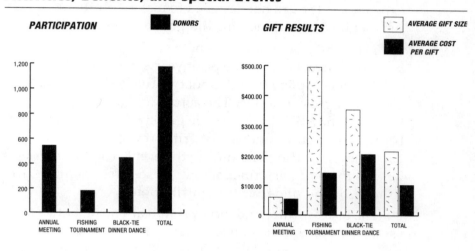

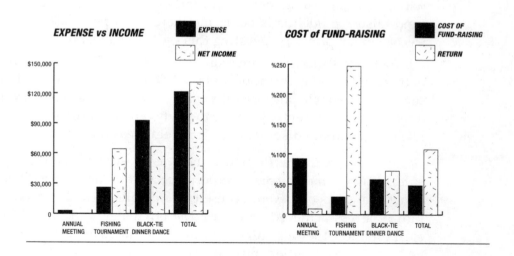

traditional activity (black-tie dinner dance). An interpretation of their results follows:

(1) The annual meeting of a membership organization is needed for business purposes (election of officers and directors, recognition and reward for volunteer service) but is not a command performance for members. To succeed with 545 participants who paid $50 each to attend suggests a committed membership. The average gift size is $59.63 because some sponsors and underwriters were recruited to help meet expenses. Although not designed to make a profit nor achieve a 50 percent net income, the meeting did pay for itself.

(2) The fishing tournament is not yet a high-volume attendance event, but it did attract 82% of the prior year's participants to return.

A strong sponsor and underwriting effort is evident from the $90,176 in gross revenue. The actual fee to fish in the tournament is $185, not the $495.47 the average gift size suggests; this figure is high because of sponsor and underwriter revenue plus extra income from auctions and raffles held during the event. The cost of fund-raising (at 29%) is the best performer among these three examples, thanks again to sponsor and underwriter contributions.

(3) The black-tie dinner dance was well attended, but its $92,651 in necessary expenses in hotel fees, a banquet, beverages, decorations, dance band, and other entertainment, and $205.89 average cost per gift, consumed a lot of its revenue. The average gift size at $354.08 is close to the $350 per couple admission price, which probably cannot be increased without causing some decline in participants. The 50 percent cost of fund-raising guideline is being met here at 58 percent together with $66,685 in net profits, suggesting this event remains profitable.

(4) Together, these three functions assembled 1,177 people in the name of this nonprofit organization and provided a total of $131,118 in net income for charitable purposes at a cost of fund-raising of 53 percent and a return of 90 percent. However, to study only net proceeds or bottom-line figures would disguise a few problem areas that need attention.

The nine-point performance index is most effective when the results of two or more years of experience are available for each activity, benefit, and special event. These extra details provide added insight into progress achieved alongside the efficiency and productivity of each function; they also highlight any difficulties in performance, suggesting where attention must be applied in the future.

Action Plans

Success with benefits and events will be made from a variety of perspectives. Some donors will wonder whether it was worth the extra money, while others will focus on whether they had a good time, sat with the "right people," or will get their picture in the paper. Only the committee and staff will be concerned about bottom-line net proceeds for charity because that is their accountability. The value of a critique with committee members is to gather public opinion and evaluate what changes may be required to satisfy more participants next time.

The keys to success are soliciting sponsors and underwriters and management of the expense budget. A dozen sponsorships in the $2,500 to $5,000 range can guarantee fiscal success to nearly any benefit. Volunteers work hard for success, and one or two last-minute decisions to rent a dozen trees for decoration or add a live auction to the program (with professional auctioneer and purchase of all the prizes) can ruin the bottom line in a hurry. Strong leadership to hold the budget is important; volunteers have been known to ignore the advice of staff.

Every organization should be cautious about adding new activities, benefits, and special events simply because another organization had great success with theirs. What appears to work best is to select a program whose unique features can be related closely to the mission of your nonprofit organization.

Related Benefits

To look on activities, benefits, and special events only as a source of money is a mistake. They attract volunteers, who represent potential workers for several other programs at a nonprofit organization, including a variety of other annual giving solicitation activities. The opportunity to train and develop volunteers through activities, benefits, and special events also is a valuable related benefit. Public functions also can enhance the marketing, advertising, and public communication objectives of your organization because they are visible, receive media attention, focus on specific programs and services as priority needs, and advocate the mission of the organization. They can build relationships with corporations and businesses through the personal involvement of their officers and employees as volunteers and participants. The general public can be invited to join in as well, sometimes without any fee or admission charge, to become better informed about the organization and the various programs and services it offers for public benefit. All in all, these are the most visible and participatory of all the programs a nonprofit organization can offer to interact with the public.

9

Volunteer-Led Solicitation

Face-to-face visits constitute the most effective solicitation method in all of fund-raising practice. If enough time and trained volunteers are available, your organization should hold personal meetings with all donors at least once a year. If time and volunteers are limited, these efforts must be directed to your biggest and best donors.

The solicitation activities described in Chapters 3 through 8 are designed to initiate donor giving, invite them to renew (and increase) their gift, ask them to join a membership organization or donor club to enjoy special privileges, call them about renewing and upgrading their gift, and invite them to work on or attend activities, benefits, and special events. You will develop a sizable pool of donors from all this effort. Has anyone met with any of them yet? Donors are the best friends a nonprofit organization can hope to have, so becoming personally acquainted provides added value. The best way to do this is through a volunteer-led personal solicitation annual giving campaign, which is a once-a-year face-to-face meeting with your biggest and best donors.

Because costs to support a volunteer-led solicitation are low, their productivity and profitability are the best of any annual giving solicitation activity. The equation is quite simple. If 25 volunteers each meet with between 3 and 5 prior donors, a total of 75 to 125 donors will be seen. If their average gifts are $100, total gifts will range between $7,500 and $12,500. Most will give again, and some may even increase their annual gift if asked to do so. Consider the result if 50 volunteers are at work. The numbers of donors seen jumps up to between 150 and 250, and with average gifts at $100, total gifts of between $15,000 and $25,000 will be received.

Purposes

The purposes of a volunteer-led solicitation activity are to meet with donors, thank them for their past support, answer questions, bring them current information, invite them to continue (and perhaps increase) their contribution, and thank them for their decision. Another purpose for organizing a volunteer-led solicitation activity is to recruit and train people who will perform personal solicitation. Every nonprofit organization needs experienced solicitors, people willing to ask friends of the organization for money. Volunteers who are willing to speak up for an organization are an exceptional asset because of their commitment and enthusiasm for the mission, purposes, goals, and objectives of "their" nonprofit organization. Their very attitude is infectious. To recruit such individuals to a volunteer-led solicitation committee is to forecast success.

The advantages and attributes, goals, and objectives of a volunteer-led personal solicitation annual giving campaign can be summarized as follows:

1. It tells current donors that they are appreciated for who they are and valuable for what they have done.
2. It identifies and recruits volunteers who will ask their friends for money.
3. It identifies and recruits leaders who are able to direct others to perform a specific assignment by a deadline.
4. It asks current donors to increase their level of annual support.
5. It invites current donors to become volunteers and actively help their nonprofit organization.
6. It identifies major and planned gift prospects.
7. It proves that personal solicitation is 16 times more effective than direct mail and 8 times more effective than the telephone.
8. It proves that personal solicitation, at $0.05 to $0.10 to raise $1.00 (or less), is the most cost-effective method of solicitation available.

Preparation

A volunteer-led solicitation activity will not take much time to complete; preparation is where the time is needed. Begin with a simple structural plan to illustrate a clear picture of authority (who reports to whom) and define the task each level has to perform. Create a committee like the one outlined in Exhibit 9.1. Committee work allows everyone an equal and fair share of the work required and includes a shared accountability for performance, plus the comfort that no worker is without help and support from others on the committee. The committee system spreads the work around so that each volunteer solicitor is asked to solicit between three and five prior donors; each team captain is assigned only three to five workers to supervise, and each vice chair is responsible for only three to five teams. This structure has another advantage, a built-in leadership development program where a vice chair can become chair the next year, team captains can move up to vice chair, and workers can become team captains.

Where does an organization find volunteers for this assignment? With a variety of annual giving solicitations activities in progress, volunteers are available from three sources: the board of directors, volunteers helping other programs, and current donors. Leadership for volunteer-led solicitations should begin with board members, who also

Exhibit 9.1

Organization Chart for a Volunteer-Led Solicitation Committee

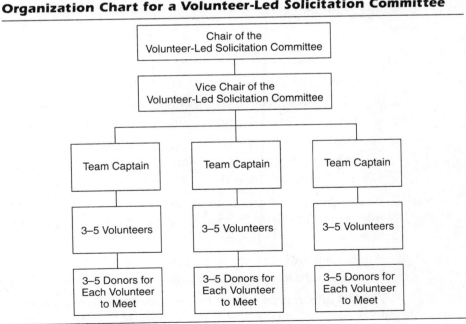

need to make their own annual gifts. Giving and "getting" are standard board duties and helping the volunteer-led solicitation program is a perfect way to meet this obligation. Candidates can be found among the volunteers who are helping other programs, such as by serving as leaders in the membership and donor club programs, joining in telephone solicitation, or serving on one of the committees preparing an activity, benefit, or special event. Current donors are excellent candidates because their interest and enthusiasm have been well developed through other annual giving programs. It is logical to ask them to volunteer for the personal solicitation program. The best way to invite them is to go see each candidate.

The most encouraging fact to share with a prospective solicitor is that everyone they will meet is already a donor, just as they are. Those selected to be seen will be among the most faithful and committed donors to the organization, people who have qualified for a personal meeting because of their demonstrated interest and level of generosity. In fact, it is because of their record of support that they deserve to be seen.

The next step is to prepare this annual solicitation activity as a mini-campaign, an efficient and effective fund-raising strategy where everyone works together at the same time for the same objective. Here are the ingredients necessary for a successful annual giving campaign led by volunteer solicitors:

1. An adequate supply of current donors with a known potential for increased levels of participation and support.
2. An adequate supply of well-trained volunteer solicitors to represent the nonprofit organization while acting as its public solicitors.
3. A few identified leaders who are experienced in organizing and directing volunteers and in motivating them to complete their assigned duties on schedule.
4. A well-prepared campaign plan managed by experienced fund-raising professionals in whose advice and counsel leaders and volunteers will have confidence.
5. A tracking and reporting system to evaluate the campaign's performance and to keep everyone informed of progress throughout.
6. A recognition program to honor donors for their achievements and to reward volunteers for their accomplishments.

Not everyone will be a candidate for personal solicitation. Many donors are quite comfortable with their current relationship, gift amount, and involvement level. The most likely candidates for personal solicitation are those who stand out among all the others because of two features: They give often during the year, and they give more money. The following behaviors indicate donors' growing interest:

1. Made repeated personal gifts each year.
2. Increased their annual gift levels or joined the membership organization, donor club, or support group.
3. Asked about commemorative giving or made a gift in memory or in honor of someone.
4. Attended one or more activities, benefits, or special events in the past year.
5. Brought friends as guests to one or more activities, benefits, and special events in the last year.
6. Requested additional information, whether asking for themselves or "for a friend who wants to know."
7. Volunteered to do some work for the organization outside the fund development program.
8. Volunteered at another nonprofit organization, possibly in a fundraising assignment.
9. Nominated by a board or staff member or by another donor.
10. Came forward on their own and asked how they could help.

Some major gift prospects (prior gifts of $1,000 and up) also may be found in any group of current donors. These donors deserve extra care in planning their resolicitation including the possible assignment of the same volunteer (or team of volunteers) who met with them last year.

You need to develop a volunteer orientation and training program. Every volunteer should attend. The program should take the form of a seminar or workshop. A sample agenda is provided in Exhibit 9.2. Also prepare an information kit for each volunteer (Exhibit 9.3).

Although the training program should be developed as a formal activity, some informality will encourage audience participation, especially if you use "role-playing" exercises to show how a solicitor might carry out a meeting with a donor. Limit attendance at each session to 25 or 30 people and schedule the planned presentation to last only 30 to

Exhibit 9.2

Sample Agenda for One-Hour Orientation and Training Session for Volunteer-Led Solicitation Committee

1. Welcome and introductions	Chair, Volunteer-Led Solicitation Committee
2. Importance of annual gift support: results of last year's campaign	Chair of the board or President/CEO
3. Annual goals and objectives: the project that needs support	President/CEO or senior professional staff member in charge of the project
4. The campaign plan, timetable, visit reports, gift reports, staff support	Chair and Vice Chair of the Volunteer-Led Committee
5. Introduction of team captains and prospect assignments	Chair and Vice Chair of the Volunteer-Led Committee
6. The art of asking for money ("role-playing" exercises)	Team captains along with successful volunteers from last year's campaign
7. The Information Kit	Fund Development staff
8. Discussion: Questions/Answers	Chair and Vice Chair of the Volunteer-Led Committee
9. Adjournment to refreshments	

Exhibit 9.3

Contents of a Volunteer Solicitor's Information Kit

1. Project fact sheet and key points
2. Organization chart of volunteer-led solicitation committee
3. Roster of members of volunteer-led solicitation committee
4. Basic fact sheet on the nonprofit organization
5. Sample questions and answers
6. Assigned donor gift history and brief personal profile
7. Most recent annual report and newsletter sent to donors
8. Supply of stationery and envelopes for thank-you notes to donors
9. Supply of contact report forms
10. Supply of postage-paid reply envelopes to send in gifts and visit report forms

40 minutes; leave the rest of the hour for questions and discussion. The training site should be conducive to training purposes (e.g., a conference room rather than the board room). The final goal is to prepare each volunteer with the following:

1. Complete instructions on the project, how the funds will be used, how those served will be helped, and how the mission will be advanced.

2. The list of benefits to the community that will result from meeting this priority need.

3. Why it is essential to meet with each donor and an explanation of how to present the project fairly, without overstatement.

4. Instruction on how to ask for a gift without implying any coercion.

5. Information on how to invite donors to join in support of the project as a means of helping those in need.

6. Details on the donor recognition program prepared for donors at all levels.

7. An explanation (followed by solicitation) of why each volunteer's own personal gift decision must be made *before* they ask someone else for their annual gift, and why this gift decision must be made as soon as possible.

8. Information on how the campaign is organized, who are the people in charge, which team captain will work with them, when the campaign begins and ends, and how they are to report back after each solicitation.

9. Details on how the results will be reported, the schedule of report meetings (they are to attend every one), how the overall program will be evaluated, and how their performance will be measured.

10. An honest sense of how important this assignment is, that their efforts are deeply appreciated, and that there will be recognition and reward for their service.

The next step is to assign each volunteer the names of the three to five prior donors he or she is to meet before the campaign ends in the next three to four weeks. It bears repeating that each assignment is a current donor who is favorably inclined to support the organization. The purpose in visiting them is out of respect for their previous generosity, to bring them information about current activities including the current priority project, and to invite them to continue their support.

The donor record given to each volunteer needs only limited information: the donor's name, address, and telephone number to make an appointment, the donor's gift history, and any comments from the last person who met with the donor.

Finally, tell volunteers how to report the results of each donor meeting. The donor's gift decision is important, but so are the questions donors ask, requests for more information, and hints of where their interests lie that allow for a follow-up to send them what they requested. These details should be reported to the team captain or fund development staff so that they can be entered on the donor record. Include a supply of meeting report forms and postage-paid reply envelopes in the worker's information kit along with all the other information they are likely to need.

Budget

The costs to prepare and conduct a volunteer-led solicitation activity are minor compared with the annual giving methods described in previous chapters (see Exhibit 9.4). The materials contained in the worker's kit are inexpensive, and most are general purpose "off the shelf" documents. Arrangements for orientation and training sessions may require room rental and audiovisual fees as well as light food and beverages. If possible, hold these sessions at the nonprofit organization, perhaps near the area where the priority project is carried out so that brief tours can be conducted after the training session. Recognition for volunteers does not have to be elaborate or expensive but should express sincere appreciation for their help. Report meetings can be breakfast or luncheon sessions. Usually two or three are needed between a campaign's start and finish. Other costs will be for the "kickoff" event and the victory celebration; both might be held as a cocktail reception in the early evening.

Budget preparation should include an estimate of expected revenue. This figure may be proposed to the volunteer committee as a goal based on the total prior gifts. Goals are valid when based on prior results, not wishful thinking.

Execution

For many volunteers who are soliciting donors, the actual "moment of truth" can be a stumbling block that seems to cause the words to stick

Exhibit 9.4

Sample Budget Worksheet for Volunteer-Led Solicitation

A. Cost Elements	Estimated Cost
Recruiting/Invitation letters	$200
Donor research	400
Donor assignment cards	100
Orientation meeting:	
Facilities/PA system	500
Light food/beverages	1,500
Volunteer worker kit	1,500
Campaign kickoff meeting	1,500
Campaign report meetings (3)	4,000
Campaign victory celebration	2,500
Volunteer recognition	2,500
Total	**$14,700**

B. Revenue Sources	Revenue Estimate
Prior donors	$220,000
Qualified prospects	50,000
Upgrading activities	25,000
Subtotal	**$295,000**

C. Net Proceeds	$280,300
D. Percent Proceeds	95%

in their throat. The orientation and training session will show them how to do it and give them the words, but the act itself still may be hard to do the first or second time. After that, it does become easier. Volunteers need to feel comfortable in meeting with prior donors; both have a common interest in the same nonprofit organization, which is always a good topic to bring up at the start of the meeting. It also helps to advise volunteers that every solicitation is unlike all the others because different people are involved; there is no single method or approach that works every time. The following guidelines on personal solicitation may be helpful to volunteers:

1. Each person they see is already a donor, just as they are.
2. Whether the donor knows the volunteer or not, both have positive feelings about the organization they are supporting.
3. The face-to-face meeting is essential for success.
4. A telephone call is the usual way to make an appointment to see a donor. While not preferred, the donor may not believe a meeting is necessary and choose to decide on their gift over the phone. Accept their decision and thank them for their support.
5. Each donor has thoughts and opinions; invite comments that can be shared with the organization.
6. There is no "easy way" to get this job done; anything other than a face-to-face meeting will not be as successful.
7. Offer to meet when and where the donor prefers.
8. The organization cannot hope to call on all its donors; only volunteers can complete this important contact each year.

When volunteers are comfortable with their assignment and have all the information they need in their worker's kit, they make appointments to meet with their assigned donors. The annual fund committee chair, vice chair, and team captains should encourage volunteers to do this right away. Report meetings should be held every week or two during the campaign period. These meetings will motivate volunteers to see their donor prospects so they have some progress to report when everyone else is reporting. Report meetings sustain the momentum of all volunteers, even if a bit of negative motivation is involved (threat of embarrassment). Report meetings also bring everyone up to date on results, reveal the number of gifts and pledges received, team performances, and other positive facts that encourage everyone to keep working. Once volunteers have met all their assigned donors, they will enjoy these meetings because of their "100 percent of calls completed" report. If there are any unassigned donors that remain, the team captains should ask these volunteers to select two or three more donors to see, but only after completing all their original assignments.

The campaign schedule usually lasts four to six weeks following the kickoff. Allowing more time tends to lull volunteers into a "do it later" state of mind. The times of year most often selected are the fall and spring months, October and November or April and May. Some committees plan their personal solicitation campaigns at less busy times for volunteers and donors alike, which may be from January to March. Whatever the time, the campaign needs to be efficient in its preparations and firm about its deadline to complete all the assignments. If any donors did not give, were not assigned, or could not be seen, they can be reserved for the follow-up campaign period, which should be scheduled to follow fairly soon. Two backup plans are available; to organize a second campaign or to fall back on telephone solicitation to be sure each donor is contacted. A letter request is least effective, as a last resort. It is important that every donor receive an invitation to make his or her annual gift sometime within each year.

Recognition is important, especially for volunteer solicitors. Their good efforts to meet and talk with prior donors must be given high praise because they are representing the organization to those who are investing in its current priorities and future plans. Report meetings, the victory celebration, and other public occasions, such as the organization's annual meeting, all offer opportunities to recognize the volunteer solicitors publicly. Nonpublic recognition begins with thank-you letters from team captains, the committee, and the annual giving chair. Awards are also appropriate to commemorate volunteer service.

Analysis

Several performance areas can be measured during and after the campaign. Each of these evaluations and their criteria should be defined in positive terms because volunteers and donors are important people. Routine gift reports will provide basic details, such as the number of donors who made gifts, their gift amount, and average gift size. Other details, such as whether donors were asked to increase their gift amount or how many donors declined to give, will come from the visit reports and will be evident in the comparison with prior year results. Exhibit 9.5 provides a comprehensive summary report form that stresses the positive results that were accomplished. This report also reminds everyone that some good donors were not seen, which should prompt the question—how and when can they be asked to join with everyone else? The answer will be to schedule a second volunteer-led solicitation campaign, perhaps in a few months, to be certain everyone is invited to make their annual gift.

Exhibit 9.5

Evaluation Form for Annual Giving Campaign Performance by a Volunteer-Led Solicitation Committee

			Prior Gift at $100	Prior Gift at $500
1. Number of qualified prospects and volunteer solicitors available	Prospects	=	250	250
	Volunteers	=	50	50
2. Number and percentage of prospects assigned to volunteers	Number	=	225	225
	Percent	=	90%	90%
3. Number of calls made, number of gifts received, and the ratio (%) of calls made to gifts received	Calls made	=	200	200
	Gifts made	=	175	175
	Ratio	=	88%	88%
4. Average gift size for prior donors and average gift size for renewed donors	Average (old)	=	$105	$525
	Average (new)	=	$110	$580
5. Number of upgraded gifts received, percentage of donors who upgraded, and average size gift for upgrades	Number	=	35	35
	Percent	=	20%	20%
	Average Gift	=	$125	$650
6. Number of prior donors assigned who did not renew their annual gift, percentage, and value of their lost gifts	Number	=	50	50
	Percent	=	22%	22%
	Value	=	$5,000	$25,000
7. Number of prior donors who were not assigned but who did make their annual gift after a telephone or mail request, percentage, and average gift size	Number	=	25	25
	Percent	=	40%	40%
	Average Gift	=	$75	$250
8. Number of prior donors who did not make their annual gift, the percentage, and value of their lost gifts (candidates for follow-up solicitation campaign)	Number	=	50	50
	Percent	=	20%	20%
	Value	=	$5,000	$25,000

The comments on the volunteer visit reports should be reviewed with care. This information will provide clues on donor interests and may help to explain responses encountered by other solicitors. For example, if several volunteers report that the project was not easy to explain, that donors were reluctant to meet with them, or that media coverage on another topic caused donors to hesitate in supporting this year's project (a change of leadership at the organization, a scandal, or

Exhibit 9.6

Criteria for Volunteer Performance Evaluation

		SCORE			
	low				high
1. Attended committee meetings	1	2	3	4	5
2. Made a personal gift	1	2	3	4	5
3. Accepted assignments	1	2	3	4	5
4. Read the information provided	1	2	3	4	5
5. Did the work on time	1	2	3	4	5
6. Cooperated with volunteer leaders	1	2	3	4	5
7. Cooperated with staff	1	2	3	4	5
8. Responded when called upon	1	2	3	4	5
9. Reported results	1	2	3	4	5
10. Offered suggestions for improvements	1	2	3	4	5
11. Advocated the cause to others	1	2	3	4	5
Median Score					

a feature story about another project), these facts should be evaluated for their impact on overall results and the details shared with volunteers at the report meetings.

There is merit in conducting performance evaluations for volunteers as well. Exhibit 9.6 provides a reasonably nonthreatening checklist of criteria that can be completed by the volunteers themselves. Job descriptions, which are recommended for the volunteer-led solicitation program, can use these 11 criteria to describe their duties and assignments; next year, all volunteers can be informed of these criteria as the campaign begins. Finally, so that every area of the campaign can be evaluated for its performance, volunteer solicitors should be asked to critique their own experience using the following checklist:

1. Preparations (goals, leadership, documents).
2. Recruitment (identification, approach, appointment).
3. Orientation and training (time, place, agenda, speakers, assignments, donor card information, worker's kit).
4. Kickoff meeting (location, style, agenda).
5. Volunteer support (leadership, team captains, staff).
6. Campaign operations (budget, report meetings, gift reports).
7. Donor relations (contact reports, benefits, thank-you letters).

8. Staff support (to leaders, volunteers, and donors).

9. Recognition and reward (donors and volunteers).

10. Victory celebration (location, style, agenda).

Volunteers should be encouraged to share their ideas on how to make the campaign more successful next time. Critique reports should concentrate on volunteer and donor performance and areas for improvement. Everyone learns from experience; critique comments should not be used to find fault or point fingers at anyone or anything. If errors were committed, they should be noted along with suggestions on how they can be prevented next time. A summary report on the campaign should be prepared and shared with all volunteers as well as with the board of directors, who otherwise will only be aware of how much money was raised.

A second summary report on the rate of growth in giving, to compare prior campaign results with the most recent experience is also recommended (see Exhibits 9.7 and 9.8). Careful monitoring of the number of donors and volunteers participating is just as important as tracking their dollars given. Other details, such as comparisons of average gift size and budget expenses, should also be included to demonstrate the efficiency and profitability of the volunteer-led personal solicitation campaign.

Exhibit **9.7**

Summary Report on Rate of Growth in Giving for Volunteer-Led Solicitation Annual Giving Campaign (Prior Gift at $500)

	Two Years Ago	Last Year	Annual Rate of Growth (%)	This Year	Annual Rate of Growth (%)	Cumulative Rate of Growth (%)
Number of donors	125	150	20	175	17	18
Number or volunteers	30	40	33	50	25	29
Number of dollars	$62,500	$77,250	24	$91,875	19	21
Budget	$6,500	$7,500	15	$8,500	13	14
Average gift size	$500	$515	3	$525	2	2
Average cost per gift	$52.00	$50.00	-4	$48.57	-3	-3
Overall fund-raising cost (%)	10	10	-7	9	-5	-6

Exhibit 9.8

Rate of Growth in Volunteer-Led Solicitation Campaign

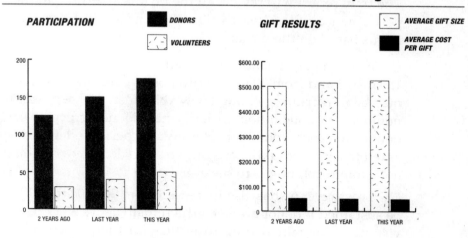

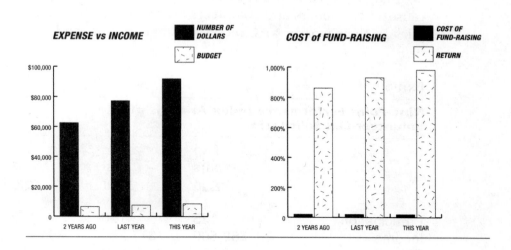

Summary Interpretation

The final report will review all the results according to the nine-point performance index (see Exhibits 9.9 and 9.10). Here are some comments based on these examples:

(1) The number of donors and volunteer solicitors has increased from 125 to 175 and from 30 to 50, with positive results. The only limitation may be in recruiting enough new volunteers to keep pace with donor numbers so solicitation assignments do not creep over five prior donors for each volunteer. However, experienced volunteers can be asked to consider taking one or two extra donors to call on if there are not enough volunteers to see everyone.

(2) Gross revenue has also increased from $62,500 to $91,875 and may be sustained if donor average gifts remain above $500 and if sufficient volunteers remain willing to meet with them. Income can increase from the same donor pool if requests for larger gifts become more frequent, which also helps to preserve the current gift level.

(3) Budget increases are modest ($6,500 to $8,500) and go up only because added donors and volunteers are involved who need more supplies in their worker kits; increase attendance at the kickoff, report

Exhibit 9.9

**Nine-Point Performance Index Analysis of
Volunteer-Led Solicitation**

	Two Years Ago	Last Year	This Year
Participation	125	150	175
Income	$62,500	$77,250	$91,875
Expenses	$6,500	$7,500	$8,500
Percent participation	63%	75%	70%
Average gift size	$500	$515	$525
Net income	$56,000	$69,750	$83,375
Average cost per gift	$52.00	$50.00	$48.57
Cost of fund-raising	10%	10%	9%
Return	862%	930%	981%

Exhibit 9.10

Illustration of Nine-Point Performance Index Analysis of Volunteer-Led Solicitation

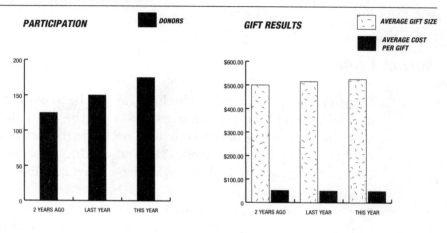

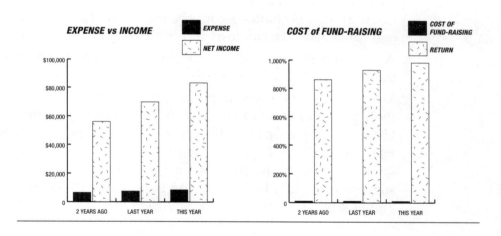

meetings, and victory celebration; and add to the number of recognition items for all participants.

(4) Average gift size has increased from $500 to $525 due to the renewal of faithful donors, more donors in the pool, and effective upgrading requests. If average gift size begins to decline, careful attention to external conditions and volunteer solicitation techniques will be necessary.

(5) The average cost per gift to produce these dollars is modest ($50), which is reflected in the cost of fund-raising (10%), certainly the most efficient of any annual giving solicitation method yet presented in this workbook.

Action Plans

Identify groups of donors who have not yet been asked to renew their annual gift and were not assigned during the campaign or were not seen by their designated solicitor. Also identify donors whose gift pledge has not been received. Plan and conduct their renewal solicitation by the most efficient and effective means possible:

1. The best plan is to schedule a second volunteer-led solicitation campaign a few months later. Using trained volunteers on the solicitation committee will be most productive because they are already well versed in the project and in the personal solicitation technique, certainly more able than an entirely new group of volunteers. However, a new group of volunteers could be recruited and trained for the second campaign, who can use this activity to gain some experience.

2. As an alternative, organize a telephone campaign to try to talk to as many of these donors as possible.

3. Mail them a first-class, personal letter inviting them to continue their generous level of support. A letter cleanup campaign is the last resort, but even this effort has a good chance to succeed if you use first-class postage and send personal letters to each prior donor that mentions their last gift, discusses the project briefly, suggests a slightly larger gift, and is signed by the committee chair and vice chair.

Donors and volunteers should be added to the mailing list for regular newsletters and reports to keep them informed of the progress of their nonprofit organization. Remember to send them birthday, anniversary, and season's greetings cards. Invite them to all the regularly scheduled public activities and special events, especially those offered to everyone else in the community. These invitations tell donors and volunteers they are being remembered as friends, not just as a source of money.

Related Benefits

Personal attention to donors and volunteers will benefit the nonprofit organization in several other ways, beginning with reliable financial and volunteer support each year. It will also be beneficial in the future, when the organization will search out its best prospects for a capital campaign. Planned giving and estate planning services can be offered to donors and volunteers as a retirement planning service, not as just another solicitation tactic. If the need arises for the organization to call on community residents to advocate its mission for a special purpose or to help in a legislative or regulatory matter where expressions of public support are essential, it can turn with confidence to its best friends, its faithful annual donors, and its many volunteers.

10

Annual Giving Summary Evaluations

The annual giving programs presented in Chapters 3 through 9 in this workbook are a large area of fund-raising practice. Nonprofit organizations can use all of these solicitation activities to raise the money they need with efficiency and effectiveness. The use of only one of these solicitation activities is not an annual giving program and does not have much potential to benefit the organization. The challenge is to integrate all of them into a comprehensive and vigorous series of solicitations, which will take years, and to continue working toward increased productivity and profitability.

Annual giving programs are the front lines of every organization's year-long effort to raise the money it needs for operating purposes. Annual giving is how and when most people become involved with nonprofit organizations, where most giving takes place, and where the greatest variety of fund-raising methods and techniques are in active practice. For some organizations, annual giving represents the entire public solicitation program; they have not begun to invest in any major gift or planned giving areas.

Annual giving combines identifying and recruiting new donors with renewing and upgrading previous donors. Annual giving also is the means to expand donor and volunteer involvement and participation in personal relationships through membership associations, donor clubs, support groups, activities, benefits, and special events, and volunteer-led, personal solicitation activities. What is constant is a relentless effort at identification and recruitment of new donors alongside promoting the continuous commitment of prior donors; and these activities all depend on friend-raising and relationship-building operating at their peak through the use of every one of these public participation opportunities. A comprehensive annual giving program is a well-oiled machine capable of steady and reliable service, day in and day out, year in and year out.

Annual giving must be annual. If solicitation is suspended even for one year, restarting the program and bringing it back to its former level of productivity can take two years or more. Each year's effort repeats all the work of soliciting for the first time. The key to success year after year lies in the nonprofit organization's ability to achieve coordination, cooperation, and communication between volunteers and donors. Annual giving offers a diversity of activity to large numbers of people. A highly coordinated effort can make it effective, efficient, productive, and profitable, and allow it to continue again the next year, and the next, without faltering.

Annual giving programs can occur once a year or all year long. Most nonprofit organizations appear to the public to be constantly asking for money. This perception can cause concern among board members and management if they believe overly aggressive behavior is present. Such an approach might offend those being solicited, which could hurt the organization's chances for raising the money it needs. The defect in this concern is that annual giving is not a once-a-year activity; its whole purpose is to ask for gifts in multiple ways throughout the year.

You should understand three special features about annual giving if your organization is to use this technique at its full potential and capacity:

1. Think beyond one year at a time.
2. Pressure to produce cash only is destructive.
3. There are many benefits other than money to be attained.

Annual giving solicitation activity can deliver other benefits besides necessary cash. It includes opportunities for volunteer recruitment and training, leadership identification and development, new client recruitment, new donor acquisition, market penetration, expanded public exposure, increased business contacts, and improved community relations. Perhaps its greatest benefit is that it also builds a cadre of faithful, committed donors, most of whom are willing to give again, year after year. These donors will be the same people who, with time and attention, may agree to commit major assets acquired over their lifetime as a major gift to the nonprofit organization that spends some time maintaining their friendship.

Purposes

Annual giving solicitation programs are an organization's building blocks. Each solicitation activity is one part of a whole, and when all are assembled together, they represent substance and structure. This structure is exemplified in the pyramid of giving (Exhibit 10.1) where the results of annual giving provide the foundation for solicitation programs for gifts of size through major and planned giving activities. This overall design completes the primary and continuing objectives of every annual giving program, to:

1. Identify and recruit new friends and donors.
2. Build lasting relationships through gift renewal and volunteerism.
3. Raise the money needed each year for priority projects.
4. Expand the relationship between community and organization.
5. Improve public understanding of the mission.
6. Increase public confidence and trust in the organization.
7. Fulfill the promise to make maximum use of gifts received by rendering quality services for public benefit.
8. Provide honors and recognition to faithful donors and volunteers.

Look carefully at whether your organization's present annual giving programs are on track with the amount of friend-raising, relationship-building, and reliable gift income productivity it should expect. Annual giving is not the source of all the money an organization can raise. What can be expected of annual giving is dependable net revenue. Annual giving solicitation has five primary objectives:

1. Acquire new donors.
2. Renew current donors.
3. Upgrade existing donors.
4. Coordinate together for donor advancement.
5. Maximize the methods used.

Exhibit 10.1

Pyramid of Giving Illustrating Annual Giving Solicitation Programs

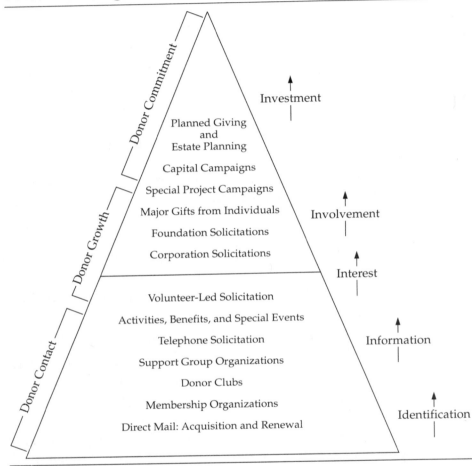

Application of these objectives will provide most of the friends and annual funds an organization needs. Predictability may be the best of annual giving's attributes. Reliable donors and faithful volunteers combined with effective and efficient solicitation activities are the source of annual wealth many an organization enjoys. Why? Think of annual gifts as the equivalent of investment earnings from a permanent endowment 10 times their size.

Annual giving programs are expected to do more each year, as though such improvements were inevitable. Many factors that affect success are outside the direct control of a nonprofit organization, its volunteers, and donors. When estimating future results, include an analysis of public acceptance of the message, the communications medium being used, and the project chosen to receive the money raised.

Preparation

Coordination for every annual solicitation enterprise must be carried out not as the fiscal or calendar year begins but throughout the entire year. The results of one program can affect all the others; flexibility is required to keep every program on its track, following its best plan, yet able to adjust where and when needed to respond to a changing public as well as the changing needs of the nonprofit organization.

Leadership is the key to success in every fund-raising activity. Nonprofit organizations with strong and effective leadership will be able to attract and maintain the levels of public support they need each year. Volunteer leaders have to be found, educated, and trained and given experience to grow with an organization and remain committed to its future. This same commitment must be given to the professional and support staff in the fund development office. Leaders in some organizations may not appreciate the concept of investing adequately in their fund-raising office and in the traditional, proven solicitation practices described in this workbook. Their emphasis may be too much on the money to be raised. These leaders may be fair game for quick fixes, "easy money," or other schemes that promise to deliver whatever money can be found. As a result, no broad-based annual giving program of substance or duration will be designed, or nurtured toward its potential to serve this nonprofit organization that needs and deserves better.

Leadership in annual giving begins with the board of directors and the CEO. Their vision of the mission, purposes, goals, and objectives of their nonprofit organization motivates annual giving's volunteer leaders and staff, prospects, and donors.

Because annual giving solicitation activities must be carried out each year, some thought and preparation must be given to how best to use these successful techniques over and over again. In and of themselves, they can quickly become stale and uninteresting. What stimulates them and excites their audiences are the projects and priority needs they support. The nonprofit organization that has a multiyear vision of its future, expressed in its master plan or strategic plan, will have more than one project or priority need to choose from as the special focus of its annual giving programs each year. With this vision in mind, your organization can evaluate a series of objectives each year (see Exhibit 10.2).

When people hear reports of how funds raised last year were used and how this year's contributions will be added to that same project or to another more current priority, the results of these effective programs serving community needs become the central focus, not the money needed to maintain the programs. Reporting what prior gifts have already accomplished is just as important as reporting what the money yet to be raised will do. These messages work in harmony to report on progress already achieved thanks to donor generosity; this is a success story. Linking annual projects with the master plan allows donors, who often think and act like private investors, to keep track of the progress their funds are helping to make possible each year. They are advancing the organization according to its plans. When a new year arrives with a new project, the donors are more than willing to continue their investment of time, talent, and treasure.

Many annual giving programs appear to be pressured to make as much money as possible, as quickly as possible, and in any way possible. Their goals do not emphasize recruiting and renewing donors who

Exhibit 10.2

Criteria for Measurement of Annual Giving Objectives

		low		SCORE		high
1.	Develop the image linked to the mission	1	2	3	4	5
2.	Obtain friends to support the mission	1	2	3	4	5
3.	Identify and acquire new donors	1	2	3	4	5
4.	Continue to renew most prior donors	1	2	3	4	5
5.	Build relationships with donors	1	2	3	4	5
6.	Identify and involve volunteers	1	2	3	4	5
7.	Develop and train future leaders	1	2	3	4	5
8.	Raise money in a cost-effective manner	1	2	3	4	5
9.	Communicate and inform donors	1	2	3	4	5
10.	Recognize and reward donors	1	2	3	4	5
11.	Develop major and estate donors for the future	1	2	3	4	5
12.	Build confidence and trust in the organization					

Median Score _____

have contributed dollars year after year although this is where progress and profits truly reside. Unrealistic expectations in the form of arbitrary goals do not allow program improvements to be implemented because program objectives must be sacrificed in the quest for dollars. Goal setting should be based on reliable data, careful analysis of prior results, attention to external conditions, and more, not an arbitrary figure based on how much money is needed.

Organizational needs must be balanced realistically against what can be raised in the current year given the maturity of the organization, the productivity of each of its annual solicitation activities in use, leadership from the board and other volunteers, acceptance by the community, and how effectively and efficiently these and other factors are working together. Goals should be understood by management and volunteers as target objectives, not fixed figures. They represent a "package" of purposes and dollar objectives, strategic plans and projected outcomes, public benefits and fiscal realities, and more. Their combination must be where the emphasis is placed, not how much money can be raised by Friday! Remember, too, that this same organization must return next year or next month to ask again.

Budget

Individual budgets for each annual giving solicitation activity have been presented in the preceding chapters. Together, these solicitation activities represent a substantial effort and an important level of commitment in an organization's operating budget.

A nonprofit organization should expect a reliable level of annual gift income from a reasonable investment of its operating budget. Expected income should be based on prior performance. Annual giving results seldom differ dramatically from year to year. Steady growth can be expected except when new solicitation activities are introduced, which may take two to three years to achieve their levels of maturity in performance and productivity.

When budgets have to be cut back during the operating year, this decision can affect more than revenue production and performance. The relationship between budget and results is tied to expenses, based on each programs's maturity and previous performance. If the budget is cut $10,000, this amount can be taken from one annual giving solicitation activity but it may not be fair to expect it to produce increased net income. The performance measurements provided in this workbook clearly show how results are linked to effort in each method of solicitation activity. If the decision is to cut $10,000 in donor acquisition by mail, the number of new donors who will be available for renewal and upgrading to all the other programs in the future will decline. If the cut is applied to membership association benefits, donor club privileges, support group programs, or to an already successful benefit event, this decision could result in lost donors as well as less revenue. The impact is hard to calculate.

Budget preparations should be guided by analysis of prior performances and the costs to achieve them. Using only one year's bottom-line figures of total revenue received against total budget consumed can be a misleading and inaccurate way to estimate the budget for the following year. Annual giving solicitation activities are designed to stimulate large numbers of donors; they depend on lots of participants as evidence of public acceptance and responsiveness. Net dollars raised, average gift size and average cost per gift, are additional signs of a program's level of productivity and profitability. Hard data help everyone to understand where more budget should be invested because of the potential to return a higher profit at a better cost of fund-raising and return percentage.

Execution

Each annual giving program can add all these solicitation activities that match with the organization to form a comprehensive annual giving program. But your organization may not be able to offer all of the annual giving methods described in this workbook. If so, you can use the following additional forms of solicitation, although you should be aware that they are not as effective or efficient as those already described:

1. Advertising and coupons.
2. Commemorative and tribute giving.
3. Commercial sales, cause-related marketing, and affinity cards.
4. Door-to-door and on-street solicitation.
5. Federated campaigns.
6. Gambling and games of chance.

7. Multimedia options (other than letter-call-letter).

8. Premiums and "give-backs."

9. Television and radio solicitation.

10. Previews, open houses, grand openings, exhibits, and special shows.

Calendar control can be used to coordinate events throughout your organization. A master calendar can keep track of all mailings, public activities, benefits, and special events and can include notes on all the holidays and related off-site programs to avoid head-to-head conflicts whenever possible.

The following guidelines will serve as a checklist:

1. Keep doing what you are doing, especially if it is effective and efficient.

2. Study all performance data to learn where improvements lie.

3. Report results to others and explain their interpretations.

4. Define options for improvement and be willing to risk investing in them.

5. Prepare an annual business plan for each annual giving solicitation activity.

6. Propose changes based on performance plus improvements tested, and forecast the likely results.

7. Prepare a three-year business plan for each solicitation activity and for the combined annual giving program.

8. Ask for more budget to implement those programs that can be expanded, based on reliable forecasts of increased net revenue.

Finally, with 365 days in the year, there are 365 occasions when donors or volunteers can be thanked again for what they have done for a nonprofit organization. Try not to forget anyone else who was part of the annual giving program, including board members, management and professional staff, employees, vendors, suppliers, and more. All were needed; all played a part in achieving success. These extra "thank-you" messages can be made as announcements at public functions, printed in one or more of the organization's newsletters, publications, or annual reports, or contained in a special year-end letter of appreciation.

Analysis

Several new criteria apply to performance measurement of annual giving solicitation activities as a comprehensive and collaborative enterprise (see Exhibit 10.3). Professional and support staff in the fund development office should be included in these annual performance reviews.

You should also evaluate the office staff and systems on whose support all the annual giving solicitation activities depend for success. Ten support areas are proposed for this review:

1. Relationships and support from board, CEO, and employees.
2. Management of changing annual priorities.
3. Delivery of timely and accurate gift reports.
4. Adequate budget preparation and management.
5. Meeting cost-benefit standards and guidelines.
6. Timely program performance measurements.
7. Office functions, operating procedures, and computer support.

Exhibit 10.3

Evaluation Criteria for Measurement of Overall Annual Giving Solicitation Activity

			SCORE		
		low			high
1.	Comparison with prior-year results	1	2	3	4	5
2.	Growth in donor universe	1	2	3	4	5
3.	Penetration of new markets	1	2	3	4	5
4.	Quality of effort	1	2	3	4	5
5.	Leadership development	1	2	3	4	5
6.	Consistency and personalization of all messages	1	2	3	4	5
7.	Regular reports and analysis of results	1	2	3	4	5
8.	Staff training and development	1	2	3	4	5
9.	Matching institutional needs (dollars deliverd on schedule)	1	2	3	4	5
10.	Forecasting future income and each program's performance	1	2	3	4	5

Median Score _____

8. Training for all staff members.

9. Financial accounting and reporting.

10. Donor and volunteer recognition and reward.

Last but not least, you should analyze donor relations, recognition, and reward. Donors and volunteers deserve the most attention, and special privileges are reserved for them in accordance with their gift levels and voluntary roles. Many recognition opportunities are available throughout each year that can be measured (see Exhibit 10.4).

Summary Interpretation

Finally, assemble the results of every annual giving solicitation program for a group summary analysis (see Exhibits 10.5 and 10.6), to trace the progress of each fund-raising method during the past three years, adding net revenue received plus cost of fund-raising and return percentages. Based on this reliable data, add a forecast of the next year's performance for each of these solicitation activities. Such a forecast can be accepted with a high degree of confidence and reliability because of

Exhibit 10.4

Donor and Volunteer Recognition Opportunities Based on Participation in Annual Giving Solicitation Activities

	SCORE				
	low				high
1. For every gift (new, renewed, upgraded)	1	2	3	4	5
2. For membership organization gifts (new, renewed, upgraded)	1	2	3	4	5
3. For donor club gifts (new, renewed, upgraded)	1	2	3	4	5
4. For each response to an activity, benefit, or special event (new, renewal, upgraded)	1	2	3	4	5
5. During each event, benefit, and special event	1	2	3	4	5
6. For each committee leader and volunteer worker	1	2	3	4	5
7. At annual meetings and other offical gatherings	1	2	3	4	5
8. At grand openeings, dedications, and other occasions and ceremonies	1	2	3	4	5
9. In news releases, brochures, newsletters, magazines, case statements, and annual reports	1	2	3	4	5
10. Whenever you see a donor in person	1	2	3	4	5

Median Score _____

Exhibit 10.5

Three-Year Performance Summary of Annual Giving Activities with a Reliable Forecast of Next Year's Results

	2 Years Ago	Last Year Actual	This Year Actual	Estimated Next Year
Contributions Income				
Direct mail (acquisition)	$102,580	$125,875	$152,669	$170,000
Direct mail (renewal)	12,450	24,550	31,064	40,000
Membership dues	79,600	86,300	91,400	100,000
Donor club gifts	465,200	498,600	528,550	550,000
Support groups	472,500	496,800	531,750	550,000
Telephone solicitation	109,250	118,550	136,468	150,000
Benefit events (3)	219,500	231,600	252,762	275,000
Volunteer-led personal solicitation	62,500	77,250	91,875	105,000
Subtotals	$1,523,580	$1,659,525	$1,816,538	$1,940,000
Solicitation Costs	$479,850	$492,775	$505,457	$525,000
Net Income Received	$1,043,730	$1,166,750	$1,311,081	$1,415,000
Cost of fund-raising	31%	30%	28%	27%
Return	218%	237%	259%	270%

results already achieved and the knowledge of how these results were accomplished. Here are some observations based on these examples:

(1) This overall annual giving program is inspiring for its size, scope, and overall productivity. These data were drawn from the results presented in Chapters 3 through 9, and while each had its separate performance, their combination is impressive and even a bit overwhelming. To raise a net of more than $1.3 million as this year's actual results at a cost of fund-raising of 28% is compelling evidence of a mature annual giving program operating at a high level of efficiency.

(2) The forecast estimated for each program's production next year is conservative yet continues to predict improvements for each solicitation activity. Given the level of maturity these data demonstrate, gains are reasonable. Unknowns can have a negative effect on this forecast, which justifies its modest assumptions. Examples of unknowns include the next list of priority projects that may or may not excite these donors and others to the same degree, changes to volunteer leadership or staff,

Exhibit 10.6

Illustration of Three-Year Performance Index Analysis of Annual Giving Solicitation

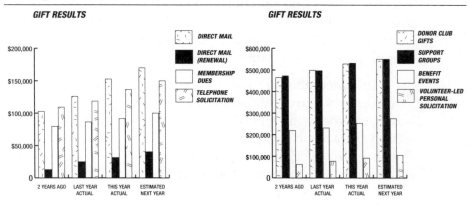

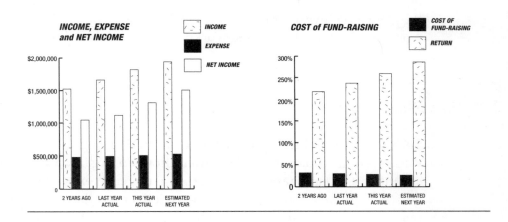

economic downturns, natural disasters, and national elections; all these can and will happen although we hope, not all in the same year. Positive events happen too. One of the organization's departments with an active donor club and support group wins a national award for excellence, a major title sponsor for one of the benefit events commits to a major underwriting gift and a three-year partnership—such well planned or lucky incidents boost everyone's spirits as well as their participation and net income.

(3) Budget expenses have increased slightly (about 5%), which is reasonable. However, overall scope of this annual giving program is demanding on professional and support staff in the fund development office. There is no equation to determine what number of donors, what volume of benefit events, what number of volunteers would suggest it is time to add staff to be able to continue to provide all the support this annual giving program requires.

It is incumbent in the nature of fund development work that it is active, very active. It also places demands on this staff for total accuracy in processing and recording of every gift, for smooth functioning of every activity and special event, for training effective volunteers who fulfill all their assignments, and for keeping donors happy and satisfied. Given this much activity, there are a lot of areas where errors can be made. Any program intensely involved with a volume of people and personalities, handling their money and their feelings, has risks and the potential for offending someone, whether or not any offense was accidental or in fact occurred. When errors and complaints begin, they must be investigated, and this is a good time also to look at staff workloads, support systems, workplace stress, and other factors that can affect performance.

Action Plans

Because of the volume and variety of annual giving solicitation activities, systems must be in place that allow an organization's leaders, volunteers, donors, and staff to profit from each experience. Annual giving's greatest asset is its ability to deliver a reliable repeat performance, which is also where its risks occur. A constant review of performance must begin soon after each form of solicitation begins, not 12 months later, because the annual giving program plan calls for a series of solicitations to follow one another within this current 12-month period.

The intent in being watchful is not to oversupervise or be overbearing, but to be alert to how each solicitation activity is being received by the public. Being alert to anything that can affect the public's ability and willingness to respond to a well-planned sequence of solicitation activities is essential; any major change may require modifications in the entire plan, schedule, and more as the program progresses during the year. Monitoring progress also is excellent preparation for making next year's plans, which leads to a more reliable forecast of likely performance and results.

Related Benefits

Reliable net income, committed donors, and experienced volunteers are valuable enough, but are all the other potential benefits being achieved? Several related benefits have been described in the preceding chapters. These include building and enhancing the image of the organization, marketing and communicating its quality programs and services, recruiting and training its future leaders, and improving its relations with community residents. It is valuable to review progress in each of these areas as well as to count donors and dollars.

As Part II of this workbook is concluded and Part III begins its concentration on solicitation programs for gifts of size, added benefits for major gift activity appear. Who among these annual donors are likely to be qualified donors for major gifts? How many experienced volunteers are available? What knowledge about the organization has been achieved by annual giving donors and volunteers to help prepare them for future projects?

PART 3

Solicitation Programs for Gifts of Size

Major giving is different from annual giving in several ways. More emphasis is placed on essentials such as prospect research, cultivation, personal solicitation, and recognition. New features are introduced, too, including the use of multiyear pledges, planned giving, endowment, strategy, and tactics. Perhaps the greatest difference will be the role of the "case" (the specific interests of the donor and the organization's goals that will be emphasized in soliciting the donor) and the size of the gift.

A "case statement" contains a summary of the mission, purpose, and vision for the future of a nonprofit organization. The case documents the plan to move the organization and its programs forward from accomplishments already achieved to higher levels of service, greater quality, even excellence. The case statement defines specific projects and priorities alongside projected outcomes to be realized for public good; includes an awareness of the unique timing, relevance, and urgency each project offers; and is possessed of sufficient size and scope to inspire attention and command respect. There is the possibility that a few major gift donors can turn an opportunity into a significant reality; they become catalysts for both action and accomplishment. They share the vision and, by their decision, invest themselves in its potential for success. When major gift donors and forward-thinking organizations join together, they truly can make a difference.

Corporations and foundations often make major gifts tied to the current and future plans of nonprofit organizations. These donors often prefer to use their limited resources for specific purposes closely matched to their own priorities, and then move on to fulfill their objectives with other nonprofit organizations. Nonprofit organizations can work with corporations and foundations for major gifts when these donors' priorities and purposes come closest to the nonprofit organization's own mission.

Perhaps the most striking difference between annual giving and major giving is tactics. Annual giving concentrates on groups of prospects and donors in mailings or by using membership organizations, donor clubs, benefits, and special events as the common attraction. Major giving must concentrate on individual prospects one at a time after the solicitor has spent time on research, rating, and evaluation; defining interests and strategy; and engaging in cultivation before actual solicitation. Solicitation itself may require multiple visits, teams of solicitors, and thorough consultations with tax, accounting, and financial planning experts.

Tax deductibility has its strongest application to major gift decisions where multiyear pledges and carry-forward deductions are allowed, even encouraged. Planned gifts and estate planning contributions incorporate lifetime decisions with the remaining years a donor may live and include gift decisions made now that will take place after the donor's death. Major gift decisions merit enhanced forms of recognition and continued donor relations.

There is one place where the group tactic applies to major giving. It is the capital campaign where the objective of a special project or building campaign is to solicit several major gifts for a common objective larger than any single donor might ever contemplate.

Performance measurement of major gift solicitation activities will be conducted in the same manner as described for annual giving solicitation activities, including the nine-point performance index. Some analysis will be more subjective than objective, some more qualitative than quantitative. The amount of money raised and its cost of fund-raising are not the only indicators of effectiveness or efficiency; quality counts in major gift solicitation as does achieving compatibility with donor aspirations. Adequate preparations are required by both parties. No individual, corporation, or foundation will make a major gift to a nonprofit organization without their own extensive investigation of every aspect of its present capability, leadership, reputation, financial position, and more.

To be prepared to meet these and other tests of quality preparation and presentation for major gift solicitation will require the serious attention of a nonprofit organization's board, management, and volunteer leadership; anything less will be inadequate to the success they seek. The challenge of major gift solicitation is to do all the homework first, so that an individual "strategic action plan" for *each* major gift prospect can be prepared. This action plan will match well-qualified and well-prepared major gift prospects with the most exciting, inspiring, and worthwhile priority projects that can be offered to them, and that will include consideration of each prospect's own interests and capacity.

Preparations for major gift solicitation lie in the broad-based annual giving program that identifies qualified donors and develops experienced volunteers. A major gift program also must be matched with a thoughtful and thorough plan for the future of the nonprofit organization. This vision provides answers about where an organization is going, what it intends to do, how it will achieve its goals, the outcomes it promises will benefit the community, and more. Further, this vision is a master financial plan that specifies how much money will be required to achieve each objective, how it will be developed, when it is needed, and where it will be spent.

11

Corporate Solicitations

Soliciting corporations for charitable dollars and other forms of support is one of the more challenging areas of fund-raising practice. Any corporation, business, firm, or partnership is first committed to its own financial success and must provide a profit to the owners. When it is profitable, there will be extra money for community service and extra time for active participation in civic and charitable affairs. Most corporate donors will want to know how their participation will provide some return to benefit their business. Executives and employees of companies and firms are less likely to respond to requests for support if the solicitor cannot understand that their priority for survival and self-interest must prevail in their gift decision. An understanding of these basic business principles will help you appreciate how corporate decision making will affect charitable giving.

Many corporations have more than one source of support for nonprofit organizations. The corporate contributions budget is one source; others include funds budgeted for advertising, human resources, marketing, and research (see Exhibit 11.1). You should try to match community needs to these alternative sources.

There are other resources to be shared with nonprofit organizations. Corporations and businesses are full of bright, resourceful people whose own interests and abilities should not be overlooked or go unsolicited. Most nonprofit boards of directors include representatives who have been chosen for service because of their established professional competence, business management skills, and willingness to share their time, talent, and energy with one or more community organizations.

Exhibit 11.1

Sources for Corporate Support to Nonprofit Organizations

Source	Description
1. Outright gift	A direct contribution or grant
2. Matching gift	A gift to match an employee's personal gift to a qualified non-profit organization
3. Advertising and marketing budgets	A gift for public visibility or for a cause-related marketing campaign
4. Research and personnel budgets	A grant to support company product development or to benefit the employee relations program
5. Corporate partnerships	Joint ventures or contracts where programs and services are arranged for employees or customers
6. Employee volunteers	Time, talent, and expertise shared by employees
7. Equipment and service donations	Use of facilities, equipment, and professional services on a pro bono basis
8. Facilities	Access to buildings, telephones, printing and copying machines
9. In-kind donations	Delivery of products without charge or purchase
10. Corporate foundations	Separate granting vehicle for gifts and pledges

A corporate solicitation program requires attention to detail, good preparation, continuous contact, a degree of aggression in wanting to solicit companies, and a positive financial statement.

Purposes

To seek corporate support is not just to search for needed dollars; there must be valid reasons for both parties to work together. A common purpose is to address community needs. The strongest case for support that a nonprofit organization can make is its own expertise in providing quality programs and services that make a difference in the community, especially when those programs and services relate in some way to the success of the company, its products, and its employees. Not every nonprofit organization will qualify for this perfect match of common objectives. When they cannot, they should look to other sources of gift support beyond corporations for the support they need.

America's social and welfare agencies are fortunate in their long-standing ties to corporations through the United Way and Federated Campaign movements, for several reasons. These include permission for annual giving campaigns conducted through in-plant and in-office solicitation (few other nonprofit organizations are permitted this privilege), personal leadership from business executives, and direct corporate grants. This arrangement has its negative side, too; members of federated campaigns seldom can approach these same companies for separate grants because they made their gift decision in the combined campaign. Conversely, some nonprofit organizations may be disqualified from corporate grants because they are not members of a federated campaign.

Those nonprofit organizations who succeed in achieving corporate support have learned where the company, its products, and its people can be matched to their needs. Finding this match and building a relationship around these common objectives is the best method to pursue. To establish such a relationship between two such different entities is never easy; their separate needs for this relationship are surprisingly different (see Exhibit 11.2). However, common areas can be found with effort and understanding.

Exhibit 11.2

Separate Needs for Nonprofit Organizations and Corporations*

What Nonprofit Organizations Need	What Corporations Need
Revenue for current operations	Support business-related community infrastructure
Predictable cash flow	Social investment
Seed money for new programs	Doing good while doing well
Broadening of the resource base	Marketing
Credibility and stature	Influencing public policy
Entry to other funding	
Noncash contributions	

*Lester A. Picker, "The Corporate Support Marketplace," in *The Nonprofit Management Handbook: Operating Policies and Procedures*, Tracy Daniel Connors, Ed. New York: John Wiley & Sons, 1993, pp. 604–607. Reprinted by permission.

Once in place, a strong relationship can continue for many years and withstand changes in top leadership for both organizations as well as occasional decreases in profits. Much of the effort to build and maintain such a partnership must come from the nonprofit organization. A corporation can justify its continued support only as long as the benefits it receives remain valid and those in positions of authority remain committed to the partnership.

Preparation

To find out which businesses and corporations can become candidates for a relationship with a nonprofit organization, begin with basic research to find those whose mission purposes, products, and services are a reasonably close match with the mission and purposes of a nonprofit organization. Only a few dozen are needed, and only a few hundred are likely to be found. Begin with those closest to where the nonprofit organization's facilities are located or near sites where its programs and services are provided. Identify programs and services that are being provided to employees of nearby companies.

Some communities will be fortunate enough to be the headquarters site of one or more national corporations that have established a charitable contributions committee or corporate foundation. Study these firms, their products, and their services; learn how many employees they have, where their employees live, and where they give. If any written purposes or actual gift decisions match what your organization is doing, learn the details of those contributions programs, their policies and procedures for application and deadlines, where they have made grants, and the amounts and purposes of those grants. If the mission and purposes of your organization are consistent with the program areas established by the company for its contributions, find out who makes their contributions decisions. Inquire if any of your organization's board members, volunteers, and donors have any contact or knowledge about the company and its employees.

The next step is to learn how the company is doing in its business. Ask to be placed on the mailing list to receive their annual report. If the company is a public company, ask their agent or a broker friend for their stock prospectus and other public information. The reference section of any public library holds a supply of excellent resource books, but there are thousands of businesses, corporations, firms, and partnerships in existence. Only a few will have any interest in a single nonprofit organization. Begin with those who are local; there is no good reason to begin with Exxon, General Motors, or Microsoft unless your organization is located near one of their major facilities and has some contact with their employees. The nonprofit organization needs, first of all, to find the match of interests both can share. Other essential data include the roster of officers and directors, most recent revenue and sales figures and dividend details, number of plants and offices in the immediate geographic area, product lines and services at those local sites, number of total and local employees, and fiscal year-end data.

To learn the contribution's history of a company will take more digging. What you need is information about their priority interest areas for giving, procedures for application, name of the contribution committee manager, prior giving history (especially to like organizations), the amounts and purposes of gifts, and type of projects supported. This corporate profile can change quickly, and continuing work will be required to maintain current details, another reason to research only the most promising prospects.

Often the best resource for information about corporate giving comes from volunteers and donors. In addition, they are the people who can provide access to many companies because they live and work in the same community as do company employees. The connections that exist between volunteers and donors and the employees in local businesses, corporations, firms, and partnerships constitute the best path to pursue to begin and maintain a relationship for the benefit of both organizations.

Volunteer service opens the door for direct access to the corporation. Many nonprofit organizations seek out volunteer representatives from companies with whom they want to build a relationship.

A final suggestion. Fiscal management is a common area where there is strength and sophistication among for-profit employees; this is an area where nearly all corporations and business enterprises excel. For this reason, a nonprofit organization should be on a sound fiscal footing before it approaches a company for financial support. Business executives can evaluate the fiscal condition quickly and will be leery of providing their time much less their company's money to an organization that is at risk. A balanced annual operating budget and audited financial statement will be a solid starting point. No investor, corporate or otherwise, should spend resources on a poorly run organization.

Budget

Costs associated with a corporate relations program can be broken into three broad areas: (a) prospect research/proposal preparation/staffing, (b) direct solicitation activity, and (c) donor relations. Most of the time required will be needed for research and proposals. There will also be travel costs to meet with corporate officials. After a gift occurs, a donor relations program will be required to maintain and expand the relationship. A full-time corporate relations program (manager and secretary) working with more than 100 corporations a year (local and out-of-town) might require a budget approaching $100,000 per year, whereas a part-time assignment could cost half that amount or less, depending on the organization, its location, and potential for corporate support (see Exhibit 11.3).

The size and scope of a corporate solicitation program will depend on where corporate policy on social responsibility matches with the type of nonprofit organization and its program and service priorities. Corporations favor education, especially higher education, because they can justify "investing" corporate dollars in training future employees, keeping up to date with research developments, meeting employee training requirements, benefiting employee families, and the like. Health and human services represents the second largest area of corporate giving because most large companies participate in United Way and other federated campaigns with both corporate gifts and employee support. Other areas that usually qualify include civic and community projects, culture, and art.[1]

Execution

The initial contact can be made by mail, telephone, or personal visit, as in all other forms of solicitation activity. Personal visits remain the best and will be most useful during cultivation and solicitation. To be successful, a request must hit the bull's-eye and do it in the first sentence of the proposal or verbal appeal, which also must be delivered to the right person.

Get to the point, explain the benefits of participation to the company, and ask for their support. If a letter is required as an introduction, it should be no longer than two pages in length. Don't waste time on extra information the corporation does not need to know about

Exhibit 11.3

Sample Budget for Corporate Solicitation Program

		Estimated Costs (full-time effort)
A. Prospect Research/Proposal Preparation/Staffing		
Taft Corporate Giving Directories		$250
Foundation Center Corporate Grants Directories		250
Proposal preparation and supplies		500
Administrative support		2,000
Staff salaries/benefits		65,000
(Manager/Secretary)		
	Subtotal	$68,000
B. Direct Solicitation Activities		
Local travel (cabs, parking, meals)		$600
Prospect cultivation/entertainment		500
Long distance travel		
Airfare		4,000
Cabs or car rental		1,000
Parking/Meals		750
Accommodations		2,000
	Subtotal	$8,850
C. Donor Relations		
Donor Club certificates/plaques		$2,000
Donor Club directory/newsletter		1,000
Annual report/newsletters		1,000
Invitations/Reservations		1,000
Corporate Technology Seminar		4,000
Annual meeting honors and awards		1,000
	Subtotal	$10,000
	Total	$86,850

your organization. Concentrate on explaining areas of joint interest and valuable returns to the company if they join with this nonprofit organization. Once a match is made, there will be time to expand this knowledge with details about the people who deliver programs and services and the quality of their work, which provides value to company employees and products.

Once qualified companies and contacts have been identified, prepare materials and meet with corporate representatives. Like the introductory letter, the request document or proposal needs to be brief (two pages single-spaced) and to the point. Few business executives have the time to read a lengthy proposal documenting the history, list of service programs with their descriptions, letters from satisfied clients, and copies of every publication the organization has ever produced. Including such extraneous material can damage the request; stick to the points of purpose of the grant, amount required, and value to the company and its employees. The proposal should contain:

1. Cover letter.
2. Proposal summary.
3. Problem and needs statement.
4. Project description and objectives.
5. Benefits to the corporation.
6. Budget requirements.
7. Support documents:
    a. Proof of tax exemption.
    b. Most recent audited financial statement.
    c. Roster of board members and affiliations.
    d. List of other corporate donors and amounts.
    e. Other documents as required.

If a personal visit is possible, plan the meeting with precision: Start by selecting the best team matched with the level of company representative to be seen. Allow only 10 to 15 minutes for actual presentation about the problem or project and the capability of the organization to address it. Focus on the relationship of the project to the company. Leave the balance of time for questions and discussion; being a good listener counts here. Thank the company representative for setting aside the time to consider this request, hand over the formal proposal, offer to provide other details at any time, and depart, all within 30 minutes. Send a follow-up note thanking the person for the visit, and enclose any added information that was requested.

Corporations are capable of quick decisions on requests for gift support; they make business decisions every day. If a contributions committee or foundation is involved, it will likely follow a deliberate process of evaluation to assess the benefits accruing to the company, what other companies have done, and their own availability of funds. The internal process for decision may take a few weeks or months, depending on the meeting schedule of the contributions committee or corporate foundation board of directors. Some corporate contributions managers have discretionary powers to make decisions on their own authority for a limited amount of funds, based on well-established qualifications. Corporations rely on this manager to screen all applications and to bring forward only those that are complete and well-matched to corporate priorities. The manager also adds analysis and recommendations based on all the information received and personal contact with the applicants.

Currently, cause-related marketing proposals are popular with many companies. The concept is to link the reputation of a corporation with that of a nonprofit organization to a sales promotion of company products in a joint advertising campaign. A portion of the sales is promised as a grant to the nonprofit organization, adding the motive of charity to help stimulate customers to buy the product. Visibility for the nonprofit organization is greater than it could ever hope to buy for itself. Your organization may have to pay a tax on this unrelated business income. The businesslike partnership between the company and the organization is the basis for their relationship, but only for the purposes of a joint venture. This concept only works if sales increase; when they decline, the company pulls out.[2]

Use activity reports to keep track of the several corporate solicitations in progress, proposal preparation, next steps in cultivation, and their expected decision dates (see Exhibit 11.4). Those corporations who become donors also require continued attention, not just to maintain their current relationship but to expand their participation in the nonprofit organization if such is possible. It is appropriate to ask a company representative about the firm's interests in other program and service areas and to introduce them to other solicitation activities that may have added value for the company, such as a sponsor or underwriter visibility at one of the organization's benefit events. Inviting employees to become volunteers also will be valuable to both parties.

Each corporate donor should be treated to all the benefits and privileges their gifts deserve within the donor recognition program. There may be merit in setting up a corporate donor club or corporate membership plan to recognize their gifts and allow for an annual meeting, facilities tour, and access to products and employees. The key to keeping corporate gifts coming is a well-prepared corporate relations program.

Exhibit **11.4**

Corporate Solicitation Activities Report

	Last Year	This Year
Research and Preparation		
Number of companies researched	80	105
Number of qualified as prospects	60	82
Number with contacts identified	40	60
Number without contact identified	20	20
Cultivation and Solicitation		
Number of companies with cultivation strategy	40	65
Number of companies without cultivation strategy	20	22
Number of volunteer solicitors trained	10	20
Number of company meetings held	18	40
Number of company meetings scheduled	10	14
Number of company meetings to be scheduled	12	10
Proposal Status		
Number of proposals in preparation	32	48
Number of proposals delivered	18	40
Value of proposals outstanding	$135,000	$255,000
Number of corporate gift decisions	12 yes/6 no	34 yes/6 no
Value of proposals funded	$120,000	$200,000
Number of pledges received	2	5
Value of pledges received	$15,000	$55,000
Support Activities		
Number of companies on the mailing list	80	100
Number of company officials on the mailing list	120	145
Number of invitations sent to benefit events	80	105
Number of replies that purchased tickets	30	35
Number of replies as sponsors or underwriters	18	21
Value of replies as sponsors or underwriters	$62,000	$95,000
Number of company employees attending	62	84
Number of volunteer invitations sent employees	12	30
Number of employee volunteers responding	6	15

Analysis

There are many areas in a corporate solicitation program for performance measurement. The number of qualified companies developed from research can be tracked with the number actually solicited and gift decisions achieved. Proposals can be evaluated for brevity and clarity. Evaluating direct contacts is important; this program does not progress unless volunteers and staff meet and talk with company officials. Meeting visit reports should be reviewed.

Exhibit 11.5 can be used to examine the entire solicitation process. Involve the volunteers who helped with corporate solicitation in this review and seek their candid answers.

Summary Interpretation

The nine-point performance index will report results achieved and analyze them with previous results (see Exhibits 11.6 and 11.7). Here are some observations:

(1) The number of participating companies appears small each year but has grown, suggesting either a limited number of qualified company prospects or an inadequate research effort.

Exhibit 11.5

Evaluation Criteria for Corporation Solicitation

	SCORE				
	low				high
1. Research materials	1	2	3	4	5
2. Cultivation strategy	1	2	3	4	5
3. Project match to company priorities	1	2	3	4	5
4. Presolicitation contacts	1	2	3	4	5
5. Proposal document	1	2	3	4	5
6. Solicitation meetings	1	2	3	4	5
7. Formal proposal submission	1	2	3	4	5
8. Acknowledgment of decision	1	2	3	4	5
9. Donor recognition	1	2	3	4	5
10. Continuing contact	1	2	3	4	5

Median Score

Exhibit 11.6

Nine-Point Performance Index Analysis of Corporate Solicitations

	Two Years Ago	Last Year	This Year	Totals
Participation	22	28	31	81
Income	$18,500	$25,500	$37,500	$81,500
Expenses	$4,525	$5,850	$6,500	$16,875
Percent participation	18%	29%	30%	26%
Average gift size	$841	$911	$1,210	$1,006
Net income	$13,975	$19,650	$31,000	$64,625
Average cost per gift	$206	$209	$210	$208
Cost of fund-raising	24%	23%	17%	21%
Return	309%	336%	477%	383%

(2) The budget required to support this program is for a portion of a staff member's time plus supplies, and local travel, which may be all the commitment this nonprofit organization can afford. Should other corporate opportunities arise, added resources will be needed but should produce good results.

(3) Percent participation suggests one in three requests is successful. This may be the best clue to the balance of this report. Attention to research, projects selected for corporate giving, proposal texts, volunteer training, and solicitation methods are all areas for possible improvement.

(4) The average gift is $1,006. Perhaps this organization is too modest in how much it is requesting, or the local business community is modest in size and resources. Maintaining this level also will be important.

(5) Net proceeds after three years ($64,625) is adequate for the effort and cost involved and appears efficient enough at a cost of fund-raising of 21%. The question remains whether this organization can improve on the number of prospects it has the potential to reach.

Action Plans

Among the benefits from associating with companies is access to their people and products as well as their good name and reputation. When

Exhibit 11.7

Illustration of Nine-Point Performance Index Analysis of Corporate Solicitations

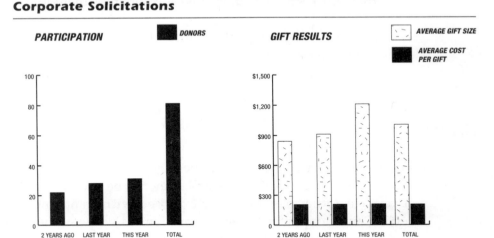

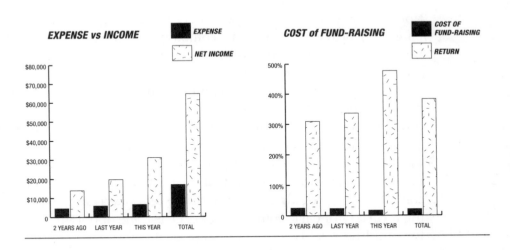

company executives' names appear on a nonprofit organization's letter-head and the corporation is on the list of event sponsors and underwriters, others consider these decisions as endorsements. Ask company executives if you can report their participation in order to influence other companies to join in support. Leveraging one gift decision to gain another is a good strategy and suggests careful thought about which companies to approach first for the biggest gifts so that all the others will be encouraged to respond in a corresponding way.

Other actions to be explored with companies include:

1. Setting an example for other corporations as well as other individuals and foundations.
2. Applying some momentum to the project being funded.

Related Benefits

Endorsements are valuable, and because many companies want public recognition for their gift decisions, they can be used by both parties to advantage. Other benefits to be explored with companies include (a) setting an example for other corporations as well as other individuals and foundations, (b) applying some momentum to the project being funded, (c) providing benefits directly to employees from the organization's programs and services, (d) inviting employees to volunteer in several areas where their time, talent, and energy will directly benefit the organization and its programs, (e) linking a nonprofit organization's name to a company-sponsored advertising and marketing campaign, (f) providing access to company facilities and possibly to its products for in-kind gifts, (g) gaining a discount privilege in purchasing the company's products and services, and more.

Companies are valuable community neighbors as well as valuable donors to nonprofit organizations. Their business and their employees provide economic benefit to the community. They also participate in community life in several ways and they depend upon community services for support of their employees and their families. Local school projects for employee dependents usually qualify for most company contributions programs along with the federated campaign representing a variety of basic community services. The opportunities are great for building relationships into active, ongoing partnerships between corporations and nonprofit organizations that, with attention by both sides, will continue to provide benefits to all.

12

Foundation Solicitations

Success in soliciting foundations will require an investment of time and money, some ability to conduct research and prepare proposals, and the management skill to administer every grant that is received. As with other forms of solicitation activity, a working relationship must be established between those foundations whose own mission, purposes, goals, and objectives are matched closely with the mission, purposes, goals, and objectives of every nonprofit organization who is an applicant.

There are four types of foundations; general purpose, corporate, community, and personal or family foundations. Together, they gave just under $10 billion to charities in 1994.[1] Their grants range in size from many millions to less than $1,000. The 457 largest foundations in asset size ($50 million or more each) made 48 percent of all the foundation grants, while total assets of all foundations exceed $182 billion and are growing. Indeed, they are a precious resource for advancing philanthropy throughout the world.

Purposes

The priorities or proposed use of a foundation's money by a nonprofit organization must match the foundation's purposes as closely as possible. Foundations have limited funds to give, despite their asset value. Nearly all are a permanent endowment of their founder's purposes, and they must manage their assets for the future as well as the present. Foundations are required by law to distribute at least 5 percent of their annual asset value, but some give more. Most reinvest unexpended dollars to preserve capital and to earn more to give later. They are also required to pay annually to the Internal Revenue Service a 2 percent excise tax on their asset value, which suggests that a strong investment performance remains one of the primary goals of boards of directors every year.

Foundations have been unjustly accused of being inflexible, mainstream oriented, ponderous, stagnant, traditional, and out of touch with grassroots responsibilities. Conservative by nature and guided by the strong presence of the Internal Revenue Service, to whom they must validate all their actions, they are unwilling and unlikely to take risks with their money or quickly change their patterns of behavior and are not persuaded otherwise by protest, influence, or even submission of the most convincing and logical of proposals.

Foundations give to a variety of nonprofit organizations in response to applications. A few, notably the Ford Foundation, define specific programs and then invite applications to fulfill that purpose. All prefer to be agents of change rather than a source for routine annual budget support; thus they favor sponsoring new initiatives, experimentation, innovation, and collaboration. After a new program has been funded and launched with their help, they prefer to withdraw their support and move on to another new project. Few want to be the sole sponsor of a single project but relish being a catalyst in stimulating others to participate.

A one-time grant is the likely result of most applications. Multiple grants to the same nonprofit organization are also possible, provided each application is highly qualified to receive support. Only the largest of grantees can expect to qualify for multiple grants in the same year. However, any nonprofit organization can qualify and receive a number of grants from the same foundation over many years, proceeding from qualified project to qualified project as the organization continues to improve and expand its programs and services to more people and causes that remain well matched to the foundation's own purposes. Such relationships bear up well under the test of time and competition, usually because the staff of both institutions have learned to work together as partners in a common cause.

Occasionally, a routine, ongoing program can attract foundation support. Established organizations who have solid experience with their programs and services are well aware of the improvements they want to add, such as expanded quality now within their ability to manage, or the capability to deliver their basic programs to more people.

Such conclusive projects can and will be funded by foundations because of a nonprofit organization's proven ability to succeed. The key to success in grant seeking is solid performance as an organization that has a continuing relationship with foundations.

Preparation

Because foundations are such an important player in the world of philanthropy, you should do your homework first. Identify your organization's goals, objectives, and future plans, and get its financial and management affairs in order *prior* to application. There is a lot of competition for grants, not only between the applicant nonprofit organizations but also between concepts, ideas, and innovative projects that foundations prefer to fund.

Preparation begins with careful research. Nonprofit organizations that do their homework will be rewarded because they will submit their priority projects only to those few foundations looking to fund those same kinds of projects. Matchmaking may be an art between humans, but it is a science with foundations. Study the published policies and procedures that most foundations make available to applicants. These procedures describe how and when to apply, whom to contact, range of grants, restrictions, roster of directors, and other instructive details, all of which should be followed with exactitude. If there is one secret to share about grant applications, it is to follow the directions the foundations have provided.

Here are a series of time-tested questions that will be helpful in selecting which foundations to approach:

1. Has the foundation demonstrated a real commitment to funding in your subject field?
2. Does it seem likely that the foundation will make grants to recipients in your geographic location?
3. Does the amount of money you are requesting fit within the foundation's grant range?
4. Does the foundation have any policy prohibiting grants for the type of support you are requesting?
5. Does the foundation like to make grants to cover the full cost of a project or do they favor projects where other foundations or funding sources share the costs?

6. For what period of time does the foundation generally make grants?

7. What types of organization does the foundation tend to support?

8. Does the foundation have application deadlines or does it review proposals continuously?[2]

Once preliminary research has identified a list of likely foundation suspects, write them and ask for their annual report and application guidelines. Read their documents carefully and follow their instructions exactly. If they ask for a two-page letter for a preliminary review, limit the text to two pages and set aside all the wonderful letters of endorsement, statistics, drawings, and photographs to share with them later. The initial contact is only to verify qualification (type of organization, deadline, priorities, amount, etc.) for the next step; don't get disqualified for failing to observe written procedures. Remember foundations have perhaps 100 times as many applications as they have money; do not give them any reason to eliminate your request from all the others.

Larger foundations have professional staff who will work with applicants. Be sensitive to their limited time to talk with everyone. Prepare the inquiry in advance by using the research data. When questions arise, call or write to ask for clarification. It is a source of continuous amazement to the boards and staff of foundations that, despite their best efforts to prepare and distribute annual reports and application instructions with full details about their purposes and qualifications, priorities and objectives, prior-year grants, names of trustees and staff, and their financial statements, 90 percent of the organizations that apply continue to fail to observe these well-publicized guidelines.

Proposal preparation is next. Once you have found a foundation whose priorities match the mission and purposes of your organization, you can prepare a grant application to present an opportunity to partner a joint enterprise. The contents of the proposal must be complete and should include the following:

1. Cover letter.

2. Introduction.

3. History and background.

4. Project description and problem statement.

5. Goals, objectives, and estimated outcomes.

6. Plan of action and project methodology.

7. Evaluation plan and reports.

8. Budget required and future funding plan.

9. Conclusion and summary statement.

10. Attachments, appendixes, and support materials:

    a. Roster of board members.

    b. Most recent audited financial statement.

    c. Operating budget for current year.

    d. Tax-exempt documentation.

    e. Curriculum vitae for program director.

    f. Charts, drawings, renderings.

    g. Other essential support documentation requested.

Each proposal also must answer all the specific information areas identified by the foundation as necessary to its evaluation.

It is a good idea to talk with other organizations who have received grants from the same foundations about the details of their application and to receive any helpful hints about areas of emphasis or sensitivity they experienced during the application and review process. Ask also about deadlines, the amount of time before a decision is known, when the funds are actually delivered, and any continuing updates and financial reports required. Many times, the research sources are two to three years behind current operations and foundations might have amended their operating procedures in the interim.

Certain qualities are preferred by foundation managers, and it is helpful to screen the final proposal text against those that are best known (see Exhibit 12.1). If the median score is not a four or higher, the content of the application needs more work to address any of its weaknesses. Another set of evaluations will be needed in the proposal document to describe how the organization will monitor its use of foundation funds toward the objectives specified in the proposal.

Budget

The direct costs to conduct a foundation solicitation program are reasonable. In fact, the greatest single expense will be people's time—lots of time to do the research, prepare and submit proposals, make

Exhibit **12.1**

Criteria for Measuring Characteristics Essential to Foundation Applications

	SCORE				
Characteristic	low				high
Accuracy	1	2	3	4	5
Brevity	1	2	3	4	5
Clarity	1	2	3	4	5
Competence	1	2	3	4	5
Completeness	1	2	3	4	5
Correct English	1	2	3	4	5
Credibility	1	2	3	4	5
Fiscally sound	1	2	3	4	5
Honesty	1	2	3	4	5
Matching priorities	1	2	3	4	5
Public benefit	1	2	3	4	5
Relevancy	1	2	3	4	5
Urgency	1	2	3	4	5
Median Score					

necessary visits to foundation offices when required or appropriate, keep track of their review progress, and if approved, acknowledge receipt of the grant with its terms and conditions, administer the money received, prepare the required periodic and summary reports, and maintain good liaison with foundation staff. Such work is often a full-time job that requires some experience as well as expertise; foundation work is not an area for part-time attention.

Direct costs other than salary and benefits of personnel assigned include basic reference works and source books, on-line computer services, postage and telephone charges plus training, some local and long-distance travel, and supplies. Indirect and overhead costs include the usual list to capture the appropriate expenses directly associated with foundation solicitation.

Each proposal also will contain a budget to define all the expense areas for the project contained in the proposal (see Exhibit 12.2); some foundations provide budget guidelines and worksheets and

Exhibit 12.2

Sample Budget for Foundation Solicitation Program

		Estimated Costs (full-time effort)
A. Prospect Research/Proposal Preparation/Staffing		
Foundation Center Directories		$500
Foundation Associates Subscription		500
Taft Foundation Grant Directories		500
Proposal preparation and supplies		1,500
Administrative support		2,000
Staff salaries/benefits (Manager/Secretary)		65,000
	Subtotal	$70,000
B. Direct Solicitation Activities		
Local travel (cabs, parking, meals)		$1,000
Prospect cultivation/entertainment		2,000
Long distance travel		
Airfare		5,000
Cabs or car rental		2,000
Parking/Meals		2,500
Accommodations		3,000
	Subtotal	$15,500
C. Donor Relations		
Accounting/Status reports		$500
Annual Report/newsletters		500
Invitations/Reservations		500
Annual Meeting honors and awards		500
	Subtotal	$2,000
	Total	$87,500

will include all the categories they wish to examine in evaluating the fiscal status of the applicant organization as well as the proposed expenses for the project.

While some staff in nonprofit organizations may believe they have unusual abilities in preparing budgets and accounting for funds, they should appreciate that foundation staff have an equal or possibly greater ability to read and interpret budgets and audited financial statements. Now is not the time for creative accounting; put most of the effort into accuracy and completeness. Consider adding a budget narrative to further explain fiscal plans; full and open disclosure is the recommended attitude. One of the most complete budget forms is required by the Kresge Foundation, whose exacting use of these data are important criteria for staff review before an application is submitted to their board for a decision.

Your organization will incur added costs in supporting projects funded by the grants it receives. These are direct, indirect, and overhead expenses that have to be met from your organization's own or other resources. Foundations prefer to avoid paying some of or all these extra costs, not because they do not accept their reality and the impact their grant will have on the operating budget of the organization but because they want to preserve as much of their grant money for as many grants to as many organizations as possible.

The best guidance for preparing a project budget is to follow the foundation's stated policies. If they are clear on whether they will pay overhead costs, follow their instructions exactly. Do not try to disguise or hide these expenses in other areas of the budget because they are likely to be challenged and may disqualify the application altogether.

Budget areas include two broad categories—salaries and benefits and the expenses for program and project operations (see Exhibit 12.3). Reasonable increases can be anticipated during the period the project is in operation. At the point of submission, it is important to anticipate how the project will progress and plan its expenses as accurately as possible. Once the grant is awarded, you can almost never go back and ask for added budget, even if based on a cost-of-living increase or an unanticipated turn of events.

Execution

Once the grant application has been completed and all details essential to the proposal are in hand, it is time for delivery. Most foundations request that the finished proposal be mailed to them, not hand delivered. Those who wish the opportunity to hear about the plans it contains will want to reserve the right to ask for a meeting to discuss these details after they have studied the document. The number of copies to submit is a detail included in the application instructions; if they ask for 10, provide 10.

Exhibit 12.3

Budget Worksheet for Three-Year Grant Application

Salaries and Benefits	Year 1	Year 2	Year 3	Total
Full-time personnel	$75,000	$80,000	$85,000	$240,000
Part-time personnel	18,000	20,000	22,000	60,000
Temporary help	0	1,500	2,500	4,000
Fringe benefits (@20%)	18,600	20,300	21,900	60,800
Subtotals	$111,600	$121,800	$131,400	$364,800

Program and Project Operations	Year 1	Year 2	Year 3	Total
Office supplies	$2,000	$2,200	$2,450	$6,650
Telephone charges	1,000	1,200	1,350	3,550
Postage/Express shipping	1,000	1,250	1,250	3,500
Printing costs	2,500	500	2,500	5,500
Books/Periodicals	250	250	250	750
Travel (local)	1,000	1,000	1,000	3,000
Travel (long distance)	2,500	2,500	2,500	7,500
Entertainment	250	500	250	1,000
Dues/Memberships	450	450	450	1,350
Conference/Training	2,000	2,000	2,000	6,000
Insurance	500	550	600	1,650
Office Rental/Lease	0	0	0	0
Equipment rental/lease	18,000	18,000	18,000	54,000
Equipment maintenance	500	500	500	1,500
Consultant fees	15,000	25,000	12,000	52,000
Services purchased	1,500	1,500	1,500	4,500
Other expenses	1,500	1,500	1,500	4,500
Subtotals	$49,950	$58,900	$48,100	$156,950
Total	$161,550	$180,700	$179,500	$521,750

Because the application is an important document and because nonprofit organizations invest a lot of their time and energy in preparing them, everyone should be anxious to present their story in the best possible way. Presentation includes three options:

1. Personal visit by important representatives of the organization.
2. The proposal document itself.
3. Informing others who may be of some influence with the foundation.

Personal visits to deliver a proposal document are usually discouraged. If personal visits are invited, they will be held prior to or at the time of submission for purposes of clarification, explanation, and information. It is worth noting that foundation staff do not take kindly to efforts to go behind their back or "end run" their role by directly influencing their board members. Although board members may be more tolerant of these attempts, they forward everything they receive directly to the staff, often with comments on their encounter with applicants. Playing by the rules is always better advice.

The final document must be able to stand alone after submission to meet the scrutiny of all who review its contents. Its presentation, appearance, completeness, readability (no jargon), and persuasiveness must work on its behalf.

The dates and frequency of board meetings are usually published. Staff try to mail out their notices of grant decisions within a few weeks after board action. Grant award notices usually require a formal acceptance of the terms and conditions, as explained in the cover letter. This notice reports dates for payment, report requirements and deadlines, public notice instructions, and other details. Take time to read this notice carefully; accepting the grant creates a near-contractual commitment.

Be certain that fulfillment is indeed possible and see to it that all requirements are met on time. The appropriate time to express appreciation and gratitude to foundation board and staff for their help and favorable decision is when you execute the acceptance. It is also correct at this time to begin donor relations activities, including honors and recognition, all within foundation policies and with preapproval.

Each rejection letter also needs careful reading. These are usually form letters and may not speak to everything that occurred in the decision. A phone call to the staff may be a good idea to learn why the request was not approved at this time. You may receive any number of responses:

- The project was disapproved, and resubmission is unwarranted (a clear "no").
- The project was accepted but insufficient funds were available at this time.
- The project was accepted and insufficient funds were available; it will be held over and included in the next review.

- The project must be resubmitted again for the next review.
- The project was acceptable, but additional details are now required in light of board review.

It is always a good idea to respond politely to each rejection letter, thanking the author for careful consideration of the request.

Analysis

An evaluation of foundation solicitation activity should measure the quality and completeness of the overall effort, including research, preparation, strategic plan, budget, submission, administration of funds received, and donor relations (see Exhibit 12.4). Because good research is crucial to foundation solicitation, analysis should review how current the details are. In a larger world, a new idea from a nonprofit organization already may have been received many times at the foundation. Preparation of proposals must be accompanied by cultivation and communications appropriate to each foundation, which must be monitored for any change in foundation process and procedure.

Foundation solicitation can be evaluated by tracking the number of proposals delivered, size of grant requests, gifts received, and average

Exhibit 12.4

Evaluation Criteria for Foundation Solicitation

Areas of Activity	SCORE low				high
Research activity	1	2	3	4	5
Proposal preparation	1	2	3	4	5
Budget preparation	1	2	3	4	5
Strategic plan	1	2	3	4	5
Formal submission	1	2	3	4	5
Administration	1	2	3	4	5
Donor relations	1	2	3	4	5
Median Score					

gift size. The nonquantifiable factors here are the quality of research and proposal preparation. Performance measurement can be a useful management tool to monitor research activity, appointments, meetings and site visits, and proposal activity (see Exhibit 12.5).

Summary Interpretation

A multiyear performance measurement using the nine-point performance index can be applied (see Exhibits 12.6 and 12.7), with the following interpretations:

(1) The number of proposals prepared and delivered each year was 100, which is a hefty pace to achieve and maintain. Successful grants received increased from 15 to 28, as did grant award amounts.

(2) Expenses to support this program began at $68,800, reflecting a full-time staff person and budget support at a cost of fund raising of 24 percent.

(3) Average gift size began at nearly $20,000 but declined to $13,750 after a larger volume of grants were received. Correspondingly, the average cost per gift began at $4,587 and declined to $3,100.

(4) A first-year net profit of $221,700 was achieved, representing a cost of fund-raising of 24 percent and a return of 322 percent, which remained virtually constant.

(5) Overall program performance was stable during the three years, while productivity increased as did net income each year. This organization has achieved a success rate of one out of every five proposals submitted for an average gift of $16,221.

To complete this assessment, it is essential to track each foundation donor for scheduled progress reports, recognition, and other continuing communications to fulfill all contractual requirements and to maintain their interest.

Action Plans

Data illustrated in Exhibit 12.6 reflect a mature foundation solicitation program that will be difficult to maintain at these high levels of productivity year after year unless the organization has significant program

Exhibit 12.5

Activity Report for Foundation Solicitation

Research Activities	Number	Gift Ranges
Prospects identified	129	$2,000 to $200,000
Annual reports/Application forms requested	110	" "
Research in progress	73	" "
Research completed	29	" "
Strategic plan completed	29	" "

Contacts and Discussions	Number	Responses
Information mailings sent	110	29
Correspondence contacts	73	10
Telephone/Fax contacts	29	10

Meetings and Site Visits	Number	Staff (S) or Team (T)
Meetings at foundation	18	S = 7; T = 11
Meetings at organization	7	S = 2; T = 1
Official site visits	3	S = 1; T = 2

Proposal Activity	Number	Grant Values
Proposals in preparation	29	$325,000
Proposals delivered	18	300,000
Proposals funded	6	100,000
Proposals denied	6	100,000
Proposals pending	6	100,000

Exhibit 12.6

Nine-Point Performance Index Analysis of Foundation Solicitations

	Year 1	Year 2	Year 3	Totals
Participation	15	18	28	61
Income	$290,500	$314,000	$385,000	$989,500
Expenses	$68,800	$76,750	$86,800	$232,350
Percent participation	15%	18%	28%	20%
Average gift size	$19,367	$17,444	$13,750	$16,221
Net income	$221,700	$237,250	$298,200	$757,150
Average cost per gift	$4,587	$4,264	$3,100	$3,809
Cost of fund-raising	24%	24%	23%	23%
Return	322%	309%	344%	326%

Exhibit 12.7

Illustration of Nine-Point Performance Index Analysis of Foundation Solicitations

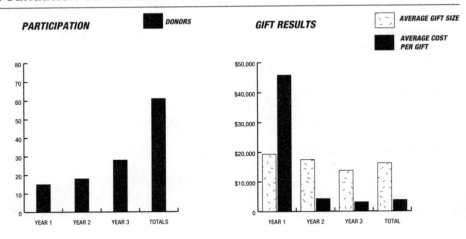

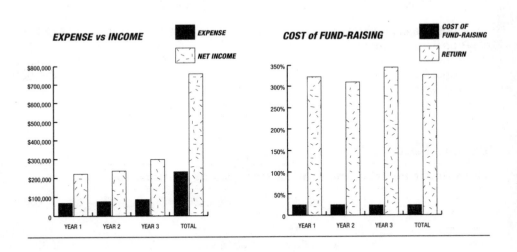

success and important new priority projects. Foundations will continue their grants on occasion but future support is neither automatic nor customary. Most prefer to direct their limited funds to other projects at other organizations. Continued contact is essential as foundations respect organizations that use their funds well and will be more likely to listen to their new ideas about new community priorities of need.

When nonprofit organizations first begin to work with foundations, they enjoy the advantage of being new. Foundations that receive the first three to five grant applications should be carefully selected as "winners" because foundation staff respect one another's evaluation techniques and decision processes. With a few grant awards in place, other qualified foundations will be more respectful of the applications they receive, provided management of grant funds is of high quality and the outcomes are well documented.

Continued emphasis on researching foundations cannot be expected to reveal new qualified candidates forever. Those that are a solid match will need constant attention to preserve the relationship. Looking at this point from the foundation's side of the coin, continued support to proven grantees is likely to be a reliable recommendation most of the time. New applicants do have to have better (not bigger) ideas with equal potential for community benefit to replace proven providers.

Related Benefits

The added benefits nonprofit organizations can enjoy from successful foundation solicitations include (a) reasonably full funding for priority projects for one year or more; (b) positive endorsement of both project and organization, most helpful when applying to other foundations, individuals, and corporations; and (c) momentum to other fund-raising programs, especially major gift activities. Grant awards can and should be reported in news releases, newsletters, and annual reports to add some public respect for the ability to win in the grants' competition arena, provided a foundation's policy does not prohibit such publicity. Quality management of grant funds with timely and detailed reports that meet foundation requirements and deadlines further enhances the chances of additional grants in the future.

Foundation board members and professional staff also appreciate personal attention and can be included as guests at benefits, groundbreaking, and dedication ceremonies, and other events linked to projects at organizations they are supporting. Managers of programs supported by foundations also should be in frequent contact with foundation staff providing update information in addition to required reports and keeping them well informed of project progress and outcomes achieved. Foundations also should be given full consideration for donor recognition alongside all other donors. All these extra efforts help the working relationship with foundation board members and staff, although they do not guarantee any more favorable treatment when the next application arrives.

13

Major Gifts from Individuals

Think of a major gift donor as an investor, someone who is interested in the outcome more than the process. Investors will do their homework to be sure the people, resources, and organization are capable of producing the desired result. They seek winners with each investment decision they make. Their judgment is based on prior experience with the project or problem, sound advice from expert advisors, personal beliefs to advance a cause, and a range of other motives from altruism and tradition to personal drives, peer pressure, and recognition.

Major gift solicitation begins with research to find individuals with the capacity to bring substantial resources to the project or cause. Next, it is necessary to recruit a team of volunteers who have access to the prospective investors and who, by their own reputation and position, command a certain respect. Their job is to explain the project as an opportunity for the investor to make a difference and to explain how the investor's decision will have a significant impact.

A special project or capital campaign is not needed to stimulate this level of gift. An organization's mission and vision of its future are sufficient, provided these are well defined and can inspire investors to action. As was true for both corporations and foundations, when interests and priorities come together between individuals and nonprofit organizations, a strong relationship can emerge to accomplish mutual goals.

You cannot time when the interests and enthusiasm of major gift prospects will peak in your organization's favor. Major gift donors make investment decisions based on a variety of motives, many of which cannot be influenced by a nonprofit organization. Donor investors are well aware of what their money can do and the attention they receive as a result. They recognize money as a source of power and appreciate that charitable giving is a means to accomplish significant good. Donor investors can be enormously persuasive in any direction they choose, and can even lead a nonprofit organization away from its own goals and objectives with their influence. You must be prepared to offer opportunities that will match an investor's goals and objectives with your organization's own mission, vision, and long-range plans.

Generous investors may learn to shift their emphasis from what they can accomplish with their money to what their money can accomplish for others, but some may not begin with that thought in mind. The nonprofit organization that can arrange both is likely to succeed in major gift solicitation.

Major gifts that require the transfer of assets other than cash can make donor investors think twice because they are transferring control over property to someone else. It is important that you be able to assure donors that their gift will be used responsibly.

Purposes

Major gift donors are not just looking to give their money away. What they are looking for are opportunities to invest their money in worthwhile projects that will deliver an important return to others and gain some personal merit for them. A donor may be interested in a gift planning program, a proposal showing them how to use several forms of giving to accomplish a series of objectives, or one or two major goals over time. This master gift plan brings together all their interests with their assets and other resources they might be willing to commit to accomplish their goals and objectives.

The stakes in major gift solicitation are quite large. The size of the gift becomes major when the investor believes the amount asked for is far more than they normally would consider for the organization. A single gift can pay for an entire project, endow a scholarship fund, even pay to build a building. The decision to invest is based on the validity and importance of the project and the influence the gift decision will have on others, including those who may be inspired to join in its support and those who will benefit from the project's accomplishments.

Preparation

The first step is to conduct some basic research to identify prospects. This is followed by rating and evaluation, which are conducted by an evaluation committee. A volunteer cultivation and solicitation team should be formed, and a volunteer should cultivate the donor. A master gift plan should be developed for the donor.

The evaluation committee should learn enough about a donor to understand how to approach the donor, what the donor's key interests are, the donor's capacity for support, and the donor's desire for attention and recognition. At the same time, the committee must respect the prospect's privacy and must ensure confidentiality. Research data takes into account:

1. The present and prior relationship with the nonprofit organization.
2. The donor's involvement and giving history.
3. Established contacts with the organization's leaders, volunteers, and staff.

After the committee has identified likely donors, it should research data that will help them match prospects with current needs and priorities of the nonprofit organization, and then define the steps in a cultivation plan that will be used to approach each donor or prospect.

The next step is to validate the research data using a rating and evaluation process, which requires the help of a few well-informed volunteers. This process assures your organization that it does not take steps that accidentally offend a qualified prospect or would be insensitive to personal situations out of ignorance. A select group of key volunteers, who may also have knowledge because of their profession as accountants, attorneys, bankers, brokers, and investment managers, can provide this service while maintaining all the professional confidences that may be involved. To maintain confidentiality, the evaluation committee should meet with volunteers who have information individually. Only a segment of the prospect list should be shared with them at any one time. Only the fund development staff will see the combined results and will use them to provide a summary for the cultivation and solicitation team assigned to meet with the prospect.

The committee should identify the organization's best representatives to meet with each prospect, guide the discussion toward known interest areas or preferences, and identify a likely gift range. The suggested gift range might not be any more specific than the following six groups, leading to a reasonably accurate "best guess" of how much to suggest to the donor as a gift amount:

1. Under $50,000.
2. $50,000 to $100,000.
3. $100,000 to $250,000.
4. $250,000 to $500,000.
5. $500,000 to $750,000.
6. $750,000 to $1 million.

With this much detail, a cultivation plan and solicitation strategy can now be prepared. The intent of this plan is to show respect for each qualified prospect by attempting to bring together the person's interests and capacity with opportunities that call for major support decisions. Cultivation is at work here, a nice word that describes the sequence of contacts, objectives for each meeting, information to be exchanged, and estimated next steps to keep the process moving toward the occasion when a reasonable direct solicitation can be made. This strategy may have a three- and a six-month series of defined steps that are reviewed after each contact. A flexible plan must find ways to keep moving without pressing for the gift decision too quickly.

Cultivation is the time for prospects to ask questions, meet with the organization's staff involved in the project, tour their facilities, and become involved in other ways. It is also a time for the organization's volunteers to ask prospects for thoughts and advice about the project being discussed, whether they wish additional details or want to meet other individuals or see other facilities. All these steps are conducted on a personal basis by members of the cultivation and solicitation team, who are encouraged to invite prospects to be their guests at one or more of the organization's activities, benefits, or special events that may occur. They also, with help from the evaluation committee, should keep track of key details in the donor's personal lives, such as birthdays, anniversaries, and other occasions of importance.

Two final preparations are required before discussions with qualified prospects can begin. These are recruiting and training the volunteers assigned to meet with each major gift prospect, and making plans for how the donor's contribution will be recognized.

Recruitment and training of volunteers for major gift cultivation and solicitation is similar to the requirements for volunteer-led annual giving solicitation activities (see Chapter 9). In fact, experienced volunteers from these annual giving ranks are prime candidates to invite to join in major gift solicitation. Their experience in preparing and meeting with important donors is the best training possible. A similar training process will be involved here, but more emphasis will be placed on the use of research information and the discipline of following the cultivation plan and solicitation strategy. A team of at least two volunteers is often recommended.

Training begins with complete orientation on the priority project being proposed and its relationship to the overall master plan of the organization. Research data and rating information are shared so the volunteer knows the donor's previous level of involvement and participation, personal interest areas, and other details essential to discussion of their future participation. The gift range to be proposed as well as the reason for the suggested amount and its place in the master gift plan will be reviewed in light of the size of the project, the donor's past giving history, and likely willingness to consider a major gift.

The overall cultivation strategy is outlined, and team members participate in developing each step as well as deciding who takes the lead to set up each appointment and lead each meeting with the prospect. Making plans for donor recognition at the outset is important, so that these answers are available when this question comes up. If the project includes a named gift opportunity, give volunteers information on how the names will be displayed or used. Also provide volunteers with plans for other forms of recognition, events, benefits, and privileges. Each of the essential elements in the cultivation plan and solicitation strategy now can be documented to be measured later for its performance each step of the way (see Exhibit 13.1).

Budget

Expenses to support a major gift solicitation are concentrated in two areas, research and donor recognition; other costs will be the time required and miscellaneous expenses to carry out each plan to its conclusion. Prospect research can be performed and maintained by fund development staff or professionals who provide this specialized service to nonprofit organizations. Some organizations purchase one or

Exhibit 13.1

Measurement of Cultivation Plan and Solicitation Strategy

	SCORE				
	low				high
1. Identify qualified donor investor and match with qualified volunteer solicitor(s)	1	2	3	4	5
2. Train volunteer solicitor(s) on the project, cultivation plan, and solicitation strategy	1	2	3	4	5
3. Volunteer team seeks appointment with qualified donor investor	1	2	3	4	5
4. Conduct meetings; answer questions and identify next steps in keeping with donor comfort and interests	1	2	3	4	5
5. Carry out next steps leading to full information to stimulate involvement and enthusiasm	1	2	3	4	5
6. Prepare for the solicitation presentation, to be ready when the "moment of truth" arrives	1	2	3	4	5
7. Solicit the gift when appropriate; confirm how the donor intends to fulfill this intention	1	2	3	4	5
8. Complete formal acknowledgments in keeping with donor's intention and timetable	1	2	3	4	5
9. Carry out donor recognition and its related benefits and privileges	1	2	3	4	5
10. Continue to maintain communications and personal contact; prepare plan for next gift	1	2	3	4	5

Median Score

more of the basic reference works, such as the Who's Who directories. Expenses may also be incurred for database searches for such public information as estimated home value from county assessor and title company records. A sample budget is shown in Exhibit 13.2.

Some funds will be required for cultivation and solicitation meetings, including local travel, lunches and dinners, and the materials to be prepared that provide the supporting details needed for an informed decision. There may be expenses to entertain prospective donors, depending on their needs and lifestyle. Costs for the donor recognition elements will complete these routine budget requirements.

Budget preparation should include an estimate of expected revenue. Because each donor investor's decision depends on several steps that may take weeks and months to complete, accurate gift amounts cannot be predicted in advance. The project to be funded is a more secure figure; whether it will require one or more major gifts and one or more years to complete is unknown.

Exhibit 13.2

Sample Budget for Individual Major Gifts Program

	Estimated Costs (full-time effort)
A. Individual Prospect Research/Proposal Preparation/Staffing	
Who's Who directories	$500
Computer level-one search of 500 donor records	12,500
In-depth level-two research of 100 qualified prospects	25,000
Proposal preparation and supplies	1,500
Administrative support	1,000
Staff salaries/benefits	65,000
(Manager/Secretary)	
Subtotal	$105,500
B. Direct Solicitation Activities	
Local travel for solicitation team	$1,000
(cabs, parking, meals)	
Prospect cultivation/entertainment	2,500
Long distance travel	
Airfare	2,500
Cabs or car rental	1,000
Parking/Meals	1,500
Accommodations	2,000
Legal/tax accounting fees	2,500
Subtotal	$13,000
C. Donor Relations	
Donor recognition/plaques	$3,000
Groundbreaking/dedication/reception	3,000
Invitations/Reservations	500
Photo album of cermonies	500
Annual meeting honors and awards	2,000
Subtotal	$9,000
Grand Total	$127,500

Execution

The well-prepared, well-rehearsed cultivation plan and solicitation strategy provides the step-by-step design leading to a major gift decision. A significant amount of time is required for donor investors to evaluate fully the opportunity being presented, measure their ability to meet the challenging sum required, balance this request and its priority against current obligations, calculate how their decision will influence others and add to their reputation, and test for the enjoyment they may experience by observing how the organization honors its other major donors. Adequate information and good presentations are not enough; there must also be a sense of involvement, excitement, even enthusiasm for the opportunity being presented.

A debriefing is necessary after each contact to review the content of the discussion, prepare responses to any requests or questions, develop immediate follow-up, and consider timing for the next step, which could be the request for a gift decision. Specific details in the official request can now be prepared so that the volunteer team will be well briefed, in case donors decide early that they want to know the details of what will be asked of them.

A master gift plan should be prepared and offered to each qualified major donor. The master gift plan defines a privileged association offered to the donor to carry out their desires through the present and into the future plans of the nonprofit organization. The plan should include recognition details, which explain how each gift will be treated and what privileges and benefits will be offered in response—always with a focus on the ultimate objective, the public benefits to be realized. Recognition details for major donor investors are worthy of an organization's best thinking, time, and the attention of its most senior volunteers and management.

A worksheet for preparing the master gift plan appears in Exhibit 13.3. The master gift plan includes three levels or phases of a donor's major gift decisions:

1. *Gifts for current purposes.* This may combine annual giving opportunities with occasional major gifts and one or more special projects and capital campaigns.
2. *Permanent support for selected program areas through endowment commitments.* Donors can restrict these gifts for endowment purposes that will perpetuate both their annual and lifelong interests.

Exhibit 13.3

Worksheet for the Master Gift Plan

Group A	Major Gifts for Current Purposes		Gift Value
	Annual giving opportunities		$25,000
	Cash or "cashed in" asset gifts		75,000
	Campaign gifts (multiyear pledges)		250,000
		Subtotal	$350,000
Group B	Gifts for Endowment Purposes (payable from current assets)		
	Cash or "cashed in" asset		$150,000
	Pooled income fund gift		$50,000
	Charitable life insurance gift (net present value)		100,000
	Charitable remainder trust or gift annuity		300,000
		Subtotal	$600,000
Group C	Gifts by Will (payable from donor's estate)		
	Transfer of cash or assets		$400,000
	Charitable trust or living trust		200,000
	Transfer to personal foundation/trust		2,000,000
		Subtotal	$2,600,000
			========
		Master Gift Plan Total	$3,550,000

3. *The estate plan.* The donor's will controls the donor's final gift decisions and completes the giving plan.

Each level of the master gift plan offers more than one gift opportunity and each opportunity requires a major gift decision. When assembled, the master gift plan is a comprehensive illustration for the major gift donor of how much the contemplated series of major gift decisions can accomplish, usually more than the person dreamed was possible.

To help guide the solicitation process and insure a positive conclusion, give considerable attention to the following four ingredients for success:

1. *Comfort.* The cultivation plan must measure how people are getting along together and the donor's comfort with the project being

presented. The volunteer team must determine if the donor likes the program, respects the team members, and enjoys the progress of discussion. Team members must also observe whether prospects are comfortable with the estimated cost or at least believe they can share in the funding required. The team must be alert to the timing of all phases of the cultivation plan and know when to move on to the next step.

2. *Anticipation.* Discussions are designed to bring the donor investor to a favorable conclusion. Donors will anticipate how much is going to be asked of them (they may know only the total amount needed) while the team is gauging what amount they should suggest.

3. *Readiness.* The plan being offered the donor calls for both involvement and investment. The project's value includes providing significant benefits to others. Details that the volunteers share with the donor suggest all is ready to begin; this shared opportunity demonstrates a high respect for the person's sincere interest and understanding of both the process and the need.

4. *Enjoyment.* Donors and the solicitation team must feel satisfaction about the accomplishments to be funded. The special treatment offered to donors in recognition of their extra generosity reflects the respect due them because of the mutual benefits they have made possible for others.

Major gift solicitation is hard work and a degree of discipline is required to keep everything moving forward. Speed is less important than taking the prepared steps in the right order and at the rate each donor finds comfortable.

To maintain an adequate intensity, use regular committee meetings and update reports circulated to volunteer teams. Fund development staff must be in constant contact with volunteer teams to monitor progress and help to adjust plans and strategy when and where needed. Staff also can suggest other activities, such as inviting prospects to be special guests of the organization at their next benefit event, to help keep the cultivation plan moving forward in a positive way.

The same care and attention to detail given to the cultivation plan and solicitation strategy must also be given to the donor recognition plan (see Exhibit 13.4), which begins immediately after the gift is confirmed. A formal recognition plan should be prepared and offered to each major gift donor. All may not accept nor wish to be honored in public. A few will request anonymity, which must be respected fully.

Exhibit 13.4

Measurement of a Major Gift Donor Recognition Plan

			SCORE		
Basic Recognition Plan	low				high
Observe honors and recognition policy with all benfits and privileges	1	2	3	4	5
Meet IRS regulations on give-backs and gift substantiation rules	1	2	3	4	5
Define a continuing program to maintain communications and contact with donors	1	2	3	4	5
Enhanced Recognition and Rewards					
Keep donor history for cumulative giving honors and recognition	1	2	3	4	5
Offer naming opportunities in keeping with honors and recognition policy	1	2	3	4	5
Provide plaques, portraits, photo albums, and other take-home symbols of appreciation	1	2	3	4	5
Perpetual Recognition					
Named major wing or building	1	2	3	4	5
Named program or service area	1	2	3	4	5
Named endowment fund	1	2	3	4	5
Median Score					

Continued communications and contact with all major gift donors is required. Making a major gift is a major experience; considerable attention was given the donor by the cultivation and solicitation team leading to their gift decision. Their gift was the culmination of several objectives for both donor and nonprofit organization and a degree of celebration followed. Once the dedication is concluded and all the recognition delivered, a period of inattention can result. It is important to continue an appropriate level of personal contact in the after-gift phase, which will not be as intense as before, but to drop all the former attention is bad manners and a grievous error. Keeping in touch is not difficult and will be appreciated by donors whose personal interests remain high. A plan for continued donor relations (see Exhibit 13.5)

Exhibit 13.5

Measurement of a Major Gift Donor Relations Program

			SCORE		
The Volunteer Cultivation/Solicitation Team Can:	low				high
Call the donor every three months	1	2	3	4	5
Visit the donor every six months	1	2	3	4	5
Escort the donor to special events	1	2	3	4	5
Subtotal					
The Project/Professional Staff Can:					
Call the donor every three to six months	1	2	3	4	5
Visit the donor once a year	1	2	3	4	5
Send activity reports at least semiannually	1	2	3	4	5
Send copies of other news at any time	1	2	3	4	5
Join or greet the donor at special events	1	2	3	4	5
Invite the donor to project activities	1	2	3	4	5
Subtotal					
The Fund Development Staff Can:					
See that volunteers keep in touch	1	2	3	4	5
See that project/professional staff keep in touch	1	2	3	4	5
Keep the solicitation team informed of all communications and any feedback from donors	1	2	3	4	5
Place donor stories in organization publications	1	2	3	4	5
Conduct receptions and donor luncheons	1	2	3	4	5
Conduct a six-month review of all the above	1	2	3	4	5
Subtotal					
Median Score					

should be prepared and followed as an appendage to the original cultivation plan and solicitation strategy.

Analysis

Performance measurement begins with ongoing attention to the cultivation plan and solicitation strategy. A summary activity report will keep track of all the major gift solicitations and related activities in progress at any one time (see Exhibit 13.6).

Summary Interpretation

The final measurement is the nine-point performance index to evaluate gift productivity and profitability. Keeping track of at least three years of a major gift program is valuable to trace progress and improvements. Here are some observations based on the data illustrated in Exhibits 13.7 and 13.8:

(1) The number of major gift donors is small but growing, as is the percent participation or response rate from ongoing solicitations (45% resulted in gift decisions). Average gifts are nearly $15,000 for the three-year period. If these improvements continue for another three years, about 100 donors will have been involved in major gift decisions representing excellent results and excellent preparation for a special project or capital campaign.

(2) The budget allocated suggests a part-time effort led by the senior fund development staff professional aided by volunteer solicitors, which accounts for the average cost per gift of a bit more than $1,000. Without knowing the organization or its local environment, it is unclear whether adding staff and budget will be able to improve this performance.

(3) Cost of fund-raising and return percentages are well within reasonable guidelines, commendable levels for a program of this size. The efficiency of this effort should be most encouraging to the board of directors and management. They should depend on this and other solicitation activities to produce reliable net income for the organization's present and future priorities, and can make future plans with greater confidence in the willingness and generous levels of support available from their constituency.

Exhibit 13.6

Activity Report for Major Gift Solicitation

	Two Years Ago	Last Year	This Year
Research and Preparation			
Number of major gift prospects being researched	135	155	202
Number of major gift prospects qualified from research	77	108	179
Number of trained/experienced personal solicitation volunteers available for assignment	14	24	48
Cultivation Plans and Solicitation Strategies			
Number of major gift prospects with cultivation plans completed	33	72	110
Number of major gift prospects with volunteer solicitation teams	27	68	85
Number of solicitation teams engaged in cultivation plans and active solicitation strategies	17	60	78
Number of major gift donor decisions	6	24	42
Number of major gift rejections	5	20	13
Value of major gifts received	$225,000	$665,000	$880,000
Value of major gift pledges received	$100,000	$335,000	$545,000
Donor Recognition and Donor Relations			
Number of donor recognition activities in progress	2	10	30
Number of donor recognition activities completed	2	10	9
Number of donor relations program plans in preparation	2	4	3
Number of six-month donor relations reviews conducted	2	14	38
Number of six-month donor relations reviews scheduled	4	10	5

Exhibit 13.7

Nine-Point Performance Index Analysis of Major Gift Solicitation

	Two Years Ago	Last Year	This Year	Totals
Participation	12	18	23	53
Income	$172,500	$215,000	$358,000	$745,500
Expenses	$16,850	$18,200	$18,900	$53,950
Percent participation	33%	46%	53%	45%
Average gift size	$14,375	$11,944	$15,565	$14,066
Net income	$155,650	$196,800	$339,100	$691,550
Average cost per gift	$1,404	$1,011	$822	$1,018
Cost of fund-raising	10%	8%	5%	7%
Return	924%	1081%	1794%	1282%

Action Plans

The analysis suggests the following actions:

1. Continued time and attention to the major gift donors will be essential to maintain their high levels of interest, commitment, and enthusiasm for the organization and its programs and services. In addition, because the size of the donor group is manageable at this time, they can be invited to be special guests at the organization's next annual meeting and honored for their generosity. This practice is recommended in future years as well. After the meeting, remember to send those unable to attend a copy of the official program with their names included.

2. A new patron or benefactor donor recognition level might be initiated for donors of $10,000 or more, which can include new levels at $25,000, $50,000, $100,000 and more for cumulative giving. Major gift donors ought to be entertained with additional gift opportunities that have enriched donor recognition benefits and privileges.

3. Each cultivation and solicitation team must be surveyed for their thoughts and suggestions about how best to maintain their relationship with each of the original donors as well as the new donors. Fund development staff can work with the department leaders and

Exhibit 13.8

Illustration of Nine-Point Performance Index Analysis of Major Gift Solicitation

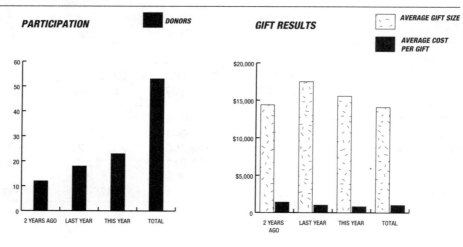

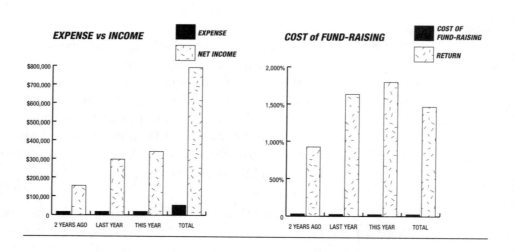

project staff where these original major gifts were directed and the money spent, to learn of any future plans that can be shared with their special donors, perhaps to suggest one or more as likely topics for beginning discussions about their next gifts.

Related Benefits

Three main benefits will be attained concentrating on major gift donors:

1. Donors will have increased their personal relationship with the nonprofit organization by at least tenfold. The attention they received leading to their major gift decision may have been one of their most enjoyable and rewarding personal experiences. If the solicitation team has maintained contact with them, these donors may still be enjoying the experience.

2. The organization has been able to advance its priority programs and services to new levels of quality and quantity, thanks to these major contributions of nearly $700,000 within three years.

3. This is an excellent opportunity for the organization to advance its image and public relations by reporting how these funds were used, how the public benefited, and how the community was served. If the donors concur, these success stories can feature their gifts as largely responsible for the progress made.

14

Special Project Campaigns

A campaign is a combination of solicitation activities assembled for a common objective. Campaigns have dollar goals and a scheduled deadline. They have a special appeal all their own, are big enough to be exciting, important, and timely, and have the capacity to stimulate, excite, and challenge donors and volunteers. They are a good idea with a respectable objective to fulfill an urgent need and can be implemented as soon as the money arrives. In short, they are special projects that command attention, with success just waiting to be claimed. A special project campaign is a combined form of solicitation activity that brings several major gift solicitation methods together.

A special project campaign serves as the bridge between an ongoing annual giving campaign, a major gifts program, and a future capital campaign. It can be used within an annual giving campaign to isolate one project and one group of donors and guide prospects toward a separate goal that represents a unique opportunity. Volunteer solicitors involved in this effort can be trained to solicit larger gifts than required in the donors' prior annual giving. A special project campaign likewise can be used within a major capital campaign, isolating one project in the overall list of campaign projects as a separate target with special responsibility assigned to a select group of donors and prospects. The special project may also be the logical next gift in a major donor's master gift plan.

One note of caution. The success of one or more special project campaigns may tempt some board members and management staff to suggest the more expensive and demanding forms of annual giving solicitation activity should be curtailed and the time and budget spent on them be redirected to more special project campaigns. This is a mistake. The success of special projects depends directly on the entire array of annual giving activities required to develop donors' interests and enthusiasm and to train volunteers willing to meet with donors to ask them for a major gift. Fund-raising practice is a continuous process of finding new donors, retaining those who have begun to give, expanding and upgrading each donor's interests and involvement through personal attention and voluntary service to achieve a level of reliability for annual revenue and the potential to meet special needs as they arise.

Purposes

Concentration on the constant demands of annual giving solicitation often limits the attention volunteers and staff can give to major gift prospects. A special project campaign can be the means to capture some of their attention and can get donors and volunteers involved in a stimulating, exciting, and challenging new opportunity. Further, it offers volunteers who are ready for something larger than repeat annual gifts a chance to be teamed together in a special assignment.

Special projects can have a unique appeal to select donors whose motives for giving place more emphasis on their personal role. The objective can become "their" project to fund with their own money or from those they will ask to participate in their program or service. Donors who are already committed to one program or service will be anxious to learn about the next opportunity to move "their" program forward and may even consider leading the effort to fund it if asked.

A special project can be an opportunity to take an unusual idea to a group of donors and prospects for their collective response. The size and scope of the project may be larger than a single donor could consider, which suggests inviting others known to have an interest in this program area to join together. Here is one occasion where individual donors and prospects may be combined with corporations and foundations to accomplish the objective. A minicampaign plan can be prepared based on their shared interests. This special project campaign will require the usual cultivation plan for personal solicitation of each gift candidate, beginning with the best prospect for the largest gift and leveraging that person's decision against the interest and potential of all the others in descending order.

Other uses of a special project campaign are:

1. To keep a major gift program in operation between major capital campaigns.
2. To keep the attention of major gift donors and prospects on their interests.
3. To keep training volunteers in major gift cultivation and solicitation.
4. To keep everyone's attention on the long-range plan and its succession of important priority projects to advance the nonprofit organization in fulfillment of its mission and vision.

Preparation

There may be one or more special project campaign opportunities in every annual giving campaign. There will be even greater opportunities for special projects in a major capital campaign. Other occasions also may lead to a special project campaign. It may even be possible to redefine a current priority or project planned for the future to coordinate with a prospective donor's preference. This kind of flexibility is desirable but must always be connected to and guided by the overall master plan of the organization. Programs and services should not be invented as special projects just because a big gift might be available.

Consider each candidate to be a special investor whose ability to fund a special project begins or extends the investor's interest and involvement with that program. Discretion is required in selecting whom to approach first. That individual should make a decision before volunteers approach the next candidate. Other special projects will require a small committee of volunteers who agree to approach a limited number of qualified candidates about joining together to meet this need. Examples include a family that wishes to honor or memorialize a family member with a group gift, or a group of former students who may be invited to endow a fellowship in the name of a favorite professor on his or her retirement.

Your organization must evaluate the decision to use a special project campaign to determine if it meets a unique need or funds an important objective. The project first must fit within the goals and objectives of the organization and then those of one or more major gift donors or prospects. Further, it must be evaluated for its influence on current solicitation activities to avoid conflicts with other priority programs that may depend on support from these same donors for their success.

Research is necessary to verify that a reasonable match exists with a group of prospective donors. You must also identify an avenue to approach them, whether through a board member, senior executive, experienced volunteer, or a team.

Next, a cultivation plan and solicitation strategy must be prepared for each qualified prospect. This includes a review of how each prospect fits within the current annual giving or major gifts program to determine the person's degree of active involvement. During this process, you should recruit experienced volunteers and review the cultivation plan and solicitation strategy with them in detail.

Budget

Direct costs to support a special project campaign will be in the range of 10 percent to 20 percent. Extra research for all major gift sources (corporations, foundations, individuals) will be required along with printing a case statement, campaign brochure, and other materials. Some administrative support will be necessary as will routine campaign committee meetings, which usually involve a breakfast or luncheon expense. Most of the effort is invested in the time of volunteers and staff to develop cultivation strategies and to implement them according to the solicitation plan. Actual solicitation activities may require more than one meeting with qualified prospects for cultivation and entertainment purposes. Recognition will require honest expenses along with appropriate groundbreaking and dedications ceremonies for new buildings or major facility renovations. It is also normal to provide a memento gift of the campaign to major gift donors ($10,000 and up), along with invitations to the organization's annual meeting for added honors (see Exhibit 14.1).

Indirect costs will be able to be absorbed in normal operations overhead. If special project campaigns become a normal feature of the fund development program, prepare a separate budget to track all these related expenses, including staff salary and benefits. A campaign goal helps to estimate the length of time required for each special project campaign. What is uncertain at the outset is how much time will be required to achieve this goal. Fund development staff also must assess the impact of each special project campaign on volunteers and donors current supporting annual giving programs and other major gift and planned giving activities. It is not unusual for a

Exhibit 14.1

Sample Budget for Special Project Campaign

		Estimated Costs (full-time effort)
A. Prospect Research/Proposal Preparation/Staffing		
Corporate research		$500
Foundation research		500
Individual major gift research		2,500
Proposal preparation and supplies		1,500
Administrative support		4,000
Case statment/campaign brochure		3,500
Campaign committee meetings		2,500
Staff salaries/benefits (manager/staff)		65,000
	Subtotal	$80,000
B. Direct Solicitation Activities		
Local travel (cabs, parking, meals)		$2,000
Prospect cultivation/entertainment		2,500
Long-distance travel		
Airfare		2,500
Cabs or car rental		1,000
Parking/Meals		1,500
Accommodations		2,000
	Subtotal	$11,500
C. Donor Relations		
Donor recognition/plaques		$3,000
Groundbreaking/dedication ceremonies		3,000
Invitations/reservations		500
Campaign memento for donors		1,500
Annual meeting honors and awards		2,000
	Subtotal	$10,000
	Total	$101,500

special project campaign to be designed to continue until the project is fully funded, which makes budget planning somewhat uncertain.

Execution

Special project campaigns should be organized around opportunities that can be created and managed. A project may come with its own deadline, such as a challenge gift to be matched by a certain date or timing with other projects that have completion dates, after which the opportunity has passed. In the examples mentioned in the Analysis in this chapter, replacement equipment or the new gymnasium, the deadline may be before the equipment breaks down for the last time or as soon as possible to replace the services it provided.

Deadlines can be useful to motivate action and attention, even to ask for a quick decision. But deadlines may not work well for prospective donors whose own schedule for decisions and access to the money can be different. People dislike being rushed into a decision. Comfort, anticipation, readiness, and enjoyment guidelines discussed in Chapter 13 apply equally to major gift donors in a special project campaign.

Because special project campaigns do not require the all-out organizational commitment, multiyear pledges, and other traditional elements and style of a major capital campaign, they can be more flexible in offering donors options for how and when they make their gifts. The project will dictate most of these details; if it is a compelling need with urgency and all is ready to begin as soon as funding is secure, the deadline is today and will be the same until completed.

Because special projects are offered to select donors and prospects, some momentum is established by bringing the opportunity to their attention. Granting them time to think about it and make their decision is both necessary and courteous, but the time comes when the opportunity may pass and a decision is required. There is the need to move on to the next best qualified candidate. Some prospects and donors are well aware of the power they and their money have to influence others and to control decisions. These circumstances can interfere with the best of plans and must be addressed with great care.

Asking for a decision is a delicate matter that requires adequate knowledge about the prospect's decision process, or at least how his or her advisers operate. Further, decisions often are a matter of timing. Donors will have other obligations and require the time to arrange funding when their resources become available or when the value of their assets reach the right market price. Their decision may be a firm commitment with the funds to follow at a later, more appropriate time. A commitment is a good faith intention and must be taken at face value; the bond of trust between donors and their chosen nonprofit organizations begins with the assumption that donors will fulfill their side of the contract. The organization must be prepared to do the same, but should wait to begin until the promised funds have been delivered.

Preparations and execution should include details about what recognition will be offered to donors. Special project campaigns offer extra opportunities to honor donors. The equipment to be replaced may be replaced again in a few years. Attaching the donor's name to the equipment will not be as lasting as placing a plaque on the wall in the room where the equipment provides its service.

Naming opportunities are common to special project campaigns and provide a valuable incentive for a favorable decision. Whatever is offered must be consistent with and fully in concert with existing and board-approved honors and recognition policy. Treating all donors fairly and equitably is essential; what a special project campaign allows is to add something extra to what is offered everyone. These donors are qualified because their major gift decision met a unique need outside the mainstream of routine annual giving and a major capital campaign; they are special and the organization must respond in some way.

Analysis

Evaluation of each special project campaign should begin with a review of the decisions to select the project offered, prospect research and preparations, cultivation plan and solicitation strategy, and recognition and reward elements. Analysis can also review what level of volunteer recruitment and training was required, campaign management, use of fund development office systems, the time required of professional staff, and cooperation from institutional staff. Continued communications and personal contact with these donors can be reviewed six months after these campaigns. Overall results can measure the numbers of donors involved and their total dollars, but likewise must evaluate and report how the money was used and what results were provided as improved programs and services of measurable benefit to the community. Comprehensive analysis permits the total story to be told, which will be of greatest interest to those who invested in making it possible.

Summary Interpretation

The nine-point performance index (see Exhibits 14.2 and 14.3) examines how each special project campaign has progressed and adds some insight into the efforts required for each to be successful. Each special project campaign can be expected to perform differently from the others because the goals and objectives, timing, and opportunity are different. Performance evaluation will help demonstrate the merits of this form of major gift solicitation activity and its unusual effectiveness and efficiency.

The examples presented in Exhibit 14.2 are Special Project 1, a family's joint gift toward the major equipment replacement; Special Project 2, a letter campaign to 250 former athletes as the emergency campaign to rebuild a burned gymnasium; and Special Project 3, a dollar-for-dollar challenge grant for $50,000 from a major donor who believes in the project and offered the challenge strategy to stimulate other donors. All three campaigns asked for gifts of $5,000 from each donor. The following observations are drawn from the results:

(1) The $25,000 family joint funding project invited all five family members to make a gift of $5,000 each. The average gift of $4,250 suggests one or more was unable to give this much money but a few gave more to achieve the goal. Net income after modest expenses of $1,450, mostly for gift recognition purposes, was $24,050, a bit shy of the true

Exhibit 14.2

Nine-Point Performance Index Analysis of Special Project Campaigns

	Special Project #1	Special Project #2	Special Project #3	Totals
Participation	5	185	11	201
Income	$25,500	$1,025,000	$60,500	$1,111,000
Expenses	$1,450	$41,550	$1,500	$44,500
Percent participation	83%	74%	61%	73%
Average gift size	$5,100	$5,541	$5,500	$5,527
Net income	$24,050	$983,450	$59,000	$1,066,500
Average cost per gift	$290	$225	$136	$221
Cost of fund-raising	6%	4%	2%	4%
Return	1659%	2367%	3933%	2397%

Exhibit 14.3

Illustration of Nine-Point Performance Index Analysis of Special Project Campaigns

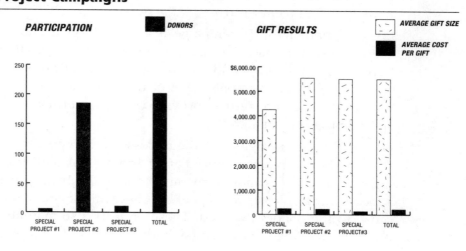

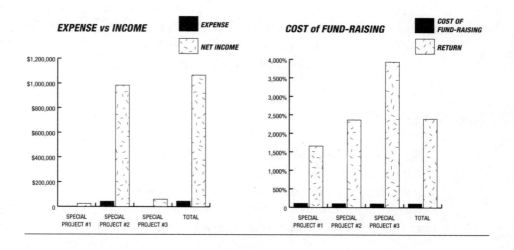

cost but over goal by $500 in income received from all five family members. Costs to conduct this private campaign averaged $290 per gift and at 6 percent is the highest among these three examples.

(2) The gymnasium project also reached its goal at a cost of $41,550 and provided net income of $983,450 for the gymnasium. Of those

solicited, 74 percent responded with gifts, for an average gift of $5,541, suggesting that several alumni made gifts larger than $5,000. Overall cost of fund-raising of this emergency campaign was 4 percent with a 2,367 percent return.

(3) The challenge gift campaign also met its goal and achieved an average gift of $5,500. Because volunteers performed all the solicitation, costs were modest and the average cost per gift was $136, the lowest of these three examples. Cost of fund-raising was 2 percent and, with a 3,933 percent return, provided the most efficient example of a special project campaign.

(4) All three campaigns met their gross revenue goal but fell slightly short of the total costs required after expenses. A reality in fund-raising is that it costs money to raise money. Each project could have added estimated costs to its goal but these might not have made much sense to the donors involved. These projects also may not have been programs included in the annual budget prepared months earlier.

(5) These performance measurements are the best yet presented in this workbook and are not accidental. Special project campaigns are unusually successful as a fund-raising tactic because of their unique nature, sharp focus, limited prospect pool, modest cost, and effective use of volunteer solicitors. The size of gifts requested, $5,000 from each donor, is again modest; yet important projects were funded and could proceed to be implemented rather quickly.

Related Benefits

Several benefits fall from the time and effort invested in a special project campaign. Donors appreciate the invitation to address a unique opportunity where they personally can make a noticeable and valued difference. Volunteers involved with a special project have a successful major gift experience to increase their confidence in personal solicitation activities. The fund development staff benefit from the added experience of researching additional major gift candidates, defining a special project, preparing cultivation plans and solicitation strategies, and arranging appropriate recognition to meet each donor's needs, all excellent experience, for a future capital campaign.

15

Capital Campaigns

Capital campaigns are the apex of the fund development program. A capital campaign is an all-out effort by a nonprofit organization designed to meet the extraordinary needs of today and to secure their future. Every solicitation activity presented in this workbook can be evaluated as a preparation for a future capital campaign. A capital campaign is the most productive, most efficient, and most cost-effective method of fund-raising practice yet invented.

If capital campaigns are all that great, every nonprofit organization should have one, right? There are certain considerations:

> One of the first questions to ask about a capital campaign is whether it is truly needed. This question deserves a compelling answer. Capital campaigns are not for raising significant numbers of gifts or significant numbers of large gifts, and not for achieving prestigious gifts or important objectives. A capital campaign is one means to financial security, but it should and, in most cases, it must, represent the studied conclusion that all traditional funding options have been exhausted and a capital fund drive is now required to raise most or all of the money needed by a certain date.[1]

Many nonprofit organizations lack the critical mass required to even consider a capital campaign. To develop this critical mass, an organization must first complete a broad-based annual giving program and then operate it effectively and efficiently. An organization must also expand to implement a major gifts program that includes personal contact with corporations, foundations, and individuals. There must be a broad base of support for most urgent priorities, as well as the internal and external expertise to succeed with major gift solicitation. Most important of all, the organization must complete an extensive assessment of community needs, refine its role in serving those needs, and measure its capacity to provide those programs and services.

Purposes

The exact purposes for a capital campaign should be crystal clear. The total list of requirements may include several facilities projects. Your organization may need to construct new buildings, renovate existing facilities, or replace equipment. You may need to improve current services and launch new projects for the benefit of the community. Programs and services are central to the list just as they are central to the story of why these needs are so urgent.

The mission and vision of your organization must be clear, and your organization should have a written master plan that has both consensus and approval throughout the organization.

Preparation

A capital campaign must meet the readiness test and be able to demonstrate credibility, relevance, urgency, and pragmatism. Without these critical ingredients, a nonprofit organization cannot defend its basic position of needing to construct more buildings, expand its programs, increase its services, improve its quality, and develop secure financing for its future. Readiness includes:

1. A thorough analysis of the organization's financial stability to conduct its present programs without interruption.
2. A realistic schedule of expanded programs and higher quality services, perhaps even new projects, consistent with the mission.
3. A future vision that is written down with ample documentation of clearly identified needs, including realistic financial, facility, and equipment requirements.
4. A well-tuned and coordinated schedule for implementation.
5. Public willingness for support that has been validated.
6. A completed assessment of every avenue of potential funding to verify the potential for success in a capital campaign, including whether adequate leadership is available to support solicitation.

7. The personal conviction and commitment of each person at the nonprofit organization who is involved with the decision to proceed with the campaign. (Your organization's board members, management, and professional staff should perform the readiness analysis in Exhibit 15.1.)

The final area of readiness analysis is to study the impact the capital campaign will have on the organization itself. Campaigns call for change and will do much more than expand the programs and services of the organization; your organization will not be the same after the campaign is concluded. The campaign will have a significant impact on current solicitation activities throughout the campaign period; they too will be changed for the better when the campaign is over.

The board and management should measure the organization's potential against the table of elements for success (see Exhibit 15.2). You should prepare a financial plan that provides complete details on the estimated costs of each project or piece of equipment, its schedule for implementation, and annual cash flow requirements in order to keep to the proposed schedule. Further, the financial plan should address

Exhibit 15.1

Internal Readiness Test for a Capital Campaign

		SCORE			
		low			high
1.	Are you convinced personally that your organization deserves to ask for leadership gifts above and beyond those sought through annual giving?	1 2 3 4 5
2.	Can you articulate that conviction to someone else?	1 2 3 4 5
3.	Can you translate your commitment into a capital gift of your own?	1 2 3 4 5
4.	Are you willing to become involved in evaluating donor potential within your organization's family?	1 2 3 4 5
5.	Are you willing to take on the extra work (or hire extra short-term staff) to keep everything moving during the campaign?	1 2 3 4 5
6.	Does your organization have or have access to the resources (books and personnel) needed to research background information on your prospects?	1 2 3 4 5
7.	Are your volunteers willing to make personal visits to your prospects?	1 2 3 4 5
8.	Do your volunteers have sufficient clout and/or access to open the doors you will need opened? If not, are they willing to approach such leadership for ad hoc involvement?	1 2 3 4 5
9.	Is everyone involved (staff, volunteers, and various institutional departments) clear about each other's roles during the campaign process?	1 2 3 4 5
10.	Does everyone understand who is to do what—and when?	1 2 3 4 5
11.	If so, then you are ready for a capital campaign!*	1 2 3 4 5

Median Score _____

*Charles E. Lawson, "Capital Fund Appeals" in *The Nonprofit Management Handbook: Operating Policies and Procedures*, Tracy Daniel Connors, Ed. New York: John Wiley & Sons, 1993, p. 553. Reprinted by permission.

Exhibit 15.2

Elements for Success in a Capital Campaign

Campaign Elements	Maximum Number of Points	Our Score
Defined institutional goals	10	
Identified fund-raising objectives	10	
Committed governing-board leadership	20	
Good prospect potential	20	
Demonstrated institutional productivity	10	
Staff capability	10	
Active cultivation process	5	
Convincing case statement	5	
Volunteer organization plan	5	
Realistic timetable	5	
Total	100 *	

*Thomas E. Broce, *Fund Raising: The Guide to Raising Money from Private Sources* (2nd ed.). Norman, OK: University of Oklahoma Press, 1986, p. 54.

the fiscal consequences of each program, service, building, and item of equipment, measure them against current revenue sources, and analyze their impact on future annual operating budgets. Forecasts of interest and investment earnings on current reserves must be calculated and may take into account the added value and income to be earned from new endowment funds.

The financial plan should include full disclosure of all the costs associated with the current fund-raising program, including the added expense of the campaign, and should be able to demonstrate that these expenses are reasonable and well within the operating guidelines of the board of directors. Lastly, the financial plan can explain how the organization can meet all these obligations within its current resources and the new funds to be delivered out of the capital campaign.

After estimated costs and timetables for implementation have been completed, you should engage outside firms to conduct three studies:

1. *Market research.* Professional firms with direct experience in conducting market research studies can assess public attitudes toward nonprofit organizations, their current programs and services, their

perceived value to the community, the reputation of their leadership and staff, opinions on current solicitation activities, etc.

2. *Development audit.* A professional firm with direct experience in conducting precampaign research studies should audit the preparedness of the fund development program to support a capital campaign.

3. *Feasibility.* A professional firm should assess from the public the extent to which funding the master plan and its fund-raising objective is feasible.

These studies may recommend changes in how the organization sees itself and talks about itself to the public, changes in the amount of the goal, delaying the campaign, developing more and stronger leadership, added research to discover more major gift candidates, and improvements to fund development staff and office systems. You should take these recommendations seriously. The objective in these studies, each well worth the investment, is to learn what must be done to succeed. In addition, they will describe each of the steps to take to prepare and to conduct the campaign successfully.

The studies should provide the following information:

1. Likely response with campaign gifts.
2. How much each audience might give.
3. The identity of major gift prospects.
4. The identity of leadership candidates.
5. Problem areas (case, timing, image, leadership, staff, systems, others).
6. An overall campaign objective (goal).
7. Specific goals for each giving audience available.
8. A timetable and sequence for solicitation.
9. Elements of the case statement and all support documentation required.
10. Staffing and budget required.
11. Public relations support plan.
12. Where and how campaign counsel will continue to be needed.

Two other areas that are important in the preparations phase are campaign counsel and a campaign gift table or gift range chart. Not even the most experienced fund-raising executive can afford to risk not using professional campaign counsel when their organization's future depends on a successful campaign. Professional consultants should be invited to assist as early as possible so the fund development office can be guided as it begins its extensive preparations. These consultants may be from the same firm or firms that conducted the market research, development, and feasibility studies. Campaign counsel can start prospect research as soon as the hint of a coming capital campaign is formalized. Prospect research is a highly complex area and a service provided by most consulting firms, whose staff includes specialists trained to these duties. Not many nonprofit organizations have the capability for this all-important function but they can be given these tools and trained to use them.

The gift table or gift range chart is a strategic tool to help everyone understand the essential key: capital campaign success comes from one simple fact—concentration on the top gifts. The gift table sets the standard for giving or a quota system with the number and size of gifts required for success. What the gift chart illustrates is that nearly all the money needed, as much as 90 percent, will come from only a few donors, perhaps as few as 10 percent of all those who participate in the campaign.

Another formula is to follow the "rule of thirds," which says that the top third of campaign gifts will come from a small number of people, the second third from a number 10 times the first group, and the remaining third from everyone else (see Exhibit 15.3). Another method to predict success is to follow the 80/20 rule, with 80 percent of the money to come from 20 percent of the donors. Decades of campaign experience have proven each of these strategies to be successful.

Another successful approach is the dual strategy of "top-down" or sequential solicitation, to secure the largest gift first, then the next largest, and so on; and "inside out," to begin the campaign inside with the board, professional staff, and employees along with donors who are considered family, and then go outside to ask the public for the rest of the money.

Each of these basic guidelines makes the same point; concentrate first and foremost on the largest gifts. If success is realized here, the rest of the campaign will be a success. If the campaign fails to secure the top two thirds or 20 percent of the donors who agree to provide 80 percent or more of the money, the campaign may not succeed.

Some routine campaign elements are known in advance and can be made ready before the campaign starts. Every capital campaign begins

Exhibit 15.3

The Gift Table or Gift Range Chart (The Rule of Thirds)

Number of Gifts	Dollar Amount	Goal	Comments
1	$1,000,000		
2	500,000	$3,000,000	Top 8 gifts (0.5%)
5	200,000		
10	100,000		
20	50,000	$3,000,000	Next 70 gifts (4.8%)
40	25,000		
60	15,000		
100	10,000		
125	5,000	$3,000,000	All other gifts
250	1,000		(1,385) (94.7%)
350	500		
500	100		
Total 1,463		$9,000,000	1,463 gifts (100%)

with leadership. Nothing of importance will happen until these few but absolutely key people are in place. These leaders must be able to make their own major gift and solicit others for their major gifts. They must be well organized, resourceful, aggressive, and committed to the successful completion of the campaign, not just overseeing its operation for two or three years.

You can also prepare printed materials, including:

1. Case statement.
2. Brochures.
3. Pledge forms.
4. Volunteer kits.
5. Volunteer training programs.
6. Donor recognition plans.

These are the same kinds of requirements for annual giving and major giving solicitation activities described earlier in this workbook.

Budget

Most of the expenses to conduct a capital campaign will be used in the preparation phase. The market research, development audit, and feasibility studies are highly professional products. All three can cost from $15,000 to $30,000 each and, with routine support expenses, can be estimated to total as much as $60,000 to $100,000 depending on the size of each study, amount of preparation time required, and the number and types of personal and telephone interviews and focus groups that are needed.

After all the studies are completed, the next major area will be the writing, designing, and printing of all the campaign publications. There must also be extensive prospect research, recruiting and training volunteers and staff, and meetings to prepare and bring every phase of the campaign on line at its appointed time for action in the campaign. Some travel and related expenses can be expected along with a campaign kickoff, regular report meetings, and supplies for mailings, copies, and other basic support. The final budget element consists of the cost for complete donor honors and recognition program, select donor receptions, dedications, and grand openings.

There is no easy formula to estimate how much it will cost to carry out a successful campaign. The old cost guideline was between 5 and 10 percent of campaign goal, depending on the number of years required. Competition for funds has increased with growth in the number of new nonprofit organizations and the maturity of others. This requires more detailed planning, greater prospect research, and more recruitment and training of volunteers. The new guideline suggested as a rough budget estimate is between 10 and 20 percent of campaign goal.

Growth in professional competence among fund development office staff, many with campaign experience, has decreased the use of on-site counsel to manage daily operations for an entire campaign. Professionals from campaign firms continue to be necessary to guide and direct overall campaign activities but are more often scheduled to provide this valued service by visiting the organization regularly (e.g., from one day a week to a few days once or twice a month).

Execution

Major capital campaigns take on a life of their own, and few act like any of the others. The elements in the preparation phase are routine, but the similarity stops when the advance gifts phase begins with the first level of solicitations for the largest gifts called for in the gift table.

Because of the high degree of selectivity with qualified prospects at this point, there is not much of a visible appearance of campaign activity. Solicitation also begins for the board of directors and their goal of 100% participation and leadership gift decisions, again a small group. The next groups to be invited to participate are members of the "family," professional staff and employees and those best of friends in the prior donor pool who have the capacity and commitment to make their all-important early major gift decisions.

Others invited to join in at this early stage are the units of the annual giving solicitation program. A major decision is going to be required here: Will annual giving programs continue their daily activities outside the campaign because the organization depends on their cash each year to maintain current operations, or will each annual giving unit be invited to consider making additional gifts, above their annual gift levels, toward the campaign goal? These gifts can be in the form of personal "something extra" contributions at the time of their annual gift renewal. If the program or service receiving their regular annual support can be matched with a campaign goal, these annual giving activities can consider their own multiyear pledge as a major contribution goal to the campaign. In this fashion, their donors will be able to count their annual and any additional gifts toward the campaign goal.

Do not under any circumstances suspend or curtail the annual giving program during a capital campaign. Some nonprofit organizations have believed it was necessary to concentrate all their annual giving volunteers and donors plus their budget and staff on the capital campaign, but regretted this decision later. Yes, the campaign can be expected to weaken their performance because it will recruit from among their best volunteers and best donors and will move them up to campaign levels. Yes, annual goals and priority projects may not compete well with the high visibility and excitement surrounding the capital campaign. Nonetheless, keep the annual giving program going. Use one or more of the several options just suggested to make it as much a part of the campaign as possible.

The effort and expense to rebuild an annual giving program to its present levels of effectiveness and efficiency will be lost overnight if it is suspended. Two to three years will be required to restart and recapture the prior levels of productivity and profitability. They are just too valuable to let slip for even a minute.

Most other campaign work is done behind the scenes with prospect research, rating and evaluation, preparation of all the campaign materials, recruiting and training of volunteers, and the like. When success with the first two-thirds or more of the gift table is in sight and all the family of donors has been solicited, the balance of the campaign comes to life. If all has gone well, two-thirds or more of the total goal is already committed. The balance of the entire effort is now directed to the final third of the goal, where the greatest number of donors will be needed to achieve success.

Preparations will need to be made when the campaign is coming to a close. These activities will include completing all the honors and recognition for qualified donors. Plans will be needed for the victory celebration to recognize the generosity of many campaign leaders, donors, and volunteers instrumental in achieving success. Lastly, spend some time near the end to plan the transition out of the campaign and back into the still active, still necessary world of annual giving, major giving, and planned giving solicitation activities.

Because of its magnitude and the variety of details, there is much to evaluate in a capital campaign. Begin performance measurement during the preparation and advance gifts phase to prevent serious errors at this most critical time in the campaign (see Exhibit 15.4). Fully two-thirds or more of the goal must be achieved during this period. The second phase or final third of the campaign is the public segment whose success depends on advance gifts performance, so it is reasonable to split the two for measurement purposes (see Exhibit 15.5). The final phase is where most campaign volunteers will be active in helping to solicit identified public sources for the balance of funds required. Much of what the public knows about a campaign is disclosed during this period because all current and past annual giving donors plus newly identified prospects are invited to help "put us over the top" of the campaign goal.

Summary Interpretation

The nine-point performance index is valuable to perform for many sections of a capital campaign, but it is hard to separate them due to their close dependence on one another's success. Also, overall results in a multiyear campaign should be reviewed on completion rather than after each fiscal or calendar year as different activities are at work throughout the campaign to limit a fair comparison of overall campaign results

Exhibit 15.4

Measurement of Campaign Start-Up and Advance Gifts Phase

	SCORE				
	low				high
1. Readiness Factors					
a. Credibility	1	2	3	4	5
b. Relevance	1	2	3	4	5
c. Urgency	1	2	3	4	5
d. Pragmatism	1	2	3	4	5
2. Institutional master plan					
a. Mission statement	1	2	3	4	5
b. Vision statement	1	2	3	4	5
c. Strategic plan	1	2	3	4	5
d. Financial plan	1	2	3	4	5
e. Facilities and equipment plan	1	2	3	4	5
3. Assessments and Analysis					
a. Market research study	1	2	3	4	5
b. Development office audit	1	2	3	4	5
c. Feasibility study	1	2	3	4	5
4. Campaign Preparations					
a. Prospect research	1	2	3	4	5
b. Leadership recruitment	1	2	3	4	5
c. Volunteer recruitment	1	2	3	4	5
d. Volunteer training	1	2	3	4	5
e. Campaign materials	1	2	3	4	5
5. Advance Gifts Phase					
a. Gift range table	1	2	3	4	5
b. Lead gift solicitation	1	2	3	4	5
c. Second level gift solicitation	1	2	3	4	5
d. Board solicitation/participation	1	2	3	4	5
e. Management/Professional staff	1	2	3	4	5
f. Employee solicitation	1	2	3	4	5
g. Best donors solicitation	1	2	3	4	5

Median Score _____

Exhibit **15.5**

Measurement of Campaign Operations to Completion

	SCORE				
	low				high
6. Individual Major Gifts Phase					
a. Current donors	1	2	3	4	5
b. Past donors	1	2	3	4	5
c. Newly qualified prospects	1	2	3	4	5
7. Foundation Solicitations					
a. Largest gift prospects	1	2	3	4	5
b. Local gift prospects	1	2	3	4	5
c. Newly qualified prospects	1	2	3	4	5
8. Corporation Solicitations					
a. Largest gift prospects	1	2	3	4	5
b. Local gift prospects	1	2	3	4	5
c. Newly qualified prospects	1	2	3	4	5
9. "Every Member" Campaign					
a. Annual giving donor participation	1	2	3	4	5
b. Prior donor invitations	1	2	3	4	5
c. Newly qualified prospects	1	2	3	4	5
10. Campaign Wrap-Up to Victory					
a. Revisit areas below goal	1	2	3	4	5
b. "Challenge Grant" option	1	2	3	4	5
c. Revisit early donors for 2nd gift	1	2	3	4	5

Median Score

at any point along the way. There are two phases in each campaign that can be measured separately: campaign start-up and advance gifts, and campaign operations and completion (see Exhibits 15.4 and 15.5).

It is also valuable to compare the results of several campaigns rather than to pin too many conclusions on just one. If the same organization has conducted one or more recent campaigns, these results will help evaluate the new one. And, if the information is available, comparisons with recent campaign results from other local nonprofit organizations, especially if the same type organization (college, hospital, museum, theater), will be insightful. However, each campaign is likely to be quite different in its performance because priority projects are different along with volunteer leadership and donor capability, image and reputation, external economic environment, and other factors. The results of separate three-year campaigns within 12 years at the same organization are illustrated in Exhibits 15.6 and 15.7 with the following commentary:

(1) The number of participants reveals how very dependent a capital campaign is on a few large gifts; campaign 2 needed many more donors, which increased costs, because of lower average gifts.

(2) The cost of fund-raising should be in the 10 percent to 20 percent range, again pointing out the problem in campaign 2. Smaller goals are more likely to result in higher costs.

(3) Studying the number of donors participating is valuable to provide insight about how important the public believes this organization and its announced highest priority to be. Established nonprofit organizations usually have a high profile of respect and trust in the community, which aids their campaign's performance, as campaigns 1 and 3 illustrate. Campaign 3 enlisted a high volume of donors, necessary because of its high goal but also indicative of strong communitywide support for its mission and vision.

(4) Average cost per gift was highest for campaign 3 at $159 due to its involving nearly 12,000 donors, but it achieved 77 percent participation from those solicited. Conversely, campaign 2 had a lower average cost per gift of $43 and succeeded in getting gifts only 48 percent of the time. Campaign 1, while the smallest overall, illustrates reasonable success rates in all areas.

Exhibit 15.6

Nine-Point Performance Index Analysis of Capital Campaigns

	Campaign 1	Campaign 2	Campaign 3
Participation	1,422	6,075	11,829
Income	$880,000	$1,089,450	$23,450,000
Expenses	$107,550	$259,650	$1,875,750
Percent participation	59%	48%	77%
Average gift size	$619	$179	$1,982
Net income	$772,450	$829,800	$21,574,250
Average cost per gift	$76	$43	$159
Cost of fund-raising	12%	24%	8%
Return	718%	320%	1150%

Exhibit 15.7

Illustration of Nine-Point Performance Index Analysis of Capital Campaigns

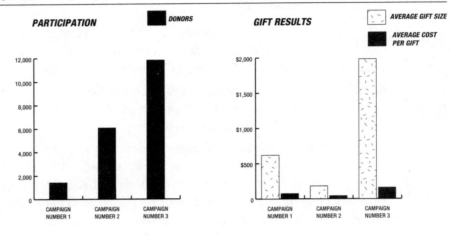

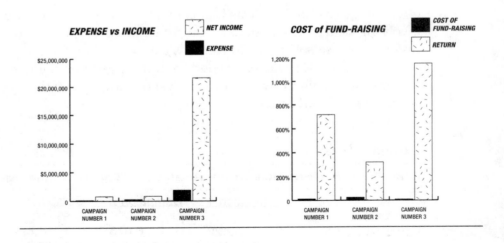

Action Plans

Capital campaigns usually require three to five years to complete and are most often staged once or twice a decade. Some larger nonprofit organizations, notably major colleges and universities, have announced billion-dollar campaigns that may require 10 or more years to complete and take on the appearance of being a "never-ending" campaign. Campaign progress in all instances remains a guide for next steps required to keep the campaign moving toward its announced goal. For example, following the top-down/inside-out design, the campaign timetable may be accelerated or slowed depending on when the largest gifts are actually received. Their best use is to leverage all other gifts to follow. The same is true within each segment of the campaign; largest corporate gift first to influence other corporate decisions, followed by largest bank gift to influence all other banks, and so on.

Because flexibility is an essential ingredient in capital campaigns along with a precise focus on major gifts, success or failure usually resides in the preparations and advance gift phase. Measurements here count the most. Without a feasibility study to test the project and goal in the community that is to be invited to give, how is it possible to estimate the potential amount that can be raised, major donors who will be willing to support the project, and volunteer leaders who will be willing to serve? Without market research analysis of public opinion, it is difficult to evaluate acceptance of the organization's master plan with its assessment of the most urgent community priority of needs. Without a development office audit, it is difficult to measure the capability and capacity of staff and systems to maintain current operating areas while supporting a campaign from start to finish.

Once campaign preparations are complete and the advance gifts phase begins, much depends on well-trained volunteer leaders and their success in soliciting the best donor prospects using carefully prepared cultivation plans and solicitation strategies. Here is where top leadership of the organization must be fully involved. Here also is where activities and events such as a campaign kickoff party and groundbreaking ceremonies can be held, to build excitement and enthusiasm. As much as 80 to 90 percent of the money is the major gifts goal, which will come from as few as 10 to 20 percent of all donors to the campaign. Without this level of success at the beginning, campaigns can drag on for extra months and years as they rely more and more on typical annual giving programs and gift levels to conclude the campaign.

During the final phase of the campaign, known as the "public phase," everyone involved with the organization is invited to join in. Annual donors are reminded that their annual gifts are necessary to maintain current operations, but are asked to contribute "something extra" in addition to their annual gift. New prospects are treated to a big project initiative with its attendant excitement involving lots of people working together. Many new donors can be recruited during a capital campaign, to be retained afterward through annual giving programs.

Donor recognition programs can begin before the campaign is finished by honoring current donors at regular activities and events during the year and in newsletters and annual reports. If the campaign is for a construction project, as is usually the case, "hard-hat" tours for major donors can begin as soon as the structure is up and safe for visitors after construction crews finish for the day. Dedications and grand opening ceremonies can be planned and a few major donors invited to be on the committee making these arrangements. Once the project is finished and the campaign goal realized, the effort needs to publish its final results and declare a close to the entire enterprise.

Related Benefits

Several advantages occur during and after a capital campaign. Nonprofit organizations are not the same afterward; their master plan called for new directions, a larger vision, which is now underway. Many donors have made the largest gifts of their lifetimes and have achieved new levels of personal satisfaction. Volunteers have experienced the excitement and satisfaction of major gift solicitation and possess a new confidence in their ability and the capability of their organization to work together to meet important community needs. The expertise and confidence of the fund development staff has grown, and they are prepared to achieve greater levels of annual contributions support.

Much has been accomplished, beginning with expanded programs and services offered at higher quality and available to more people. The organization has achieved a new capability and level of confidence to meet its next challenge. The ability of the fund development staff to organize themselves to successfully petition the community for valid needs has been proven; image and reputation are their highest levels. The master plan suggests more is needed, more can be done, and planning the next campaign can now begin.

16

Planned Giving and Estate Planning

Often considered the last area of fund-raising practice, planned giving offers valuable benefits to nonprofit organizations and its dedicated donors and volunteers. A well-defined planned giving program will position an organization favorably for senior donors who will encounter difficult estate planning decisions. A well-thought-out estate plan should be designed to provide financial security and personal satisfaction by donors while also providing for their family, friends, and favorite nonprofit organizations.

There are many types of planned gifts; they can be classified in two broad categories:

(1) *Revocable gifts.* The most common form of a revocable gift is a will or living trust. By creating a will or living trust, donors provide for the special needs of their family, take full advantage of estate tax savings, handpick their executor, and select their favorite nonprofit organizations to benefit from their estate plan. Recipient organizations may receive a percentage of the residue of a donor's estate, a specific dollar amount, a selected asset, or specific property. For revocable gifts of a will or living trust, donors retain the option to change their mind about their designated beneficiaries.

(2) *Irrevocable gifts.* Irrevocable planned gifts can be created during a donor's lifetime (inter vivos) or by their will or living trust (testamentary) and, once executed, cannot be revoked. A variety of irrevocable planned gifts are available and include but are not limited to:

- Charitable remainder unitrusts.
- Charitable remainder annuity trusts.

- Gift annuities.
- Lead trusts.
- Pooled income funds.
- Life estates.

Donors using these forms of planned giving retain an income interest in the asset (that is, they receive the earnings but not the principal) and receive generous tax savings. Because these gifts are irrevocable, extensive planning and careful consideration are required prior to each gift decision.

For those donors who have been active contributors to charity, planned gifts represent a perpetuation of their lifetime of giving and are often placed in endowment on receipt by the nonprofit organization. Estate planning gifts are an opportunity to complete a gift program started earlier, such as to finish funding a long-supported project, endow a favorite program area, or memorialize a spouse or friend. Quite a few donors prefer to define these outcomes themselves rather than leave these decisions to their heirs. Some donors prefer to preserve their estate from the bite of the Internal Revenue Service, which may impose an estate tax rate as high as 55 percent.

Nonprofit organizations have incorrectly thought of planned giving as a low priority in their fund development program because of their more urgent need for operating cash. When their solicitation programs begin to achieve some maturity, they begin to appreciate the value of endowment income as an additional and reliable source of annual cash.

Planned giving is a highly technical, highly personalized, and highly structured area of philanthropic practice that is also multifaceted and (on the surface) reasonably complex to understand and use. Because planned gifts usually involve gifting of assets and not discretionary income, these gifts also are often large when compared with other contributions.

Purposes

The two main purposes of a planned giving program are:

1. To assist a donor in achieving his or her financial, estate, and gift planning objectives.

2. To assist in the long-term financial security of nonprofit organizations through gifts restricted for endowment.

As individuals approach their retirement years, they become more aware of the need to prepare their estates and financial plans. As current donors to nonprofit organizations, they are given information about planned giving and estate planning services available. Bank trust departments and insurance companies market similar services to their clients. Attorneys, accountants, and financial planners also bring up tax planning considerations in their discussions with clients who have engaged them to assist in their retirement and estate planning decisions. It has been widely reported in the media that the largest generational transfer of wealth in the United States, expected at between $7 and $10 trillion, will occur between 1995 and 2010.

Decisions about gifting assets accumulated during a lifetime also require a special consideration—donative intent. As with all charitable gifts, donors must contribute their assets to an Internal Revenue Code 501(c)(3) nonprofit public benefit corporation, which permits them to enjoy the benefits of an Internal Revenue Code 170(a)(1) charitable contribution deduction from personal income tax. Unlike other gifts, planned gifts also can offer donors a retained interest in their gift and the extra benefit of an income stream from its continued operations for the remainder of their life. Donors who lack donative intent and are searching only for a secure investment paying a high return or an advantageous income tax break may be dissatisfied with a planned gift because they must irrevocably transfer their asset. Tax planning may be secondary to the commitment to benefit others as a consequence of making a gift, but it remains a highly important element in all planned giving and estate planning decisions.

As an example of donor benefits available with planned giving, consider a couple aged 70 and 75 who purchased $100,000 in ABC company stock years ago. Their investment now has appreciated and is worth $600,000. ABC stock is paying between $18,000 to $24,000 a year (at least 3% to 4% dividend rates), all of which is ordinary income subject to income tax. If these stock owners make a gift of their ABC stock to an 8% charitable remainder annuity trust, they will enjoy the following tax and life income benefits:

1. A charitable contribution deduction in the year of the gift with a 5-year carryforward.

2. Avoidance of capital gains tax on the $500,000 appreciation.

3. An income of $48,000 every year for the rest of their lives, which doubles their income from prior dividends.

4. An estate tax deduction for the value of their trust at death.

Further, these donors can choose to use a portion of their increased income and tax savings to create an irrevocable life insurance trust that will replace their $600,000 as a gift for their heirs.

A nonprofit organization can act as trustee of each trust. If willing to do so, it assumes the fiduciary duty of administrator, investment manager, and all liability obligations of the trust. If the gift is in the form of a gift annuity, the nonprofit organization also must commit its own assets to ensure that the donors will receive their annuity payment without fail. If the nonprofit organization elects not to serve as trustee of the trust, it should offer to assist the donor in selecting a competent, professional corporate trustee. With prudent and balanced investment practices, these planned gifts will preserve principal, make all payments faithfully, and even increase the value of the original gift over the life of the trust.

Because these donors have shown such generosity in gifting their $600,000 in ABC stock, the nonprofit organization welcomes them into a stewardship program for planned gift donors. On the death of both donors, the organization accepts the use of the balance of funds in their trust as directed by the donors. Their distribution from their trust may be unrestricted and can be added to endowment or applied where the board of directors choose. If their contribution is restricted to endowment, with the income to be applied to a particular program within the organization, the funds will be dedicated to that purpose.

Preparation

The planned giving program, like every other fund-raising activity, needs a complete plan, effective leadership, committed advocates, technical expertise, competent personnel, adequate budget, consistent public exposure, and experience. Nonprofit organizations must be willing to invest a portion of the fund development budget in these forms of future gifts without the expectation of immediate returns, and to continue their commitment without interruption. The initial steps include items on the following checklist:

1. A definition of a deferred gift as it applies to the institution.

2. The rationale for establishing the program.

3. An explanation of the various forms of deferred gifts that will be acceptable to the institution (for example, the decision whether or not to establish a pooled-income fund should be a board, not a business office, decision).

4. Suggested drafts of deferred-gift forms to be used by the institution.

5. Recommendations on investment procedures, including objectives for funds, fiduciary responsibilities, and so on.

6. A suggested statement of policy governing the institution's program, including advertising, conflicts of interest, staff solicitation, and protection of donors and the institution.

7. A list of recommended institutional representatives authorized to negotiate deferred gifts (I suggest the chief executive officer and the senior development officer).

8. A request for permission to establish a deferred-gifts advisory committee, and a list of suggested members.

9. A suggested legal counsel to be retained by the institution.[1]

Add to these preparations a written policy and procedure manual to guide the organization in its decisions on evaluating each planned gift. These policies will include directions on minimum gift values for each form of planned gift, acceptable assets (not all gift forms are appropriate for every organization), toxic and environmental analysis procedures, and whether the organization will act as trustee for each form of charitable trust, gift annuity, and pooled income fund.

Once an organization begins to offer planned giving to its constituents and accepts its first planned gift in trust, it can never stop this program nor relinquish its obligation to these donors. Certain lifetime responsibilities for these donors and their assets are involved. Whether it acts as trustee of the trust or not, it is obligated to complete the terms and conditions contained in the trust agreement. Unlike annual giving and other forms of major gift development, planned giving and estate planning include the responsibility for developing the nature of each gift, maintaining a relationship with each donor, managing the assets prudently according to the terms of the trust, and fulfilling the donor's ultimate directions on use of the money at maturity of the gift. To fulfill these obligations, the organization needs access to the following skills:

1. Knowledge of the planned gift vehicles available to donors, policy, and procedure for operations.
2. Legal, tax and technical assistance in preparing gift instruments.
3. Investment management.
4. Trust management and administration.
5. Accounting and income tax report preparation.
6. Probate procedures.

After these internal preparations are complete, nonprofit organizations offering planned giving and estate planning programs to their constituency must communicate this information to them. Your organization should develop a marketing plan that is well matched to the institution, its public, and the environment in which it operates. This plan also must remain flexible to accommodate changing conditions in a manner similar to the launch of a capital campaign. It must present a professional image throughout to inspire confidence and trust. The six steps in Exhibit 16.1 can be used to develop a marketing plan.

Budget

The expense categories to support a planned giving program are similar to those of every other fund-raising activity. A few new expense areas will occur, such as extra legal and accounting fees, special software to perform calculations, real estate and other property appraisals, and support for the one-on-one personal cultivation and counseling of donors that is necessary. If you start the program by promoting bequests only, budget demands will be minimal and will consist of the cost of a basic brochure promoting the concept and the text of sample language to be added naming the nonprofit organization (using its full legal name) as a beneficiary of the donor's will or living trust. If a full-service planned giving and estate planning program is to be offered, a comprehensive budget worksheet will be required (see Exhibit 16.2).

These expenses are investments in the planned giving program that proceed completion of any planned gift agreements. Investments require patience and it often seems that planned gifts take a long time to mature. A budget investment of $175,000 per year for five years ($875,000) for a large nonprofit organization can and should produce a variety of executed planned gifts in excess of this initial investment.

Exhibit 16.1

Steps in Creating a Planned Giving Marketing Plan

1. Understanding who the organization is in relation to the marketplace. This involves demographic and psychographic studies of the potential donor base, to determine what groups of people might realistically give to the planned giving program. Not every organization is willing to pay the cost of such a study, but those who have gone the extra step have found the study to be invaluable both for delivery of services and for fund-raising.

2. Segmenting the marketplace into target markets based on identities of wants and needs of the potential donors in each of the market segments.

3. Designing planned gift strategies that may be appealing to each target market and that meet the perceived wants and needs of that target market.

4. Checking similarly situated organizations to see what the competition is doing and what outreach programs they may be planning that may overlap or conflict.

5. Developing effective outreach efforts based on the market studies done in accordance with the above steps. These will no doubt include donor and professional seminars, bequest mailings, newsletters, advertisements (perhaps), and other sources of reaching people who may be willing to commit to the planned giving program.

6. Creating effective private communications, once an individual prospect is identified.*

*Lynda S. Moerschbaecher and Erik D. Dryburgh, "Planned Giving," in *The Nonprofit Management Handbook: Operating Policies and Procedures*, Tracy Daniel Connors, Ed. New York: John Wiley & Sons, 1993, p. 530. Reprinted by permission.

The actual number of gifts and their value is impossible to predict. But it is reasonable to forecast that new planned gifts will be executed and that bequests will continue to be received during this initial five-year period. Notice of other planned gifts will be received from new donors who never notified the organization of their generosity until it announced its own program.

Should bequest revenue be measured against the current budget of the planned giving program? Yes. Bequests represent cash income received the same as every other contribution. The costs to process and record them are minimal, and these expenses should be charged to the planned gifts budget. Bequest income represents the promise of future income that every planned gift will eventually fulfill.

Exhibit 16.2

Sample Budget for Planned Giving Program

		Estimated Costs (full-time effort)
A. Prospect Research/Staffing		
Prospect research		$1,500
Computer software (one-time purchase)		3,000
Brochures (for each type of gift plan)		4,000
Newsletter (quarterly)		4,000
Planned Gifts Committee support		1,500
Administrative support		1,000
Staff salaries/benefits (manager/secretary)		65,000
	Subtotal	$80,000
B. Direct Solicitation Activities		
Direct mail/marketing/promotion		$2,500
Workshops/seminars		2,500
Local travel (cabs, parking, meals)		2,000
Prospect cultivation/entertainment		2,500
Long-distance travel		
Airfare		2,500
Cabs or car rental		1,000
Parking/Meals		1,500
Accommodations		2,000
Legal fees/appraisals/tax accountants		5,000
	Subtotal	$21,500
C. Donor Relations		
Donor recognition/plaques		$1,500
Heritage Society/Codicil Club		3,000
Invitations/reservations		500
Annual meeting honors and awards		2,000
	Subtotal	$7,000
	Total	$108,500

Newly executed planned gifts should *not* be reflected in the income statements because the assets remain in trust and have not been transferred to the organization's control, even if the organization is acting as trustee. On the death of the income beneficiaries, the trust or gift annuity transfers all its remaining assets to the organization, which then reports it as bequest income.

Planned gifts where the organization is acting as trustee *should be* reflected in the audited financial statement, as funds in trust.[2] Further, the value of each planned gift under management should be *counted* and *reported* in activity reports prepared by the fund development office. This level of productivity should be included in the performance evaluation of the planned giving program.

A common question is whether fair market value or net present value should be used in reports of planned giving results? Referring back to our donors' gift of ABC stock, they certainly believe they made a gift of $600,000; that is the fair market value of the asset when it was transferred to their charitable remainder annuity trust. But, because the gift is not yet the property of the organization, the organization cannot count it as revenue received. Further, it can be shown as a receivable held in trust but only when the organization is acting as trustee.

The net present value (in the first year of the gift) is equivalent to the charitable income tax deduction the donor receives when making the gift. The deduction is calculated using the factors of type of gift (annuity trust), age of the donors (70 and 75), the monthly applicable federal rate (AFR), and the income payout rate (8%), as illustrated in Exhibit 16.3. The amount of the charitable deduction will differ depending on the type of gift. Because they selected the charitable annuity trust, their tax deduction will be $311,604. (In any of these examples, the net present value is not calculated, nor is it the same as the charitable contribution deduction.) Net present value should be disclosed to all parties *before* any decision to execute the gift is made. This is especially true if the gift being created requires a financial commitment by the organization, such as with a charitable gift annuity, in which case the organization should be fully aware that it must have the resources to guarantee the payments from its own assets.

The final answer about the value of any planned gift is to wait for the cash amount received at maturity. Accounting guidelines may change between now and that future time, but the amount of a planned

Exhibit 16.3

Charitable Deduction Values for Different Planned Gifts*

Assumptions	Charitable Annuity Trust	Charitable Unitrust	Charitable Unitrust
Beneficiary ages	70, 75	70, 75	70, 75
Principal donated	$600,000	$600,000	$600,000
Payout rate	8%	5%	8%
Payout schedule	Quarterly	Quarterly	Quarterly
Benefits			
Charitable deduction	$311,604	$285,390	$188,646
Annual income or first year's income	$48,000	$30,000	$48,000

*Ronald R. Jordan and Katelyn L. Quynn, *Planned Giving: Management, Marketing, and Law.* New York: John Wiley & Sons, 1995, pp. 187, 189, 190. These illustrations were prepared using PG Calc's Planned Giving manager software. Reprinted by permission.

gift can always be reported accurately only when it matures. Ultimately, when a planned gift matures, the amount received by the organization becomes the value recorded for financial purposes, according to present accounting guidelines.

All forms of planned gifts will have continuing expenses after the gift is made. These include administrative, management, and investment fees, check distributions, and donor relations activities. These expenses are paid long before the gift matures. In reality, the organization has received the remainder value in full; its expenses are accounting history.

Your organization should decide at the outset, when starting its planned giving program, whether to value these gifts at net present value or fair market value. Once this determination is made, the organization should be consistent in its accounting for all these gifts. At this same time, it should also decide whether it will keep a record of revocable gifts (not their values) and maintain records of every other form of planned gift, including expectancies.

Issues regarding gift values and accounting practices are important to resolve when developing a budget that defines how a planned giving program will be managed and evaluated. There is a direct relationship between costs and results in all other areas of fund-raising and while this is also true in planned giving, the results almost always represent solicitation activities performed several budget years earlier.

Execution

Your organization will need a professional with experience in planning and managing a planned giving program, either as staff, volunteer, or consultant. A myriad of questions will require explanation and repeated presentations. Some confusion about planned giving may exist with donors and board members due to promotional hype about tax savings from these gifts. There also is a bit of mystery associated with this form of giving, perhaps because the economic benefits sound too good to be true. Other elements of the program are intimidating to many people because of their complexity.

The most valuable resource available to assist every form of solicitation activity offered by a nonprofit organization is the confidence and trust its donors already hold in the board of directors, management, volunteers and technical advisors, current investment performance, and professional staff. Once a donor decides to make a planned gift, that individual becomes an advocate of the value of this unique method of giving.

Unfortunately, there have been isolated incidents of illicit or unscrupulous behavior reported in the media in which the elderly were bilked of their life savings by an estate planning scandal, which creates suspicion and distrust in the minds of many people. There also have been a few organizations and entrepreneurs who have promoted planned gifts as "tax shelters" with high annual payout rates, which also have misled willing donors. Nonprofit organizations and their planned giving volunteers and staff must proceed with caution to preserve the quality and reputation of their organization when they promote planned gifts.

A sequence of actions will serve to introduce a new planned giving program. Begin with the board of directors, so they are the first to be well informed about basic concepts of planned giving, gift vehicles to be offered, and types of assets the organization is willing to accept. The board also should review and approve the planned giving policy and procedure manual that will govern daily operations of this program. It is appropriate at this time to ask members of the board, "Have you named our organization in your estate plan?"

Next, promote this program to current donors and volunteers. Begin with older donors (65 years and older) and those with a lengthy giving history. If appropriate, offer these same services to those who regularly use your nonprofit organization's programs and services because they have already experienced their value. The general public (and only those market research identify as qualified prospects) are the last group to approach. The amount of effort required to recruit and execute the first planned gift will be high. Generally, a planned gift is seldom the first gift a new donor should be invited to make. Begin with those who have already demonstrated their commitment to your organization and for whom the advantages of a planned gift is of value to their individual retirement and estate plans.

Many nonprofit organizations use volunteers in their planned giving program while others employ professional staff. The best method is a mix of both. For those who elect to use both, hire an experienced executive and then invite a select group of organization members whose profession is estate and financial planning to serve as the planned giving advisory and policy committee. This committee's job description calls for their technical expertise to guide the organization in formulating its policy and procedures, and in evaluating every planned gift offered. Planned gifts are seldom similar; they differ in substantial ways from the type of gift, the asset funding the gift, the amount of income desired, and the level of risk to the organization in accepting the gift.

Consider a second volunteer group, possibly called the endowment council, whose member candidates are first recommended by the advisory policy committee. These additional volunteers are other professionals whose business practice also includes estate planning, from tax accountants to tax attorneys, from stock brokers to real estate agents, from life insurance agents to financial planners. Provide them with orientation and regular training sessions along with a supply of planned giving brochures to prepare them to discuss these concepts and their opportunities with their clients. They also represent a "farm club" for future membership on the advisory committee.

A third group also will be necessary to a successful planned giving program. If not already appointed and in operation, the board of directors should activate an investment management committee. Their responsibility is to establish investment guidelines and supervise the investment performance of each planned gift in trust for each donor's lifetime. After planned gifts mature, the committee also manages the investment of endowment funds. In combination, these three committees plus professional staff constitute the expertise required to enable a planned giving program to grow to success.

This team will be tested; bet on it. Gifts will be offered in exchange for highly mortgaged homes and apartment buildings; partial ownership in commercial buildings, time-shares, and condominiums; undeveloped land (usually in a distant, often deserted location); boats, airplanes, and vintage automobiles; SEC Section 144 stock, non-publicly traded securities, and more. The team also may be offered to "purchase" a planned gift for a commission to the agent who has "developed" a donor who wants to receive the tax benefits of a planned gift. Not all such offers will make good planned gifts or even good outright gifts for that matter. In fact, a gift for sale may be in violation of the "Model Standards of Practice for the Professional Gift Planner."[3] These standards were adopted in 1991 by the National Committee on Planned Giving and subsequently endorsed by the American Council on Gift Annuities. Some additional pitfalls to be wary of include a variety of technical bear traps that will test the knowledge and skill of the entire planned giving team. Lynda Moerschbaecher and Erik Dryburgh have assembled a list of "tricky gifts" to serve as early notice to all. In no particular order, they are the step transaction or collapsible gift rule, tangible personal property, intangible assets, mortgaged property, alternative minimum tax, unrelated business income, self-dealing, and toxic waste and environmental liability.[4]

Time is on the side of the organization that actively invests in a planned giving program. Gone are the pressures of "quick fixes," and "quick bucks" to meet payroll by Friday, pressures that sometimes can test the edges of ethical practice as well as intelligent decisions. Planned giving's best features are its deliberate pace, patience, more lasting purpose (endowment), and its reliability. Nonprofit organizations must practice these same virtues, especially patience, in realizing these ultimate gifts. Planned gift donors may be few in number, but they are likely to be the largest single investors in a nonprofit organization. They also are most interested in the organization's long-term future and often become its most vocal advocates.

Analysis

Measuring the cost-effectivenes of planned giving programs is complex because costs incurred in one year to increase awareness about estate and planned giving options may not result in a planned gift decision until many years afterward, most likely when the donor is ready. Some donors require a lot of attention from planned giving staff, which takes time and some budget money but produces no new gifts. Many non-profit organizations determine the success of their planned giving program by counting the number of executed irrevocable gifts at fair market value. Others count the number of gifts in progress, attendance at workshops and seminars, mail responses, and any other activity that represents time and effort spent in support of planned giving.

Performance analysis of a planned giving program can examine several areas of activity in addition to counting the number of gifts received and their value. And, however a nonprofit organization chooses to value and account for its planned gifts, the number and value of these commitments can be quantified (see Exhibit 16.4). Several program elements can be tracked in this activity report. Counting the contacts stimulated by each marketing effort indicates know-how and identifies where these messages are being received. Each respondent should receive a follow-up call (in person or by phone, if possible), to answer questions and to explore the prospect's interest and ability to make a planned gift. Tracking also indicates which communication methods produce the most responses.

An evaluation of the costs to mount each effort and the response will yield performance characteristics for the constituency. The constant effort to recruit and manage new donors who choose charitable trusts may appear to be the most efficient and profitable because the number of donors is small and the value of these gifts is usually large. Such results may compare unfairly with all the efforts to secure a large number of new donors to the pooled income fund, gift annuities program, or life insurance plan, all of which begin with smaller gifts.

A summary report of executed planned gifts at their fair market value or net present value is valuable to present as a part of monthly financial statements, usually alongside the investment committee's summaries (see Exhibit 16.5). This report will remind board members, management, and volunteers that irrevocable gifts for the future use of the organization are in place. Current values of any irrevocable planned gifts for which the organization is not trustee can

Exhibit 16.4

Activity Report for Planned Giving Program

A. Number of Contacts Stimulated by:

	Contacts	Meetings	Gifts
Newsletter/Annual Report requests	26	6	1
Direct mail request for information	125	18	2
Seminar/workshop attendees	255	39	3
Board members	8	6	0
Development committee members	12	6	1
Planned Gifts committee members	33	18	2
Major Gifit committee members	14	6	1
Annual Giving committee members	6	0	0
Other contacts: Prior planned gift donors	6	4	2
Totals	485	103	12

B. New Planned Gifts Executed

	Number	Donor Age (estimate)	Value (est.)
Will or living trust	5	72 (avg.)	$300,000
Pooled income fund	1	65	25,000
Remainder unitrust	1	75/73	250,000
Remainder annuity trust	2	82 (avg.)	450,000
Gift annuity	1	78/74	50,000
Charitable lead trust	0	-0-	-0-
Life estate	1	82/80	750,000
Life insurance policy	1	77/72	50,000
Other	0	-0-	-0-
Totals	12	75 (avg.)	$1,875,000

C. Bequests and Legacies Received

	Number	Amount
Unrestricted bequests	1	$125,000
Restricted bequests	1	25,000
Matured charitable trusts	0	-0-
Matured gift annuities	3	78,550
Matured life estates	0	-0-
Matured life insurance policy	1	65,000
Other	0	-0-
Totals	6	$293,550

Exhibit **16.5**

Summary Report of Executed Planned Gifts

Year	Donor Age	Initial Gift	Market Value	Annual Rate (%)	Annual Income
Irrevocable Charitable Trusts under Trusteeship					
Unitrust 85-1	64/64	$90,000	$112,535	8	$4,678
Annuity 91-1	86	100,000	81,023	—	6,750
Unitrust 91-1	76	450,000	556,098	8	26,183
Annuity 91-2	77/71	200,000	194,835	—	16,000
Unitrust 94-1	59/50	182,993	186,463	8	9,746
Subtotals		$1,022,993	$1,130,954		
Pooled Income Funds					
Fund—1992	86	$10,000	$9,608	6	$684
Fund—1993	62/65	44,650	42,899	6	3,055
Fund—1994	86	20,790	19,590	6	1,395
Subtotals		$75,440	$72,097		
Gift Annuities					
1993-1	82/79	$50,000			$4,092
1994-1	72	280,000			11,136
Subtotals		$330,000			$15,228
Irrevocable Charitable Trusts Not under Trusteeship					
Unitrust 91-3	72	$150,000			
Annuity 91-3	84/83	50,000			
Unitrust 93-1	80/81	500,000			
Annuity 94-1	78	325,000			
Subtotal		$1,025,000			

Planned Gifts Summary

Trusts as Trustee	$1,022,993
Trusts Not as Trustee	1,925,000
Pooled Funds	75,440
Gift Annuities	330,000
Total Planned Gifts	$3,353,433

only be estimated, but they exist and will be received in time. What can be reported is their original value, age of the donors, and date executed.

Summary Interpretation

Exhibits 16.6 and 16.7 provide a three-year summary of a new planned giving program using the nine-point performance index. Because these results are in summary form, the relative efficiency of each of the several planned gift vehicles is not apparent. However, after only three years, the planned giving solicitation program's cost of fund-raising and return percentages, based on the nine-point performance index, are among the most productive and profitable of any solicitation activity presented in this workbook. The following interpretations are based on the data presented in Exhibit 16.6:

(1) The number of bequests received, while unpredictable, is steady for the moment. Bequest income, also unpredictable, illustrates how a single large bequest in Year 2 can distort that year's results quite easily

Exhibit 16.6

Nine-Step Performance Index Analysis of a Planned Giving and Estate Planning Program

	Year 1	Year 2	Year 3	Total
Bequests received	8	9	12	29
Bequest income received	$55,000	$870,000	$39,500	$964,500
New planned gifts written (irrevocable)	5	13	9	27
Value of new irrevocable planned gifts written	$110,000	$425,000	$375,000	$910,000
Total number of gifts	13	22	21	56
Total value of gifts	$165,000	$1,295,000	$414,500	$1,874,500
Expenses	$129,550	$165,000	$142,250	$436,800
Percent participation	38%	61%	42%	47%
Average gift size	$12,692	$58,864	$19,738	$33,473
Net income	$35,450	$1,130,000	$272,250	$1,437,700
Average cost per gift	$9,965	$7,500	$6,774	$7,800
Cost of fund-raising	79%	13%	34%	23%
Return	27%	685%	191%	329%

Exhibit 16.7

**Illustration of Nine-Point Performance Index Analysis of a
Planned Giving and Estate Planning Program**

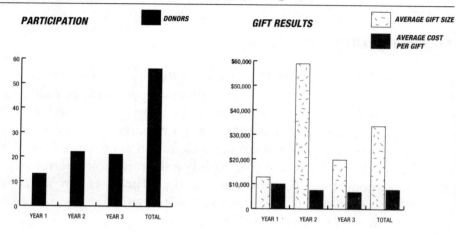

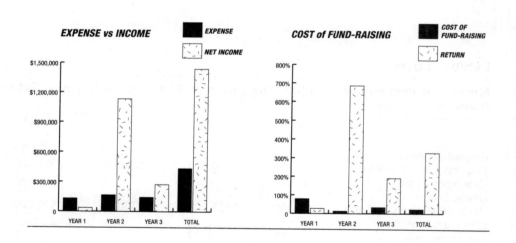

and may suggest to the casual reader that something was wrong the following year because of the serious drop in bequest income.

(2) The effort in this program, correctly, is directed toward the preparation and completion of new irrevocable planned gifts. A full-service program will offer several planned gift vehicles, including pooled funds, gift annuities, and life insurance, which are usually smaller gifts and may be the reason the value of new gifts written declined in Year 3.

(3) A planned giving program's expenses often are allocated 10 percent to processing bequests and 90 percent to developing new gifts. The budget has increased each year, reflecting increased activity and related costs associated with accounting, appraisal, legal, and brokerage fees required to execute complex planned gifts.

(4) The average cost per gift appears to require almost $8,000. With average gifts being completed at $33,473, the cost of fund-raising at 23 percent is acceptable and is likely to decrease with continued growth in the number of planned gifts executed.

(5) The conclusion to be stressed from this example is that $964,500 in bequest income has been received and should be set aside as endowment if at all possible; these gifts will never occur again. Further, future gifts have been concluded that total $910,000 and will most likely be added to endowment when they mature, for a combined total of nearly two million in present and future assets to benefit this nonprofit organization for its long-term future.

Action Plans

This planned giving program is well launched and should expect continued success. A challenge will be to continue to stimulate constituents through communications and marketing to inquire into the options and benefits of planned giving after they have all been invited several times to seminars, workshops, and briefings on the subject. The public is not easily stimulated to respond to these invitations. Further, it is easy for them to confuse programs promoted by nonprofit organizations with those advertised by the numerous estate planning counselors and advisers who use the same methods to find clients.

Continued attention must also be given to current (living) donors whose new gift plans are in operation. In addition to ensuring that their regular income checks are being delivered on time and completing their annual tax return documents, the organization must maintain donor relations. As is true of every other form of solicitation activity, present donors make the best prospects for additional gifts. Planned gift donors who are enjoying the benefits of their gifts are among the best candidates to add to their existing gift or execute new planned gifts. They are also the best advocates of this form of giving, and with their permission, their experience can be written up in the organization's publications and used in other marketing materials.

Attention likewise must be given to active supervision of the manager entrusted with investing these funds. If the organization acts as trustee of the trust, supervision must be an active part of a planned gifts program. Donors depend on solid performance for their income, and the nonprofit organization must meet its stewardship responsibilities. If the organization is not the trustee, it should make contact with the trustee to ask about performance along with donor satisfaction with both administrative and investment activities. There is no good reason to fail to monitor every planned gift to ensure protection of the donor's and the organization's future asset.

Related Benefits

Two significant benefits result from a planned gifts and estate planning program: satisfied donors and financial stability.

Most planned gift donors have entered this program late in their life, invested a portion of their life savings in one or another form of planned gift, and are dependent on its performance for a portion of their retirement income. Their peace of mind in having resolved distribution of their estate, a weighty burden to many people, allows them to enjoy their senior years with greater confidence and less worry. Satisfied donors are a precious asset any nonprofit organization would enjoy.

Nonprofit organizations that have invested in planned giving also show confidence (although their board still may worry some) about their own future. Every planned gift written is a major gift the organization will receive in time. Most will flow eventually into the endowment fund and continue their productivity for the benefit of many people for generations to come. Their very existence adds an entire level of financial security to the future of the organization. Only direct gifts to endowment make an equal added contribution to the organization they serve.

Summary Performance Analysis Techniques

Substantial information is now available for each solicitation activity in use. The multiple measurements of all these results have led to an understanding of their performance and identified where their improvements lie. These data further suggest what potential each may hold to achieve higher levels of performance in the future. Now it is time to assemble all these solicitation activities together for a summary performance measurement. Part IV will begin this summary with measurements of effectiveness and efficiency followed by an analysis of the productivity and profitability of all their results. Among the extra benefits realized will be forecasts of reliable estimates of future performance. Next, this experience will be used to establish performance standards to guide decisions on future budget investments and to monitor results that ought to be achieved.

Part IV provides a series of sample public reports to display performance that can be used to enhance public confidence and trust in the fund-raising practices used by nonprofit organizations. The future always promises some probability for change to present practices. A review of a host of challenges now on the horizon will conclude this workbook.

Nonprofit organizations and their professional fund-raising executives are being asked to defend their performance against a variety of tests. While there is merit in comparative analysis, there is no merit in holding people and programs accountable to unsubstantiated guidelines. The fact remains today that nonprofit organizations in the United States neither keep records nor report the results of their solicitation activities using consistent data elements. Until uniform criteria are accepted and put to use, comparative analysis will remain a fruitless and misdirected exercise.

What is possible now is self-assessment. Board members and management staff are becoming convinced that "cost-effectiveness analysis is a clear necessity for responsible nonprofit management," and "that the rigor involved will improve the organization's internal effectiveness and efficiency and will enhance the organization's external image."[1] Some nonprofit organizations use total dollars raised compared with fund-raising expense as their only measurement of fund-raising success. While simple to perform on appearance, this comparison can be misleading and is often misunderstood. This method is common in for-profit organizations, but it fails to provide equally clear evidence of success in nonprofit organizations. Lacking any other criteria, however, simple bottom-line cost of fund-raising ratios often are applied as a nearly infallible performance measurement.

Another incomplete analysis technique is to compare fund-raising results among nonprofit organizations. Organizations and their solicitation activities are unique. Institutions and agencies do not provide identical services to the same people in the same city at the same time with the same staff and facilities any more than they use the same volunteers to solicit the same public for the same purpose using the same fund-raising methods at the same time. Caution must be exercised in comparing fund-raising results of one organization with another, even if they are all of the same type, because environments and their use of different solicitation activities are so unlike one another.

What can be learned from studying the relationship between gross revenue, total costs, and net proceeds? Is $30,000 in net proceeds a "success" if gross revenue for the solicitation activity was $100,000 (a 70 percent cost of fund-raising)? Yes, may be the answer if this is a first-time, acquisition mailing or first-ever benefit event. No, if it is a renewal mailing or a benefit event's third year of operation.

Performance measurements should be applied uniformly to each and every solicitation activity, not just to mailings and benefit events. Assessment criteria can be defined to fit each method each time it is used, to measure the results of each against its own prior performance and to document where progress has been made and where additional improvements may lie. In time (a minimum of three years of continuous analysis using uniform criteria), performance measurements can achieve a higher purpose than to justify current budget investments. Assessments also help to define the potential and future capacity of the overall fund development program, the "vision" every evaluation exercise ought to set as its ultimate goal.

17

Effectiveness and Efficiency: Productivity and Profitability

The performance reviews in Parts II and III provide data for a combined analysis. The objective here is to achieve a comprehensive understanding and appreciation of performance. While each solicitation method has achieved its own degree of effectiveness and efficiency, the total fund development program also must be measured for its overall productivity and profitability.

Summary analysis should address:

1. Accountability for decisions made.
2. Quality indicators on performance.
3. Program assessments as to growth in numbers of donors and their levels of gift support.
4. Improved cost of fund-raising.
5. Improved return (net income).

One summary review will be to perform these measurements using the nine-point performance index.

Summary analysis also will require new instruments to expand these evaluations beyond just calculations of year-end statistics to compare performance against some level of guidelines or uniform standards. Some national guidelines are advocated by the Philanthropic Advisory Service of the Council of Better Business Bureaus and the National Charities Information Bureau.[1] Beyond this, common sense and good judgment should prevail in evaluating and reporting nonstatistical results to volunteers and donors. Fund development must also demonstrate its ability to:

1. Enhance the image and reputation of the organization it serves.
2. Advance its marketing, promotion, and community relations efforts.
3. Increase public confidence and trust in the organization and its leadership and management.
4. Achieve a higher level of effectiveness and efficiency in the quality of its programs and services offered for public benefit, including its solicitation practices.

Internal operating systems that support solicitation activities are often overlooked in summary analysis, and emphasis is placed only on results without analyzing the efforts required to achieve them. Exhibit 17.1 identifies a few summary areas where performance analysis can begin for the people involved and for internal support

Exhibit 17.1

Internal Analysis for Volunteers and Office Systems

		SCORE		
	low			high
A. People				
Board leadership	1	2	3	4	5
Board participation	1	2	3	4	5
Volunteer leadership	1	2	3	4	5
Solicitor training	1	2	3	4	5
Solicitor supervision	1	2	3	4	5
Regular volunteer performance evaluations	1	2	3	4	5
Median Score				
B. Office Systems				
Professional staff leadership	1	2	3	4	5
Prospect identification	1	2	3	4	5
Computer support systems	1	2	3	4	5
Staff training and development	1	2	3	4	5
Donor communications	1	2	3	4	5
Donor recognition	1	2	3	4	5
Regular solicitation activity performance evaluation	1	2	3	4	5
Median Score				

systems. If leadership and volunteer training score low, the balance of performance likely will be affected. If office systems and donor communications are ineffective, results will quickly illustrate these weaknesses.

Purposes

The primary objectives of a fund development program are:

1. To recruit donors and volunteers.
2. To build relationships that renew and increase their support.
3. To educate them about the public benefits of programs and services being offered.
4. To involve them in future planning.
5. To excite them about the opportunities for expansion and improvements in quality.
6. To encourage them to participate in communicating plans and priorities.
7. To invite them to help by giving and getting gifts.
8. To recognize and reward them for their commitments, contributions, and faithful service.

Evaluating these eight performance areas will require measuring more than dollars raised. Equally, analysis of these objectives should go hand in hand with assessing sound management in directing the process. Each nonprofit organization also should be evaluated on its fiduciary performance, the quality of its management of programs and services delivered, its operating systems, and its appropriate use of all funds raised, held, and spent. In combination, these measurable factors answer the public's need for assurance that what they were told was accurate, that claimed accomplishments were in fact done, that plans were reasonable and realistic, that requests for their help were valid and worthwhile, and that the outcomes delivered back to the community were beneficial improvements. To measure the increase in acceptance and confidence that a community holds for its nonprofit organizations, their programs and services, and their fund development activities is just as important as counting the number of donors and volunteers who participated and the money they gave.

Preparation

What kinds of data are required for summary analysis? Chapter 1 provided a uniform budget worksheet so all costs can be documented. Chapters 3 through 16 measured the results from each solicitation method using a consistent nine-point measurement index to provide performance yardsticks. Bringing total revenue and total costs together permits a first-level, bottom-line analysis of the overall performance of the entire solicitation program. Now you must discover what should be measured and how to interpret and use the results.

Preparation begins with report design. Basic gift reports create a summary of key data such as sources of gifts and uses of gifts received (see Exhibit 17.2). A second report will add cost of fund-raising by method of solicitation (Exhibit 17.3). These two summaries provide a wealth of data for analysis and interpretation. For example, the individual performance levels for each of the solicitation activities used in annual giving and major gifts programs are vastly different. These exhibits show that annual giving and major gifts

Exhibit 17.2

Sources and Uses of Gifts Received

		Unrestricted	Temporarily Restricted	Permanently Restricted	Totals
A.	**Annual Giving Programs**				
	Direct mail acquisition	$35,500	$ -0-	$ -0-	$35,500
	Direct mail renewal	45,500	31,000	-0-	76,500
	Membership dues	48,500	-0-	-0-	48,500
	Benefit events (3)	-0-	59,600	-0-	59,600
	Volunteer-led solicitations	15,800	38,000	28,200	82,000
	Subtotal	$145,300	$128,600	$28,200	$302,100
B.	**Major and Planned Giving Programs**				
	Corporations	$ -0-	$45,500	$ -0-	$45,500
	Foundations	-0-	65,000	-0-	65,000
	Individuals	25,000	105,500	15,000	145,500
	Bequests received	5,000	15,500	24,500	45,000
	Subtotal	$30,000	$231,500	$39,500	$301,000
	Total	$175,300	$360,100	$67,700	$603,100

Exhibit 17.3

Cost of Fund-Raising Report by Solicitation Method

	Gift Amount	Budget Approved	Budget Expended	Cost of Fund-Raising
A. Annual Giving Programs				
Direct mail (acquisition)	$35,500	$14,500	$14,798	42%
Direct mail (renewal)	76,500	1,500	1,620	2%
Membership dues	48,500	550	585	1%
Benefit events (3)	59,600	20,000	21,747	36%
Volunteer-led solicitations	82,000	1,200	1,250	2%
Subtotal	$302,100	$37,750	$40,000	13%
Direct Costs: Annual Giving				
Labor/Payroll		$62,000	$63,050	
Non-payroll costs		37,750	40,000	
Subtotal		$99,750	$103,050	34%
B. Major Gifts Programs				
Corporations	$45,500	$3,500	$3,250	7%
Foundations	65,000	3,500	2,015	3%
Individuals	145,500	3,800	4,200	3%
Bequests received	45,000	200	1,850	4%
Subtotal	$301,000	$11,000	$11,315	4%
Total	$603,100	$48,750	$51,315	9%
Net Income	$471,985			
Direct Costs: Annual Giving				
Labor/Payroll		$18,000	$16,750	
Non-payroll costs		11,000	11,315	
Subtotal		$29,000	$28,065	9%
C. Expense Summary (A + B)				
Direct Costs		$80,000	$79,800	
Indirect Costs/Overhead		$48,750	$51,315	
Total		$128,750	$131,115	22%
Return				360%

programs raised almost the same amount of money but at a much different cost of fund-raising (34 percent and 9 percent).

An accurate interpretation of the cost of fund-raising percentage is crucial to this first level of performance measurement and will be decisive because future budget allocations will be based on these hard numbers. Once multiyear data become available, assessments will help to interpret the progress achieved by each solicitation activity in use and become the critical criteria used to predict next years's likely performance.

Preparation must also include some thought to how summary information can and should be presented. The format should help inform and educate viewers about results and also aid them in interpreting what these results mean (see Exhibits 17.4 and 17.5).

Exhibit 17.4

Multiyear Summary Results with One-Year Forecast Including Cost of Fund-Raising and Return Percentages

	Year 1	Year 2	Year 3	Est. Year 4
A. Annual Giving Programs				
Direct mail (acquisition)	$27,550	$31,250	$35,500	$42,000
Direct mail (renewal)	55,880	69,500	76,500	85,000
Membership dues	40,400	44,000	48,500	55,000
Benefit events (3)	45,500	53,400	59,600	68,000
Volunteer-led solicitations	58,500	65,500	82,000	90,000
Subtotal	$227,830	$263,650	$302,100	$340,000
B. Major Gifts Programs				
Corporations	$13,500	$28,000	$45,500	$55,000
Foundations	8,000	35,500	65,000	80,000
Individuals	35,000	78,000	145,500	160,000
Bequests received	5,000	26,000	45,000	25,000
Subtotal	$61,500	$167,500	$301,000	$320,000
Total	$289,330	$431,150	$603,100	$660,000
C. Expense Summary				
Labor/payroll	$68,015	$72,100	$79,800	$85,000
Nonpayroll costs (Includes indirect costs and overhead)	39,550	46,225	51,315	50,000
Subtotal	$107,565	$118,325	$131,115	$135,000
Net Income	$181,765	$312,825	$471,985	$525,000
Cost of fund-raising	37%	27%	22%	20%
Return	169%	264%	360%	389%

Exhibit **17.5**

Illustration of Multiyear Summary Results with One-Year Forecast

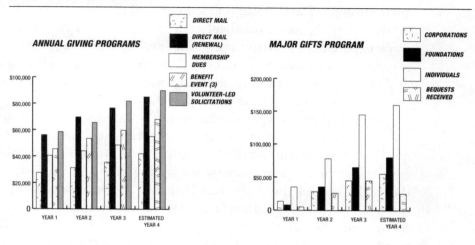

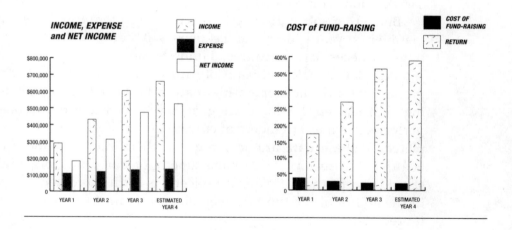

Budget

Accuracy and completeness remain the chief benefit from tracking all the expenses required to support the entire fund development program. Solicitation activities are more visible and therefore better known. The invisible parts are contained in indirect costs and overhead expenses, and while out of sight, they must also be included. Recalling that budget dollars are best understood as investments made by nonprofit organizations with the expectation of profitable returns, it is essential that all areas of expense be allocated properly to each solicitation activity and be inclusive of all the support costs required for their successful application. Documents supporting this effort are (a) budget preparation worksheets, (b) routine financial statements to track expenses, (c) accounting guidelines for consistency, and (d) audit statements to provide an independent review of operating procedures and year-long performance, all four conducted in accordance with generally accepted accounting principles (GAAP).

Nonprofit accounting standards and guidelines can and do change and require close attention for organizations to remain current with modifications and alterations to any public financial statements that result. Currently, changes enacted by the Financial Accounting Standards Board and the American Institute of Certified Public Accountants in 1993 and 1996 affect financial statement preparation, guidelines for accounting for funds raised, and the preparation of audit statements.[2] These changes will help to document the results of fund-raising because they will require more reporting on funds raised and how these contributions are spent.

Budgeting solicitation activities requires more thought than estimating next year's income and expenses. Accuracy in both these functions is necessary, of course. Fund development budgets can and should offer reliable estimates of future income alongside the cost to produce it for the next operating year, and for one to two years following that. A reliable forecasting ability is possible once consistent performance measurements of current and past year results are completed. If these data are accurate and their interpretation credible, boards of directors and management of nonprofit organizations should accept these financial projections with increased confidence in the ability of the fund development program to deliver the results it predicts.

Execution

When the measurements completed and all levels of performance are documented, the final challenge is to assess the results correctly. Each individual solicitation method has now been reviewed and its results tabulated. Each method's weaknesses and strengths, areas for improvement, and current levels of efficiency and effectiveness, productivity and profitability have been determined. The entire group of solicitation activities also have been assembled and all their data is now combined for final presentation and evaluation as the total achievement for a full operating or budget year or for a three year period. How are these one-year and three-year achievements to be interpreted and understood? How much growth, how much potential, how much capacity remains to be realized? What will it cost to achieve likely potential and how long will it take? How flexible are current programs in maintaining their present level of performance against changing institutional priorities? Can current performance be maintained (and improved) when major new funding needs arise? Further analysis will be required to interpret the ability of existing programs to meet the need for both continued levels of net income and new amounts to meet future needs. Donors and volunteers are motivated to help address needs; they are never puppets who can be manipulated to perform at will.

Summary evaluations have ten goals. The first five will provide accurate and clear demonstrations of the following characteristics:

1. Effectiveness.
2. Efficiency.
3. Productivity.
4. Profitability.
5. Predictability.

The second five will interpret performance dynamics as documented in:

6. The nine-point performance index evaluation tool.
7. Interpretations of these combined results.
8. Forecasts of future performance.
9. Setting goals and objectives against realistic standards and guidelines for future measurement.
10. Public disclosure and reports.

A description of each of these evaluations follows.

(1) *Effectiveness* The intended result of the effort can be measured by a review of several factors, most of which should be established at the outset. For example, a direct mail acquisition program attempts to re-cruit large numbers of new donors from several new or previously tested sources or lists. The mail package is designed to be opened so that the contents of the appeal will motivate the recipient to reply with a gift. Each mailing's effectiveness can and should be measured by comparing, for *each* list used, the number of replies (percent participation), and average gift size to determine how capable the list, package, and message were in stimulating the desired results. A 1 percent rate of return may be acceptable, but an average gift of $8 should raise questions about the effectiveness of (a) lists used, (b) appeal message, (c) contents, (d) timing, (e) and amount requested.

(2) *Efficiency.* After measuring effectiveness in producing the de-sired results (doing the right thing), measuring efficiency evaluates how well the right thing was done (quality). Judgment controls most fund-raising results. Continuing with the direct mail acquisition ex-ample, how well chosen were the lists used? Were reference checks on list merchants and their sources carried out? Was performance from prior users of each list known? Was adequate testing of each list car-ried out to prove the existence of a reasonable potential before the de-cision was made to invest more budget in that list?

The mailing package can contain extra information pieces, but print-ing and inserting added contents will increase assembly and processing costs. Efficiency is reduced further if the contents of the package exceed three ounces to trigger higher postage charges. Other options can affect efficiency and related cost of fund-raising percentages. Expense con-trols are related to computer-generated letters with personalization, inserting personal data to letter texts, linking various gift amounts to donor benefits, upgrade requests, use of address correction return services, asking for extra information on response forms, using third-class, nine digit, presort (ZIP + 4) bulk-rate postal services, providing postage-paid reply envelopes, and more.

(3) *Productivity.* Overall results include several measurements of the ef-fort required (output) along with its desired benefits (outcomes). Con-tinuing with a direct mail renewal example, the expectation when asking prior donors to give again is that most will continue. How many can be expected to reply? Will they give the same amount again? How many will increase their gift (upgrade) if asked? What value is there in resoliciting lapsed donors who have not replied to previous renewal re-quests? How long should they be pursued? Measurements also should take into account how overall renewal solicitations were influenced by

other activities separate from actual resolicitation requests, such as communicating with prior donors between solicitations, presenting benefits and privileges based on their last gift, providing donor access and use of any of the organization's programs and services, and extending invitations to join in other solicitation activities (e.g., buying tickets to attend activities, benefits, and special events).

(4) *Profitability.* The utility of each fund-raising program is first measured by the gross revenue it produces. Next, all of its related expenses are subtracted to capture net proceeds. Each solicitation method will have a separate "profit margin." When gathered together, they should demonstrate a balanced effort where each is profitable according to its own capability and potential. The overall result for the nonprofit organization is a reliable level of contributions income to help provide its programs and services to the public. The complete story on profitability must also address outcomes, that is, the benefits actually delivered back to community residents.

(5) *Predictability.* The first four measurements will yield a wealth of performance data that will help predict future results. Predictions are risky and can fail to deliver exactly as they foretell. However, it is quite possible to use the results of the first four measurements to estimate likely levels of continued fund-raising success.

The next five measurements will help you predict future performance with greater reliability and accuracy:

(6) *Nine-Point Performance Index Evaluation.* Applying the nine-point performance index to summary data from the entire range of solicitation activities provides a series of bottom-line performance information (see Exhibits 17.6 and 17.7). Interpreting these combined results calls for independent judgment. Comparative analysis against three years of experience will be more telling than one year of experience; comparisons for a ten-year period will provide substantial data for estimating future expectations. Results are expected to increase from year to year, but they will not be consistent. Improvements in cost of fund-raising and return percentages are also expected, but these will not illustrate other valuable achievements, such as overall program growth in numbers of satisfied donors, volunteer competency, improved image and reputation, increased public confidence, and more. Other evaluations are needed to gather these facts.

(7) *Interpretations.* Success is perceived or proven, depending on how the results are interpreted and by whom. Performance measurements are designed to be applied fairly and equitably to the entire fund

Exhibit 17.6

Summary Analysis of Nine-Point Performance Index with One-Year Forecast

	Year 1	Year 2	Year 3	Est. Year 4
Participation	1,478	3,315	4,879	5,000
Income	$289,330	$431,150	$603,100	$660,000
Expenses	$107,565	$118,325	$131,115	$135,000
Percent participation	0.064%	0.095%	0.102%	0.100%
Average gift size	$196	$130	$124	$132
Net income	$181,765	$312,825	$471,985	$525,000
Average cost per gift	$73	$36	$27	$27
Cost of fund-raising	37%	27%	22%	20%
Return	169%	264%	360%	389%

development program. Because uniform performance standards and guidelines for these assessments are lacking, interpretations will range widely depending on the organization, the depth of the analysis, and the knowledge of those who prepare and review the evaluations.

It is recommended that comparative analysis begin with measuring the prior experience of *each* solicitation method in use. Three years or more of data are recommended to achieve reliable data for comparative analysis, trends, and predictability. After these separate results are prepared and reviewed, there may be added value from a review of similar results by other nonprofit organizations, especially like organizations in the same community. In such comparisons, it is essential to learn the results of their entire solicitation program, method by method, rather than depend on only bottom-line data. It is of little value to compare annual giving methods used and their results between organizations if one has only two to three years of experience and the other ten or when the past three years have included a major capital campaign for only one, or when the other received several bequests. Apples to apples and oranges to oranges comparisons are highly desirable but seldom available, even among like nonprofit organizations because no two organizations are enough alike to gain much insight from attempting direct comparisons. There is ample room here for misinterpretation and misunderstanding from comparing only bottom-line figures.

(8) *Forecasting.* Forecasting begins following completion of two sets of performance analysis. The first set is the nine-step review of combined

Exhibit 17.7

Illustration of Summary Analysis Using Nine-Point Performance Index

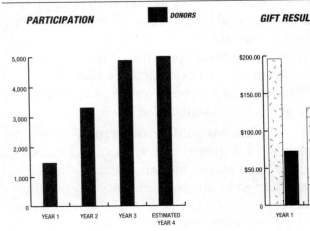

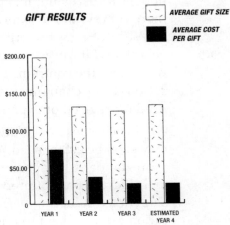

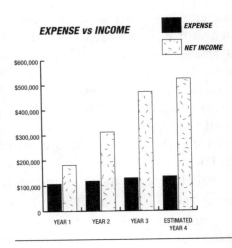

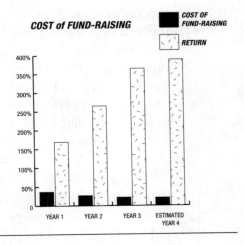

results of all solicitation methods over several years (three is the minimum), as illustrated in Exhibits 17.4 and 17.6. These data establish a degree of reliability about the relationship between results and the level of budget investments made. The second set is the completion of one or more surveys of the external factors that affect performance along with a review of how the organization used the gifts it received for public benefit and its anticipated future priorities. Rapid marketplace changes will affect the continuing solicitation activity of each nonprofit organization just as changing priorities within an organization will dictate the need for revised or expanded solicitation practices.

(9) *Setting standards.* National guidelines for fund-raising performance may soon be established. When available, they can be advocated as uniform standards for performance measurement. Uniform measurement tools like the ones offered in this book may become a standard methodology for conducting performance evaluations. Every nonprofit organization can use them to understand its own results better.

Your organization should develop performance guidelines based on its own experience, not the results of others. Of course, one goal should be to achieve continued growth at a reasonable cost. You can set standards of annual performance appropriate for *each* solicitation activity through ongoing performance analysis using consistent measurement tools. Using these tools to monitor each activity's improvements can help you identify their best levels of efficiency and profitability. Remember that results will not be the same for every nonprofit organization in every community because geography and style, competition, image and access to prospects, experienced volunteers and prior donors to solicit, to name just a few of the external factors that influence results, will always be different for each type of nonprofit organization. (See Exhibit 18.1 on page 266.) Therefore, standards and guidelines from other organizations will be of only limited value to your organization.

(10) *Public disclosure and reports.* Having completed all this good work to measure performance, why not share this success story with your public? Success is an important story to tell because it helps everyone who is involved appreciate the value of their decision to support an organization that can achieve positive results. There will always be other organizations who raise more money. That fact is less important than whether both are raising what they need, whether each is operating at its highest level of productivity that can be achieved with the present volunteers and donors, staff, and budget, and how well it uses these gift resources for public benefit.

The combined results of these 10 measurements will improve the understanding of philanthropic practice for any nonprofit organization that makes use of them.

Analysis

Finally, the performance levels illustrated in exhibits used in this chapter suggest this fund development program may have achieved its first plateau of overall productivity after an initial three-year investment. Adding the results of these three years together reveals gross revenue of $1,323,580 from an investment (budget) of $357,005 to provide net income of $966,575 (see Exhibits 17.6 and 17.7). Adding bottom-line analysis, these results were achieved with an overall cost of fund-raising of 27 percent and a return (net income) of 271 percent. The forecast for Year 4 includes net income of $525,000 at a cost of fund-raising of 20 percent and a return of 389 percent, a truly remarkable prediction for increased productivity and profitability within the next 12 months!

Can this analysis reliably predict future performance? Yes and no. Yes, if current programs continue to be well led and well supported and no external change of magnitude occurs to upset the willingness of the public to continue their commitment. Yes, if continued attention is given to performance measurement so that improvements are identified and budget is provided to capture them. No, if an abrupt change in leadership occurs, such as at the board chair, campaign chair, president, or development director level; leadership is the most significant factor in predicting the potential for success. No, if economic conditions worsen, a major disaster occurs, or a scandal implicates the organization or its leaders. So long as giving remains a voluntary act, the synergism of public confidence and trust that allows it to flourish can also be the cause for it to falter, even to fail.

Action Plans

The analysis offers considerable insight into the progress of each solicitation activity in acquiring, renewing, and upgrading donors at an ever-increasing level of efficiency. As illustrated after only three years of experience and shown in Exhibits 17.4 and 17.6, the cost of fund-raising percent by Year 3 has been reduced from 37 percent to 22 percent, and the return (net income) has increased from 169 percent to 360 percent. Further, analysis of these programs and their performance suggests an increase in net income of $53,015 will occur the following year (+10%). One interpretation of this annual giving program is that it may have reached a plateau where a reasonably steady level of performance might now be anticipated, with only modest gains in net revenue each year. Each annual giving program has a limited capacity to be able to increase its results year after year. To maintain current performance levels will require some additional creativity in program management as well as a little more budget because repetition alone will not suffice to stimulate donors and volunteers.

Major gift solicitation programs respond well to new institutional priorities. In Exhibits 17.4 and 17.6, $525,000 appears to be a reasonable level of net income to estimate these solicitation activities can provide for the next few years. The organization can plan to improve this performance with a combination of:

1. Several membership levels for the membership program.
2. A title sponsor for one of the benefit events to lift its net income.
3. Added personal solicitation activities.

The organization can also plan to identify significant community needs that the organization is prepared to address with new or expanded programs and services.

Accounting rules now require that multiyear pledges be counted in full in the year they are made, which will boost the first and second year of a multiyear pledge campaign to levels that will require careful analysis as well as accurate tracking of payments. Productivity studies during this period will be quite positive when compared with prior annual giving results. The organization should plan to continue analysis of annual giving performance because the level of productivity *after* the campaign is likely to decline to precampaign amounts.

Related Benefits

Should these figures be real, it is assumed that the board of directors, administration, donors, volunteers, and development staff of the organization should be delighted with this level of performance. These results prove the value of investments committed to a broad-based fund development program. Such levels of achievement should be reported widely as a success! "The rest of the story . . . " as radio commentator Paul Harvey often says, will be to tell how these funds were used to benefit the community. What were the actual outcomes? Did this money improve residents' lives through cultural understanding, education, health, welfare, and more? Every nonprofit organization can expect to continue to receive support from the public only as long as it delivers quality programs and services that benefit parts of this same public. It must also demonstrate that it has the ability to manage its operations, including its fiduciary duties, in a professional manner deserving of continued public confidence and trust. When all is in order and the facts made public, the combination is nearly unbeatable.

18

Forecasting Reliable Results

After completing the comprehensive analysis of total performance defined in Chapter 17, you can predict the results for each solicitation activity. Adequate details are now available to estimate future performance with reliability, especially if three or more years of data have been collected and studied. A few variable factors also must be considered, to be balanced against results and performance analysis. These factors include changing institutional priorities, changing participants (donors, volunteers, and staff), and changing external conditions. They can be balanced by the knowledge and understanding prior performance provides, which has coped with these same variables in previous years. You can include changing conditions in the forecast and estimate likely results with confidence.

Purposes

The first objective in forecasting is to provide a reliable estimate of expected results. The second is investing in those programs with an expected rate of return in net income that more than justifies the decision to commit the same or increased budget resources to solicitation activities.

Predicting gift results has seldom been a topic for academic research despite the copious computer data available within nonprofit organizations, especially at colleges and universities with their extensive alumni fund-raising records. Two current university researchers admitted that the "one variable that was never considered in these earlier studies but that was incorporated in our study was past giving.

This characteristic has been used informally by development officers over the years as the best predictor of future giving. Yet, until this study, it had not been used in formal studies of giving behavior. In our analysis, we found that it is the strongest single predictor of current giving."[1] Good news, indeed, given its appearance so late in this workbook, but all the preceding measurements and report forms were necessary. The best method to predict future giving is to study past giving records.

Forecasting fund-raising results also might be described as taking advantage of improvements. Complete assessments of the fund development operation provide the capability "to identify what is being done well and confer suitable rewards, to identify areas where improvement is possible and desirable, to assess the entire planning process and its critical assumptions, and to develop future plans, objectives, and standards."[2]

Forecasting becomes reliable after a solicitation activity has been used three or more times and the nine-point performance index has been conducted on all of its results. Based on these performances, board members and managers, donors and volunteers, and fund development staff will be able to accept predictions of future returns. Their use of these data should be to act on the most obvious improvements. The organization can continue budget support for successful solicitation activities and add more support where results demonstrate the highest expectations for increased returns. This approach produces a constant increase in level of net profits. Although the most effective solicitation activities should receive greater attention, this should not be at the expense of the basic operating areas, acquisition and renewal. If more budget is made available, there should be a clear explanation in advance of how and where it will be invested. Each alternative should be documented to prove that these additions can increase overall results. The best answers of where to invest will depend on several factors including:

- Potential growth for each solicitation activity.
- Likely net income potential to be realized.
- Strategic development in numbers of renewed and upgraded donors.
- Priority of need and pressure for cash from the organization.
- Improving quality and personalization of development office operations.

- Present staff capability to increase workload (or alleviate burnout potential).
- Anticipating changing economic trends in the community.
- Competitive strategies relating to other nonprofit organizations.

Adding budget without clear evidence of improved returns from prior performance measurement is as unwise as it will be unproductive.

Financial planning within nonprofit organizations requires accurate figures for all sources of revenue along with expenses. Contributions represent one of only four revenue sources available to nonprofit organizations. The other three are their own success in managing the operating budget to achieve a surplus or margin, interest and investment earnings from funds under management, and for-profit enterprises (borrowing is a last resort seldom to be used for budgeting annual operating purposes). Among the first four, solicitation activity represents one-half (50%) of the available options, a fact often underappreciated by nonprofit organizations. Nearly everyone forgets that the endowment was achieved as a result of solicitation from cash contributions and planned gifts that matured. When fund development is acknowledged as a reliable source of half or more than half of the alternative sources of revenue (but not half the total income), its ability to predict and deliver reliable results should increase in importance, especially when margins from operating budgets and net income from for-profit enterprises are less reliable in generating revenue at a comparable low cost in budget dollars.

Preparation

After several measurements of solicitation activities have been completed, analysis of their results points the way to forecasting future performance. An environmental audit (Exhibit 18.1) adds reality to these expectations by identifying factors that can influence results. Environment has a strong influence on fund-raising performance because environmental factors affect the potential to raise money. Rank each factor for its likely influence on current solicitation activities, which also serves to identify strengths and weakness, assets and liabilities. Invite board members, development committee members, and a selection of donors and volunteers to conduct this audit. The bonus is that this exercise will

Exhibit 18.1

Environmental Audit of Fund-Raising Potential

	SCORE				
	low				high

Group A. <u>External Environmental Factors</u>

Clear mission, purposes, goals, and objectives	1	2	3	4	5
Competition, image, and market position	1	2	3	4	5
Public confidence in programs and services	1	2	3	4	5
Board leadership and competency	1	2	3	4	5
Management leadership and competency	1	2	3	4	5
Fiscal management and profitability	1	2	3	4	5
Overall economic conditions	1	2	3	4	5
Overall political and government conditions	1	2	3	4	5
Geographic location (urban or rural)	1	2	3	4	5
Accepted style of local fund-raising practice	1	2	3	4	5
Media attention to fund-raising scandals	1	2	3	4	5

Median Scores Subtotal _____

Group B. <u>Internal Environmental Factors</u>

Type of nonprofit organization	1	2	3	4	5
Written long-range and strategic plan	1	2	3	4	5
Board leadership, background, and attitude	1	2	3	4	5
Ethics and professionalism	1	2	3	4	5
Employee wages and benefits	1	2	3	4	5
Status of debt financing	1	2	3	4	5
Pressure for cash	1	2	3	4	5
Commitment to develop an endowment	1	2	3	4	5
Volume and variety of fund-raising practices	1	2	3	4	5
Leadership development program	1	2	3	4	5
Volunteer recruitment and training	1	2	3	4	5
Availability of new prospects	1	2	3	4	5
Existing donors for renewal and upgrading	1	2	3	4	5
Access to wealth	1	2	3	4	5
Focus on major gift cultivation and solicitation	1	2	3	4	5
Professional staff and fund-raising counsel	1	2	3	4	5
Appropriate staff, space, budget, and systems	1	2	3	4	5
Operating donor recognition program	1	2	3	4	5

Median Scores Subtotal _____

Median Scores Total _____

help increase everyone's awareness of how the world "outside" can directly affect even the best of fund-raising efforts "inside." Reasonable expectations should be based on a breadth of understanding, not ancient history, intuition, or unrealistic aspirations. The environmental audit of fund-raising potential should be conducted at least once every two to three years as the pace of our world continues to accelerate and changes occur even more quickly. Organizations that do not anticipate change are unlikely to be able to make decisions based on comprehensive assessments with the speed they now require, and will quickly fall behind.

Goal setting can be included in the preparation phase. Goals should be targeted for *each* solicitation activity so that its objectives will reflect an overall effort to improve effectiveness and efficiency of operations within the next 12 months in several areas of activity (see Exhibit 18.2). Goals can reflect progress in identifying the improvements found in analysis of prior experiences. Performance will track added investments made and their achievements to compare the results as increased net returns in numbers of donors, average gift size, net income achieved, cost of fund-raising, and other measurement categories. In this fashion, each solicitation activity can continue its development to full potential within the overall fund development program. When other needs arise, the ability of each solicitation method already in place can be assessed for its ability to respond to changing priorities.

Budget

The cost to conduct forecasts is only a minimal amount of staff time. The value for this effort comes from its reliability. If no time or effort has been given previously to performance analysis for each solicitation activity, the cost in time to conduct the various measurements outlined in this workbook will be extensive and can be spread over one to two years. Building a database of performance results is recommended as the first step to integrate measurement as an ongoing management practice.

Execution

Approvals should be requested for both the budget to be invested and the goals to be attained. To accomplish all these desired results, board

Exhibit 18.2

Sample Form for Setting Goals and Objectives for a Recurring or New Solicitation Activity

Solicitation Activity: _____

_____

Current Chairperson
and Vice-Chair(s): _____

_____

_____

Proposed Next Chairperson _____
and Vice-Chair(s): _____

_____

1. Description of the Solicitation Activity:

2. The Primary Purposes/Goals/Objectives:

3. Proposed Date(s) and Schedule for Planning
   Preparation, and Implementation:

4. Estimate of Volunteers and Staff Required:

5. Analysis of Prior Experience and Results with
   Nine-Point Performance Index:

6. Estimated Budget (worksheet attached):

7. Forecast of One, Two, and Three-Year Performance:

members, management, donors, volunteers, and fund development staff all must be recruited, trained, motivated, and led. Fund development is both a contact sport and a team effort. Will everyone always perform as expected? Unfortunately, the answer is "not likely." Si Seymour predicted this outcome as "with most of the workers in most campaigns, it is usual to say that a third will perform as asked (the responsible ones), a second group will respond under pressure and prodding, and the last third, no matter what you or any one else does, will turn out to be mostly deadwood."[3]

Executing the forecast depends on several factors working together. Board members, management, donors, volunteers, and fund development staff provide leadership and direction to the entire effort of public solicitation. The advance work by the marketing and communications teams also is vital to solicitations because it depends upon public awareness of the organization, its mission and purposes, and the many contributions it has delivered back to the community. Solid management practices and sound fiduciary policies contribute greatly to public confidence and trust in the organization's use of gift dollars to the greatest advantage for public benefit. Demonstrated levels of proficiency and productivity in solicitation activities—doing the right things and doing them well—are also required of nonprofit organizations. Quality of performance in all areas of operations will demonstrate success, which is the essential ingredient for achieving continuing and improved levels of understanding, participation, and support from the public.

To achieve such willing and generous participation requires open and full disclosure of program plans and demonstrated results. The several measurement tools provided in this workbook are more than adequate to answer inquiries about the performance of every area of solicitation activity. What remains to be done is an equally solid program of public education about the uses of funds raised to benefit the public. The best opportunity for reporting this performance is during each solicitation period. Messages about current priorities, changing needs, and accomplishments for public benefit are what solicitations talk about. Regular progress reports throughout the year to board members, management, volunteers, and donors substantiate the success that the organization is continuing to achieve. Adding information about results and outcomes is an excellent opportunity to promote understanding about overall performance. Everyone involved wants to know that his or her efforts have been part of this success. Tie the results to the people who made them happen—the board and management with their decisions and leadership of the organization, volunteers for their efforts to conduct proven solicitation activities, donors for their understanding of public needs and their generous levels of participation, and all the employees for their successful implementation of programs and services delivered to the public. Everyone is a winner in this success story.

Analysis

Evaluation of the results of each solicitation activity should continue. In addition, recent performance should be measured against the forecast so that the quality of earlier analysis and their interpretations from prior experience can be measured (see Exhibit 18.3). For example, the actual increase in performance for both direct mail acquisition and renewal is 12 percent and 11 percent respectively, both commendable achievements, but these areas fell 1 percent below the forecast. This suggests the forecasting methods are quite reliable for these two areas. The performance by volunteers in their personal solicitation of prior donors increased 18 percent over the prior year and exceeded

Exhibit 18.3

Analysis to Measure Performance against Prior Year Results Compared with a One-Year Forecast

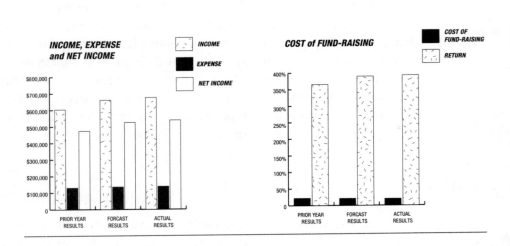

the forecast by 7 percent. This exciting news confirms several facts, including the validity of the recruitment and training programs for volunteer solicitors. More important, it proves once again that the most efficient and effective fund-raising method is personal solicitation.

A review of the external and internal factors included in the assumptions and reassessed in terms of their changes can also be performed using the environmental criteria contained in Exhibit 18.1. How accurate was the forecast in predicting the areas of achievement realized in the actual returns? Net income was increased by 14 percent, 2 percent above the forecast. Was this success due to increased numbers of donors or larger gifts from current donors (details not provided in the Exhibit 18.3 data)? It will be important to review the details to learn which solicitation activity, message, timing, and so on developed these new donors or increased current donors' gift levels so that additional attention and resources may be applied here next year. Current donors cannot be expected always to give more; there must also be a constant effort to recruit new donors. Finding the balance will require three years or more of experience. A review of expenses is just as valid, especially where staff time was allocated, to understand how much effort had to be expended to achieve these results. Both labor and nonlabor costs were 6 percent; labor was on budget but nonlabor was 6 percent above budget. Performing the same tasks each year will cost more each year in both areas. Watching the rate of growth for both will provide clues for next year's budget plan. Slowing expenses or cutting back on budget will influence overall effectiveness and efficiency; it will be important to know which programs will be impacted and to what degree. In the exhibit, nearly every annual giving activity was 1 percent below expectations, whereas individual gifts and bequests exceeded their income projections. Corporations and foundations were below expectations but proposals outstanding may produce gifts in the next operating year; attempting to forecast when these gifts will arrive is chancy at best.

Measuring performance against forecasts is valuable. This information should be monitored and reported each year using a rate of growth in giving report form (see Exhibit 18.4). Overall fund development objectives include assessing success in raising friends and building relationships along with raising money. How fast can a program be expected to expand? Monitoring overall program growth is evidence of all three. For example, this exhibit suggests that cumulative growth in number of participants is strong at 31 percent as is income received at 26

Exhibit 18.4

Report on Overall Rate of Growth in Giving Using Nine-Point Performance Index

	Two Years Ago	Last Year	Annual Rate of Growth (%)	This Year	Annual Rate of Growth (%)	Cumulative Rate of Growth (%)
Participation	1,355	1,605	18	1,799	12	31
Income	$448,765	$507,855	13	$571,235	12	26
Expenses	$116,550	$123,540	6	$131,850	7	13
Percent participation	39%	44%	13	52%	18	31
Average gift size	$331	$316	-4	$318	0.4	-4
Net income	$332,215	$384,315	16	$439,385	14	30
Average cost per gift	$86.01	$76.97	-11	$73.29	-5	-15
Cost of fund-raising	26%	24%	-6	23%	-5	-11
Return	285%	311%	9	333%	7	16

percent, while expenses have increased by 13 percent. Average gift size is declining by 4 percent, which may indicate good annual giving performance in recruiting new donors but also suggests more effort in upgrading current donors is required along with more emphasis on major gift activities. Average cost per gift (−15%) and cost of fund-raising (−11%) are declining, which suggests a level of efficiency is being achieved. The return percentage has increased by 16 percent and while positive, may be a bit slow and ties back to what signals the average gift size is sending. Lastly, these details on growth in giving also will aid in the accuracy of future forecasts.

Measurement tools are valuable for analysis of results and understanding what activities, efforts, and factors contributed to their success, but no known analysis is infallible in predicting the future. Measurements are valuable for budget preparation purposes, for identifying improvements, for demonstrating levels of continued efficiency and effectiveness along with productivity and profitability, and for aiding everyone's appreciation of what amount of effort is required to be successful with a variety of solicitation activities. All of these answers add to the knowledge of a nonprofit organization about its solicitation activities, but they are not infallible at predicting the future. Why not? Because every part of the equation is not within the control of a nonprofit organization. The great variable is people and how they behave and respond.

Giving is voluntary and never should be assumed. Honest efforts must be dedicated to solicitation activities to achieve the desired results. What can be predicted is how a well-defined effort with adequate investment of volunteers, staff, and budget directed toward proven areas of performance can and will achieve positive results. The key to success is in an accurate understanding of current performance that can be linked to continued investments that strive to achieve the improvements earlier analysis suggested was possible.

Action Steps

Several suggestions flow from the level of analysis required to forecast future results plus a comparison of results against predictions. Most important is the integrity of the process to forecast performance for each solicitation activity. Careful and thorough measurement of actual performance, application of budget to areas of success and their likely improvements, analysis of effectiveness and efficiency, and more, all help to show where continued investments in successful solicitation activities remains valid. Adding investments to likely improvements will increase overall productivity and profitability. Not every solicitation activity will perform at the level predicted and those that do can also exceed these expectations. Most ongoing programs will be able to outperform their prior year's results. This outcome is not as a result of any forecast wizardry but from the good information their prior performance suggested for continued investment so that each will continue to be effective as well as profitable. Occasionally, good fortune and a bit of luck will occur, such as an unexpected, one-time major bequest. Such gifts are windfalls and can distort the best of predictions. Despite such good news, analysis can point out the one-time nature of such gifts and factor out their likely reoccurrence in future forecasts.

Related Benefits

The greatest benefit from attention to performance measurement is increased confidence by all who witness this performance. Board members, management, volunteers, and donors do not begin with much understanding of how solicitation activities actually perform from year to year. Their focus can be expected to start with overall gift income and bottom-line analysis. Disclosure of details involved in each area of solicitation activity and its performance analysis, along with the methodology used in forecasting gift revenue, aids in an understanding of the overall fund development process. All participants should be able to see where their own efforts and those of others were necessary to the overall program and how their actions contributed to these results.

The methodology used in forecasting gift revenue aids in an understanding of the overall fund development process. Another benefit from forecasting is the level of reliability the nonprofit organization can depend on for its financial planning. A forecast of reliable contributions income is quite valuable for fiscal operations. This forecast is part of the story about the solid financial performance of the organization itself, which enables the public also to see where their money has been spent and the benefits it has provided. This leads to continued public support.

Future growth of the fund development program is directly related to the needs of the organization and must be measured against the potential for the ongoing fund development program to meet these needs. There are limits to the amount of potential growth a solicitation program can achieve in the short term that is linked directly to the needs of the organization and its ability to achieve its goals. Extensive analysis helps to define where these limits may reside at a point in time for both the organization and its solicitation program. This information also helps define how and where solicitation activities are well matched to institutional programs and services, as it ought to be. Reliable forecasting leads to the ability to establish guidelines and performance standards for each area within the overall solicitation program for its own future performance and that of the nonprofit organization it serves.

19

*S*etting Performance *Standards*

The prior experience of each nonprofit organization is the best source for setting its guidelines to measure its own results and for setting standards for its present and future performances. Your organization can use the measurements, analyses, and forecasts developed in earlier chapters to establish performance standards for each solicitation activity that has been in use for three or more years. Setting standards and establishing guidelines for solicitation activity are well worth the effort.

Purposes

Board members, management, donors, volunteers, and staff in the fund development office should all understand the expectations of the fund-raising program. Performance measurement separates realistic results from unrealistic expectations. Regular assessments of results also provide guidance and direction for future action, including how much budget will be required, what results can be expected, and what levels of performance can be achieved.

Decisions to add budget resources or to increase performance expectations must take into account prior performance, planned improvements, likely net results, and forecast information. Performance standards add target measurements of effectiveness and efficiency, productivity, and profitability.

Meeting and exceeding performance standards adds confidence to the performance measurement process and reinforces the decisions made by board, management, and staff. Reliable expectations also permit the uninterrupted delivery of programs and services.

Adding performance standards to solicitation activity compliments the efforts required to set such guidelines. Continued application of these sound decisions enhances their credibility and reliability. Every nonprofit organization aspires to the highest level of credibility in all its actions, especially those that serve the public and must stand the test of their scrutiny in fiscal matters. Nonprofit organizations are charged with stewardship of the public's money and are obligated to deliver quality programs and services that benefit the community in return. Their special privileges of tax-exempt status depend on this performance. They also must demonstrate competent fiscal performance to deserve that same public's confidence and trust in their use of gift dollars.

Preparation

The first step in setting performance standards is to identify, for *each* solicitation activity, the results achieved with corresponding details from nine-point performance index data (see Exhibit 19.1). This information suggests:

1. The level of effort (budget) required to maintain current results.
2. Where improvements may be possible and needed.
3. A forecast of what results can be expected from continued levels of effort and budget support.

The next step is to assemble this same information to illustrate just net income from each area of solicitation activity and its cost of fund-raising percentage (see Exhibit 19.2). These figures offer guidelines on what level of efficiency can be expected based on three years of experience.

Charts and graphs help to visualize the trends and directions that performance suggests are realistic expectations (see Exhibits 19.3 and 19.4). Additional information also may be brought to this final review, such as perceptions from the environmental audit (see Chapter 18, Exhibit 18.1), results of traditional market research surveys, development office audits, and pre-campaign feasibility studies. A host of

Exhibit 19.1

Summary Three-Year Analysis with One-Year Forecast Including Cost of Fund-Raising and Return Percentages

	Year 1	Year 2	Year 3	Est. Year 4
A. Annual Giving Programs				
Direct giving (acquisition)	$27,550	$31,250	$35,500	$42,000
Direct giving (renewal)	55,880	69,500	76,500	85,000
Membership dues	40,400	44,000	48,500	55,000
Benefit events (3)*	45,500	53,400	59,600	68,000
Volunteer-led solicitations	58,500	65,500	82,000	90,000
Subtotal	$227,830	$263,650	$302,100	$340,000

*Benefit event income is net of expenses.

	Year 1	Year 2	Year 3	Est. Year 4
B. Major Gifts Programs				
Corporations	$13,500	$28,000	$45,500	$55,000
Foundations	8,000	35,500	65,000	80,000
Individuals	35,000	78,000	145,500	160,000
Bequests received	5,000	26,000	45,000	25,000
Subtotal	$61,500	$167,500	$301,000	$320,000
Total (A + B)	$289,330	$431,150	$603,100	$660,000

	Year 1	Year 2	Year 3	Est. Year 4
C. Overall Performance Summary				
Labor/payroll	$68,015	$72,100	$79,800	$85,000
Nonpayroll costs	39,550	46,225	51,315	50,000
Subtotal	$107,565	$118,325	$131,115	$135,000
Net Income	$181,765	$312,825	$471,985	$525,000
Cost of fund-raising	37%	27%	22%	20%
Return	169%	264%	360%	389%

nonquantifiable criteria that also can be included are progress reports on leadership development and volunteer performance, surveys on concurrence of donor benefits and privileges, and other reviews of community changes that are always more difficult to assess and predict.

The use of an outside evaluator is often recommended—someone uninvolved in the organization who can perform an analysis unemotionally and objectively. "A valid and comprehensive evaluation is possible only if the organizational climate and culture are conducive to a candid and objective appraisal of performance. In the end, the results of evaluating any part of the organization reflect on the chief

Exhibit 19.2

Net Proceeds and Cost of Fund-Raising Percentage Summary Suggested as Standards of Performance with One-Year Forecast

	Year 1	Year 2	Year 3	Est. Year 4
A. Annual Giving Programs				
Direct giving (acquisition)	$-7,500	$-9,850	$1,200	$2,800
	(116%)	(110%)	(91%)	(91%)
Direct giving (renewal)	48,550	57,345	66,875	73,000
	(13%)	(17%)	(17%)	(14%)
Membership dues	34,500	37,075	40,175	43,500
	(15%)	(16%)	(19%)	(19%)
Benefit events (3)	45,500	53,400	59,600	68,000
	(58%)	(55%)	(51%)	(48%)
Volunteer-led solicitations	55,250	61,950	77,690	84,500
	(6%)	(5%)	(5%)	(6%)
Subtotal	$176,300	$199,920	$245,540	$272,800
	(13%)	(14%)	(19%)	(20%)
B. Major Gifts Programs				
Corporations	$11,750	$24,750	$41,550	$51,750
	(13%)	(12%)	(8%)	(6%)
Foundations	4,200	30,750	58,550	74,900
	(47%)	(13%)	(10%)	(6%)
Individuals	28,950	76,800	129,800	148,600
	(17%)	(2%)	(10%)	(7%)
Bequests received	4,800	24,500	42,500	24,500
	(4%)	(6%)	(6%)	(6%)
Subtotal	$49,700	$156,800	$272,400	$298,750
	(19%)	(6%)	(9%)	(9%)
	========	========	========	========
Total (net income)	$226,000	$356,750	$517,940	$471,550
Cost of fund-raising	(22%)	(17%)	(14%)	(14%)

staff officer, and that person must be willing to embark on the evaluation with an open mind."[1]

Budget

Little direct cost is required to develop performance standards other than the time and people to do the work. As with forecasting, most of this effort is assigned first to the computer. Volunteers and staff are

Exhibit 19.3

Illustration of Net Income Summary Results with One-Year Forecast

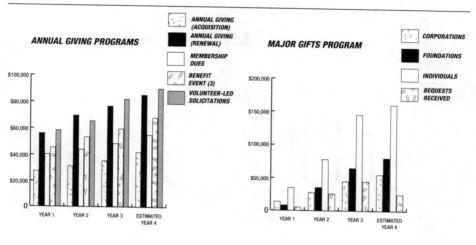

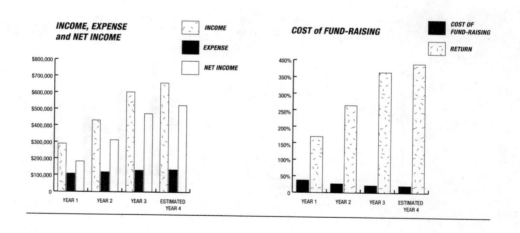

needed to evaluate performance data to arrive at recommendations on guidelines to be applied to every area of solicitation activity. The added expense is the independent evaluator, who may be a professional fund-raising consultant with extensive experience in auditing fund development programs. The value of their findings will exceed whatever fees are involved if credible standards are defined and accepted as a result of their support and provide the critical details for fund-raising programs

Exhibit **19.4**

Illustration of Cost of Fund-Raising Summary Results with One-Year Forecast

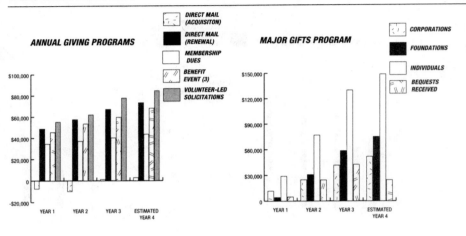

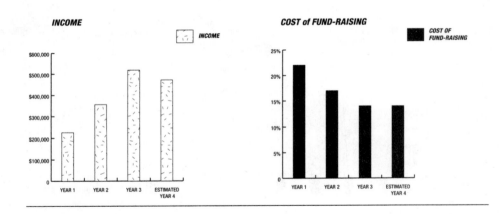

to improve their performance. The immediate application of performance standards to the overall budgeting process is a benefit that balances against the time invested to develop the standards.

Execution

Because nonprofit organizations are not the same in how they conduct solicitation activities, and because solicitation activities do not perform the same for every organization, it is difficult to attempt to define uniform performance standards that apply to all. The recommendation is to establish only those relating to your organization's own programs.

Prior results and cost of fund-raising analysis demonstrate the direct relationship between expenses and net income realized for current programs. This experience will serve as the foundation for calculating a standard for each activity. The first guideline is to continue each solicitation activity at the level of its own standard. For example, if donor clubs and membership associations attract the same number of donors each year, expenses will creep up due to inflation and erode revenue.

Reasonable cost guidelines for solicitation activities have been developed (see Exhibit 19.5) from some national studies and from years of experience. They refer to a current level of achievement for a solicitation

Exhibit 19.5

Reasonable Cost Guidelines for Solicitation Activities

Solicitation Activity	Reasonable Cost Guidelines*
Direct mail (acquisition)	$1.25 to $1.50 per $1.00 raised
Direct mail (renewal)	$0.20 to $0.25 per $1.00 raised
Membership associations	$0.20 to $0.30 per $1.00 raised
Activities, benefits, and special events	$0.50 per $1.00 raised (gross revenue and direct costs only)**
Donor clubs and support group organizations	$0.20 to $0.30 per $1.00 raised
Volunteer-led personal solicitation	$0.10 to $0.20 per $1.00 raised
Corporations	$0.20 per $1.00 raised
Foundations	$0.20 per $1.00 raised
Special projects	$0.10 to $0.20 per $1.00 raised
Capital campaigns	$0.10 to $0.20 per $1.00 raised
Planned giving	$0.20 to $0.30 per $1.00 raised

*Sources: For direct mail guidelines—Direct Mail Marketing Association. For planned giving—Norman S. Fink and Howard C. Metzler, *The Costs and Benefits of Deferred Giving.* New York: Columbia University Press, 1982. For capital campaigns—American Association of Fund Raising Counsel, New York. The balance are derived from the author's direct experience, research, and publications.

**Benefit event cost allocations: To calculate bottom-line total costs and net proceeds from a benefit event, calculate and add the indirect and overhead support expenses to direct costs incurred and subtract from gross revenue.

activity that has been in active use for a minimum of three years. None of these have been subjected to extensive public testing or academic scrutiny to prove their projections. With this standard as a first level of assessment, performance measurements for each activity can then be measured using the nine-point performance index.

The next step is to interpret the results and apply their conclusions to determine how to improve the effectiveness and efficiency of current solicitation activities. Interpreting the results of solicitation activity does not come easy; not everyone studying the same facts will reach an identical conclusion.

Analysis

Analysis can begin with just three basic figures—number of donors, gross revenue, and total cost. Not every organization collects or reports these data for *each* solicitation activity they conduct; neither do they calculate percentage response, average gift size, or average cost per gift. An important limitation remains because uniform guidelines from accounting professionals on collecting and allocating fund-raising costs are not yet available.

One solicitation activity that is a frequent target for close study is direct mail acquisition, which can experience cost of fund-raising percentages of 125 percent to 150 percent. Such performance attracts well-intentioned questions to challenge such percentages. Again, solicitation activities must be analyzed based on at least three years of performance and direct mail ought to be seen as a combined effort, acquisition and renewal together. Acquisition is designed to be an investment in constituency building rather than fund-raising. Although initial results from a direct mail program appear poor, renewals can yield a response rate of 50 percent or better at higher levels of gift income and at a cost of fund-raising of 20 percent to 25 percent.

Separate evaluation of direct mail acquisition and renewal is important, but they can also be measured together to understand their maximum potential as a solicitation activity. First measure each mailing (acquisition and renewal) separately to assess its performance. Also evaluate each group of acquisition mailings conducted as a package, as well as each group of renewal mailings. Acquisition and renewal efforts also should be consolidated to appreciate the overall effectiveness and efficiency of direct mail for solicitation purposes.

The value from evaluation is to use its findings in making future solicitation decisions. Effectiveness and efficiency studies show which efforts were "the right thing to do" and which were being "done well."

Experience suggests that consistency of performance is identical to the degree of commitment achieved by each donor. Be sure to measure what every solicitation must contain that is essential to its success—available suspects, prospects, and donors matched with people who can be recruited and trained as volunteers who ask for their help in addressing urgent and relevant community needs. "Total dollars raised alone is no test of the potential for efficiency and effectiveness of the methods and techniques being used."[2] We must remember that solicitation activity is a social exchange between people who care about helping other people through the good works performed by nonprofit organizations.

The data in Exhibits 19.1 and 19.2 contain several details for further study. Net income and cost of fund-raising percentage for each solicitation activity points up most clearly their disparity in performance, but this result is expected. Direct mail acquisition and renewal solicitations are unlike corporate and foundation solicitations, although both actually deliver their requests by mail. No one would expect a 1 percent or a 50 percent response rate from proposals sent to corporations and foundations, but what response rate should be expected? Nonprofit organizations that depend heavily on grants to fund their annual operations need a high rate of return on their investment in seeking government grants and contracts as well as corporate and foundation gifts. You should decide, based on the needs of your organization, whether each of these three sources should be evaluated separately and whether each source should also be held to the same or to separate response rates. The application of a universal standard is not possible, nor would it be a reasonable guideline for everyone's use.

The group of annual giving activities perform differently from the group of major gift programs, which concentrate on larger, one-time gifts from individuals, corporations, and foundations. However, the results of both could report nearly identical net income (see Exhibit 19.1). In setting performance standards, your organization should decide how it wants to answer the following questions:

1. Should the performance ratio between annual and major giving groups be assumed to be different?

2. Should expectations be based on net profits from each in a 50–50 ratio?

3. Should the ratio be 60–40 in favor of major gifts, 80–20, or even higher?

4. How should planned giving and estate planning be reviewed in this comparative analysis?

5. Are there other criteria that should be used to evaluate the performance between solicitation methods?

6. What criteria should be used to decide where to invest time and budget to achieve the highest net revenue next year and after three more years?

These questions bring back the issue of single, "bottom-line" comparisons of results between nonprofit organizations. The impetus for such comparisons often comes from board members, donors, and volunteers, who want to be assured their investments of time, talent, and treasure are being well spent on the organizations they support.

Action Plans

Setting standards provides immediate guidance to the budgeting process. Standards also reinforce forecasts of future performance. Nonprofit organizations can rely on these forecasts because they were derived from their own results. What they ought not to do is become overconfident that results will happen as predicted; a lot of effort will be required every year to achieve these goals. And, likely as not, something will happen during the year to interfere with these assumptions. With good data and a flexible attitude about change, assumptions can be reworked using the standards and a range of forecasts offered in adjustment. Nonprofit organizations should never spend any projected net revenue before it arrives, although some do commit these resources in advance.

Among the advantages of the information now available should be confidence and trust in the fund development program's ability to provide reliable amounts of revenue. Reliability adds financial security and flexibility to the organization's financial planning.

Standards also can become part of the annual goals and objectives that solicitation teams are given to achieve. They know the results they have to produce, the resources given them to achieve them, the deadline for completion, and the level of quality expected in their performance. Volunteers and staff also hold a high degree of confidence in action plans prepared for each solicitation activity because they know their track records, they have been part of earlier performances, they have participated in all the evaluations, and they know their community and its residents. In fact, they often want to exceed the prior year's performance and set higher standards of achievement for those who follow them. Volunteers know their nonprofit organization and those whom it serves are the ultimate beneficiaries of their increased efficiency and effectiveness and also can take the greatest amount of pride in exceeding the goals set for them.

Related Benefits

Those who use the report forms and measurement tools presented in this workbook will enjoy a greater understanding of present solicitation activities. Reporting the results to others, including the public, increases credibility in the organization's self-assessment process. This will enhance public acceptance of future requests for their participation.

20

Public Reporting and Future Challenges

Nonprofit organizations prepare and distribute several reports that are available to the public and confirm their stewardship in management of resources and effective fulfillment of their mission. The purpose of these documents is accountability to retain public confidence and trust by displaying efficient stewardship and accurate fiscal management. Three public reports are available on request from any nonprofit organization:

1. Audit statement.
2. Annual reports.
3. Tax returns.

In addition, the Internal Revenue Service and state authorities may conduct investigations to ensure that the organization is complying with government regulations and meeting disclosure requirements.

Several challenges, however, may cause changes in how nonprofit organizations conduct their operations and how they report their results to the public in the future.

Audit Statement

The board of directors should review financial reports and fiscal management practices every month. In addition, it should require annually an independent audit of financial activities performed by a certified public accountant hired for this express purpose. This examination will result in an audit statement conducted in accordance with generally accepted accounting principles. Four major benefits can be realized from this audit exercise:

1. Credibility of the financial statements.
2. Professional assistance in developing meaningful financial statements.
3. Professional advice on internal control, administrative efficiency, and other business matters.
4. Assistance in tax reporting and compliance requirements.[1]

Annual Report

The annual report is a valuable publication that summarizes activities and accomplishments and may include lists of donors as an added expression of appreciation for their support. Annual reports should provide a financial digest that presents:

1. Sources and amounts of revenue received.
2. Statistics on programs and services rendered.
3. Categories of expenditures.
4. Status of funds held and invested.

These data are interesting but hardly the ingredients of a best-seller, and annual reports too often are destined for crowded coffee tables, storage shelves, and the trash basket.

What if annual reports were required to disclose specific information about how nonprofit organizations manage themselves? Would they be willing to submit to a critical analysis of their performance against defined community standards judged by local residents? What if continued tax-exempt status depended on passing such a community benefits test? Would this level of disclosure and performance measurement cause nonprofit organizations to operate any differently than they do now?

Publishing annual reports that may or may not discuss program performance is optional for most nonprofit organizations, but one change has already begun. The Commonwealth of Pennsylvania now

Exhibit 20.1

Commonwealth of Pennsylvania Characteristics of a "Pure Public Charity"

	SCORE				
	low				high
1. Advance a charitable purpose	1	2	3	4	5
2. Render gratuitously a substantial portion of its services	1	2	3	4	5
3. Benefit a substantial and indefinite class of persons who are legitimate objects of charity	1	2	3	4	5
4. Relieve government of some of its burden	1	2	3	4	5
5. Operate entirely free from private motive	1	2	3	4	5
Median Score					

requires certain nonprofit organizations to document the extent of public benefits delivered to the community in order to retain their exemption from paying property taxes. To prove their charitable purpose, nonprofit organizations in Pennsylvania must meet the five characteristics of a "pure public charity" (see Exhibit 20.1) or pay a property tax or a negotiated assessment fee.

This movement should be of concern to every nonprofit organization in every state in the union. Not because a valid exemption is being threatened, which it is, but because the government that granted these privileges also can take them away. What is the purpose here? It is not to put nonprofit organizations out of business but to gain new revenue to meet the needs of a deficit-burdened government.

Annual Tax Return

This annual report is required of all nonprofit organizations and is filed with the Department of the Treasury, Internal Revenue Service. The IRS calls this document the "Uniform Charities Annual Report" and the "Return of Organization Exempt from Income Tax," but it is better known as IRS Form 990. IRS Form 990, like all IRS reports, is a financial summary of revenue received, functional expenses, balance sheet, analysis of income-producing activities, compensation, and more. It also requests information about activities such as the amount of interaction with other nonprofit organizations, lobbying, and solicitation activities. Anyone who wants a copy of the IRS Form 990 for any nonprofit organization may ask IRS for a copy or ask the organization. Corporations, foundations, and government agencies also may request that a copy accompany each funding application as a condition for making any grant awards.

Nearly all 50 states have an annual registration and report requirement for those nonprofit organizations operating within state boundaries or soliciting the public inside state lines. State annual reports ask for data similar to that requested by the IRS and most will accept a copy of the IRS Form 990 to meet these requirements. Some further require a separate report to capture additional details required by state regulation, with the obligatory IRS Form 990 as a supplemental document. In addition, a few states (notably California, Connecticut, and New Jersey) are publishing reports based on state information and IRS Form 990 data. One report they all prepare discloses the fund-raising performance of paid solicitor firms (also called commercial or professional solicitors) showing total revenue received, fund-raising expenses, and net proceeds delivered to the nonprofit organization. The intent of this report is to improve public awareness of the sometimes expensive financial practices and deceptive solicitation methods used by a few of these firms.

Nonprofit organizations completing the IRS Form 990 encounter several problems. Most board members, management staff, and fund-raising professionals know little about this tax return and do not take this document seriously, which is unfortunate. IRS studies reveal that as many as half of all returns are inaccurate and incomplete; one sample found 81 percent contained one or more significant errors. There is also a poor attitude about filing deadlines, where late filing penalties begin at $10 per day and can grow to $5,000. Because filing tax returns is a legal requirement, filing an inaccurate or incomplete Form 990 is virtually the same as not filing at all and is subject to penalties, including a prohibition from soliciting any additional contributions.

IRS Special Emphasis Program

The Internal Revenue Service does review 990 returns and will select a few nonprofit organizations for a full-scale audit. A separate "special emphasis program" has been in progress since 1990 to audit compliance by nonprofit organizations with several IRS regulations resulting from new legislation. These audits investigate unrelated business activities where taxable events may occur, joint ventures where private inurement may be possible, compensation practices involving top executives and agreements with solicitor firms, charitable gambling practices, extent of lobby activities, travel tours, thrift shops, disclosure of the quid-pro-quo exchange on gift amounts for donors participating in benefits and special events, and (added in 1993) substantiation letters or receipts for goods and services received for every gift of $250 or more.

There are many people who will ask for copies of audit statements, annual reports, and IRS Form 990 data, beginning with the media, whose reporters have easy access to these documents at state offices. Charity watchdog agencies, such as the Council of Better Business Bureaus and the National Charities Information Bureau, ask for and use these documents in their evaluations. They also recommend that donors ask for copies before making gift decisions. A few states require that all fund-raising appeal literature include a statement that copies of audit statements and IRS form 990s are available on request from either the nonprofit organization or the state agency.

IRS Intermediate Sanctions

The Internal Revenue Service has given this rather nasty title to a potential revision to federal tax law allowing IRS to penalize a nonprofit organization for serious misdeed. At present, the only punishment or enforcement power IRS has is to take away tax-exempt status, which it has rarely done. Something short of revocation is an intermediate sanction.

The stimulus for this proposal began with questions in Congress about private inurement, or self-dealing, a special circumstance where individuals could benefit personally and financially from their relationship with a nonprofit organization. This concept has expanded to include excessive lobbying, most types of political campaign activity, questionable lending practices, and what legislators call excessive perks, defined as luxury cars, country club memberships, and lucrative severance packages.[2] Perhaps the most troubling allegation surrounds "excessive compensation" for executives of nonprofit organizations, where excessive means salaries of $100,000 or more. A related development mentioned earlier in this chapter is the Pennsylvania "pure public charity" test, where the penalty or intermediate sanction is to pay property tax or an assessment fee.

Public Accountability

To be accountable to the public requires open and full disclosure of financial and other performance details. Nonprofit organizations remain a bit reluctant to reveal their financial details. Some fear the data will be used against them, to deny contributions or to impose regulatory penalties, because both have been known to happen. Some are reluctant because nonprofit accounting standards are different from for-profit accounting standards; the information may not be understood and could be misinterpreted, which also happens. Others are embarrassed at their results, not because their figures are inaccurate or their financial controls are not in order, but because they may be unable to manage their budget successfully and ended the fiscal year in a deficit position. These are reasonable concerns, but they are reasonable areas for improvement as well.

The public (especially those donors who are investors) is interested in the financial health of its nonprofit organizations. With government cutbacks, communities are increasingly dependent on charitable institutions and agencies to meet local social and welfare needs, maintain quality education and healthcare, offer cultural events, sponsor causes advocating improvements to society and the environment, and much more. Because churches and religious organizations are exempt from filing these financial reports with federal or state agencies, a similar level of accountability and disclosure is not as available to the public except when the information is volunteered. The opportunity for improved public education about the financial management of nonprofit organizations awaits those organizations who are willing to disclose their details to improve their credibility with the public and increase trust in their actions as "pure public charities." What is it that's private about a nonprofit, public benefit organization anyway?

Future Challenges

This workbook's discussion about fund-raising cost effectiveness has brought a number of related subjects to the table. Many have had influence on the management of fund-raising practice; others require close attention to prepare for and respond to additional changes on the horizon. The demand for increased disclosure and accountability to the public continues. This demand is due in part to scandals and con

Exhibit 20.2

Future Challenges to Fund-Raising Cost-Effectiveness Practice

Accounting guidelines and standards	Licensure and certification
Aging population	Loyalty
Coalitions and collaboration	Management efficiency
Confidence and trust	Mission and vision
Disclosure	Profitability
Ethical fund-raising practices	Quality (TQM and CQI)
Flat tax and other tax reforms	Technology
Globalization	Telemarketing
Judicial intervention	Underserved people in need
Leadership development	Values and vision

artists, fraud and abuse, and other illicit practices that continue to happen and receive wide media attention. It is also due to the growth of the third sector in the United States, represented today by more than 1 million nonprofit enterprises of whom nearly 600,000 are public charities. Requests for more information is further due to the desire by generous donors and people who volunteer their time, talent, and energy for charitable purposes based on assurances that their efforts are respected and their money is not wasted. There are several areas of potential change, special challenges that can influence how nonprofit organizations engage in solicitation activities (see Exhibit 20.2). A brief summary on each of their relationship to fund-raising cost effectiveness follows.

Accounting Standards and Guidelines

Major revisions to accounting standards used by nonprofit organizations to report contributions and to prepare financial statements were issued by the Financial Accounting Standards Board (FASB) in June 1993, to be effective for fiscal years beginning after December 31, 1994. The American Institute of Certified Public Accountants (AICPA) next revised their audit guidelines for nonprofit organizations and issued new instructions in 1996 based on FASB's pronouncements. The immediate benefit from these pronouncements is increased disclosure about contributions received and used, but it will take a few years until every organization learns how to apply these guidelines.

The absence of professional accounting standards and guidelines on how to allocate fund-raising costs remains a problem. This deficiency is a serious handicap for nonprofit organizations who wish to provide authenticity to their performance measurement for all the solicitation activities described in this workbook. How to allocate fund-raising costs is also a problem for state regulators, as Connecticut's Assistant Attorney General, David Ormstedt, has observed:

> If the fundraising law limits could not be changed, the next best strategy was to change how fundraising costs were calculated. Since the fundraising percentage is determined by dividing fundraising expenses by total contributions, the percentage can be altered by changing the numerator. That is precisely what was accomplished when the American Institute of Certified Public Accountants promulgated Statement of Position No. 78-10, later amended with cosmetic changes as No. 87-2. It permits charities to liberally allocate the costs of an activity between fundraising and program. Almost always, the program allegedly accomplished i[t]s education of the public. Thus, what heretofore had been fundraising costs now became program expenses. For many charities, especially those delivering little or nothing in the way of tangible services, the new rule of accounting resulted in a lower fundraising-to-revenue ratio and, conversely, a higher program-to-revenue ratio. That change not only virtually eliminated the threat of state sanctions for having high fundraising costs but also improved the image of the charity as seen through its state and general purpose financial reports.[3]

Aging Population

Improved living conditions and quality healthcare result in longer lives for Americans. But an aging population places new demands on a society that is unsure how to treat its senior citizens, especially the oldest. Healthcare is a major preoccupation and expense; so is housing, whether independent living or nursing and retirement homes. These and other services for the elderly are provided by nonprofit organizations that partially rely on their ability to raise the gifts they need to maintain quality facilities that will provide humane care for ever-larger numbers of older people.

This same population has accumulated enormous assets and wealth, estimated at between $7 and $10 trillion, and has begun to transfer it to their heirs, to their favorite charities, or to the government.

Planned giving and estate planning programs will benefit greatly from this opportunity, but the operating expense (and patience) required to manage these relationships will continue for many years before these gifts mature.

Coalitions and Collaboration

Sometimes more than one nonprofit organization is attempting to provide similar programs and services in the same community. Unnecessary duplication of services is an unwise use of limited resources. Competition, heralded in the for-profit world as good for business, usually is counterproductive for nonprofit organizations. Financial pressures from changing economic conditions can be the cause for joint efforts to meet common public needs. Because resources are limited, it makes sense for organizations to band together where appropriate, sacrificing a little ego and independence to the higher goal of better service to meet community needs. Words like merger, acquisition, and buyout are threatening; affiliation, association, and partnership are more comfortable terms. Whatever the arrangement, organizations that join together will want to be ready with a lot of answers for questions about the disposition of previous gift funds and how future gifts will be administered. More complex questions about contractual agreements specifying ultimate beneficiaries named in various forms of planned gifts and estate plans already in place will need to be answered with care. Solicitation activities may become less expensive from centralized services, but increased gift support may not be achieved until volunteers and donors understand exactly where the money will go and who will control its use.

Confidence and Trust

Fund-raising cost has become a popular focal point for public scrutiny of nonprofit organizations and their operations. Everyone has a figure or a percentage in mind they believe is a reasonable amount to spend. In the absence of national studies or comparative data based on broad experience, there is no standard or guideline that can be used to measure every organization and its fund-raising program. The absence of this standard can cause a loss of confidence and trust in solicitation practices when the figure appears high and the reasons why are not well explained. This workbook advocates that every organization measure its own performance for *each* of its solicitation activities and, using the nine-point performance index, set its own reasonable cost standards based on three or more years of experience.

Disclosure

Nonprofit organizations have a lot of information about public needs; it is their business to know and their mission to respond to them. Likewise, they are expert in how to use their programs and services to make improvements and know how to measure the results. To help to fulfill their mission, they must be willing to be more forthcoming about what they know, how these organizations function, and what financial requirements are necessary to get the work done. Open and full disclosure about their activities and operations will help to increase public confidence and trust in their efforts; withholding information appears to justify rumors and myths and can cause additional skepticism. No organization under suspicion can carry out its assigned purposes with any expectation of success from public gift support.

Ethical Fund-Raising Practices

There are two areas for mischief—during solicitation and in the use of funds after they are received. The first is about fund-raising practice, the second about proper management. Any fraudulent behavior is damaging to public trust and to the legitimate practice of public gift support, and is to be avoided. Adequate laws and regulations are present to encourage correctness and to prosecute violations. What must be improved is the supervisory attention of those in charge to both solicitation and management of the public's money.

When scandals occur, such as the 1995 pyramid investment scheme operated by New Era for Philanthropy, fund-raising practice was blamed even though no public solicitation activities were involved. It was the boards of directors and senior managers of participating nonprofit organizations who made the decisions to invest some of their organization's money in New Era, believing the promise they would double their money in six months. "Institutional and staff ethics and credibility will become an even greater issue in the future. . . . Honesty in how you deal with the public and donors isn't the best policy—it is the *only* policy. The public will scrutinize your records and demand impeccable integrity from the staff, complete credibility from the institution, and unfailing stewardship from the board."[4]

There are other examples of misconduct by people associated with charitable giving who may be willing to bend the rules a bit or agree to a questionable gift plan because of pressure to produce revenue. "Easy money" and "quick fixes" are never good decisions for nonprofit organizations and should be avoided. Gray areas involving ethical conduct can be guided by traditional principles of honesty, integrity, promise keeping, fidelity, loyalty, and fairness. Forms of "slippage," as identified by Michael Josephson of the Josephson Institute for the Advancement of Ethics, include creative accounting, misleading results, overstatement of case, marketing hype, deceptions to influence others, concealment of bad news, and false credit for others' work, all of which can lead organizations in wrong directions. Among the advances in fund-raising professionalism is the project completed by the National Society of Fund Raising Executives (NSFRE) to develop formal statements of a Code of Ethical Principles and a Standards of Professional Practice (see Appendix B) that further includes an enforcement policy and procedure. This guideline will benefit all who practice public solicitation; it may have less influence on those responsible for proper management of funds raised.

Flat Tax and Other Tax Reforms

Every time Congress says the words "tax reform," the pace of contributions slows as donors wait to see what changes will be made in their ability to make gifts and to claim a portion as a deduction from their taxes. The flat tax proposal appeared again in 1995. One version would eliminate all deductions, including charitable gifts, while others would retain the charitable deduction as is. The same Congress is reviewing legislation to bring back the tax deduction for donors who do not itemize their taxes, an earlier benefit that was removed by the Reagan administration in 1984.

Tax deductibility is important to all Americans and to their nonprofit organizations, not to escape paying taxes but because it is the government's formal endorsement of giving. But, when this same government is burdened with a huge deficit, it appears willing to sacrifice one or more of its more hallowed sanctions as a short-term solution. Removing the tax deduction will reduce giving. Further, it will increase the cost of soliciting contributions because greater efforts will be required to persuade donors that their time and money are still essential and valuable, even if the government takes away the benefit of tax deductibility.

Globalization

As the world continues to shrink due to instant communications, solicitation activities have increased. Nearly every nation possesses some form of charitable activity where people are helping people, whether these practices are a homegrown variety or imported from another country. The success of philanthropy in the United States has been transplanted around the world and has proven its principles by working well everywhere. Some nonprofit organizations are expanding their solicitation activities overseas. Can American nonprofit organizations be as efficient and effective in soliciting contributions from foreign sources as they are at home? It is too early to compare their performance against similar results at home. What is clear is that nonprofit organizations around the world can use these same fund-raising methods and techniques to develop their own constituency of friends and relationships to produce reliable donors and dollars. In time, they too must develop their own standards of measurement to ensure efficient and cost-effective solicitation practices.

Judicial Intervention

Every so often, court decisions provide new directives for nonprofit organizations and their solicitation activities. Several cases a year are brought to state courts to challenge existing solicitation and reporting regulations or to prosecute those who would disobey the law. Several such cases in the 1980s relating to state authority to administer solicitation activity based on the percentage of expenses to dollars received resulted in three U.S. Supreme Court decisions that reduced the states' authority to regulate fund-raising practices.[5] These three landmark cases stemmed from the use of professional firms who were engaged in public solicitation for nonprofit organizations whose expenses to net proceeds ratio was considered too high. Other state regulations and local ordinances already in place require nonprofit organizations to pay fees for permits to conduct charity benefits and special events, review copy used in telephone solicitation, ask for supplemental financial statements when gambling activities are conducted, and more, all of which adds to the administrative burden and management cost of solicitation activities as states attempt to reduce fraudulent practices.

Leadership Development

Volunteers are an all-important resource for success in solicitation activity. Volunteers deserve to be well informed about the organizations they serve, including details about financial operations and the cost-effectiveness of fund-raising practices. Men and women from all walks of life can appreciate that it costs money to raise money; they also can understand the relationship between revenue and expenses and good judgment applied to how money is spent to achieve the best return for the organization. Involving volunteers in budget preparation for solicitation activities, in changes to plans and strategies with cost considerations in mind, and in performance measurement will increase their awareness of these realities and improve their ability to assist the organization in making the best decisions possible. Future leaders with direct experience in budget planning and cost-effectiveness analysis can help with allocation decisions at the board level that will achieve the best value with budget dollars invested in solicitation activities for every organization they serve.

Licensure and Certification

No license is now required to solicit the public for contributions. Professional consulting firms and paid solicitor companies are required by most states to register their firm, to contract for their service, file a copy of their agreement with state authorities, and report their financial results. Employees and volunteers at nonprofit organizations need not meet this or any other requirement, hold any academic degree, or demonstrate any prior experience to be hired or assigned to work in fund-raising. Most practitioners learn their craft through on-the-job experience, a good teacher but not always the most effective nor efficient method.

Proposals calling for licensure are handicapped by the absence of professional training opportunities except those offered by fund-raising associations and societies. Academic preparation has only just begun to be offered in U.S. colleges and universities, encouraging news but inadequate to meet the demand for trained fund-raising and consulting staff for the more than one million American nonprofit organizations actively soliciting gifts. Discussions about licensure requirements have not clarified what amount of knowledge and experience will be defined as adequate preparation. Licensure will require some authority (either government or voluntary) to administer applications, certify qualifications, conduct examinations, maintain records, perform recertification, and discipline the entire process, all with fee levels high enough to cover these operating costs. Some form of apprenticeship permit will be needed so individuals can gain experience and continue their training; classroom instruction is no substitute for on-the-job experience with boards, volunteers, donors, and prospects.

Voluntary accreditation and certification have been in place with the Association for Healthcare Philanthropy (AHP) and the National Society of Fund Raising Executives (NSFRE) for many years. Both these associations operate a certification program that requires at least 5 years of experience to apply for the first level. An advanced level for senior professionals that requires 10 or more years of experience is also available. Further, AHP and NSFRE have developed a consolidated baseline certification program for practitioners with 5 years of experience that is now in process of final resolution. These voluntary accreditation programs have been successful. They demonstrate a personal commitment by the candidate who submits to an application and review process plus a four-hour written examination at the first or "Certified" level. Those who pass have verified they possess a basic knowledge of solicitation activities and their management requirements, professional standards of ethical practice, and knowledge about cost-effective performance measurement and reasonable cost standards.

Loyalty

Unrelated to licensure and certification is the observation that fund-raising professionals appear to change jobs all too often. The reasons for career moves in the field are the same as everywhere else; newcomers may learn early they are not well suited to the work or need to change jobs to gain wider experience and receive promotions. Most fund development offices are small, three to five people or less, and their solicitation programs are often confined to annual giving activities because the organization's priority need is for operating cash. There is little time available for prospect research, cultivation planning and solicitation strategy, donor relations, and performance measurement. These intense working conditions—usually accompanied by limitations in compensation, operating budgets, and support services—require a high level of loyalty, commitment, and dedication that can burn itself out after a year or two. Loyalty is more often attainable in larger, more stable nonprofit organizations where personal and professional growth are possible and where experienced professionals are available to mentor newcomers. Investments in solicitation activity made by organizations likewise are investments in the staff who supervise and conduct fund-raising programs. Length of service benefits the employer in several ways, not the least of which is consistent program performance at higher levels of cost-effectiveness and efficiency.

Management Efficiency

There is more to fund-raising than raising money. Building and maintaining relationships with volunteers and donors is crucial to the continued success of every solicitation activity. Managing budgets and personnel and supervising gift processing, bank deposits, and fund accounting records are necessary skills. Senior staff often are responsible for the management of multiple areas of solicitation activity plus donor relations; accounting and investment of funds raised; and the development committee with its subsidiary committees and support groups, all reporting to the board of directors.

Quite a few fund-raising professionals are given other assignments. These may include areas of activity compatible with fund development, such as public relations, publications, volunteers, community relations, and the like. Other collateral duties may be less compatible, such as personnel, planning, marketing, and government relations. Whatever the assignment, these skills need academic or other training plus some experience in their management. Multiple assignments tend to receive part-time attention, not the best arrangement of full-time responsibilities.

Mission and Vision

Solicitation activities are seriously handicapped without a clear statement of how current programs and services represent a nonprofit organization's charter or mission. Solicitations are hindered further by the absence of any vision for the future, a master plan that reflects the organization's long-range view of unmet needs and how it intends to address them. Without a written mission statement and future plan, fund-raising is only about money-raising, not charitable purposes intended to benefit others. Solicitation activities should be included in the text of every mission and vision statement. Public gift support is a major resource needed to accomplish these objectives and deserves to be part of the long-range or strategic plan as a means to enable the organization to perform all of its needed services.

Profitability

The word "profit" is not often used when referring to financial operations of nonprofit organizations. Success is described by citing results and accomplishments rather than being displayed in a profit and loss statement. However, professional business and financial practices are everyday functions of nonprofit organizations who purchase supplies; invest employee pension funds along with cash, fund depreciation reserves, and endowment; manage facilities; maintain equipment; and conduct other business activities. Management of a nonprofit organization is a complex responsibility and requires professional training and experience. Senior management staff work closely with the volunteer board of directors and their committees in directing daily operations according to professional business practices. Financial management objectives are the same as those of for-profit enterprises, to operate within available resources and to complete each fiscal year without a deficit or red ink. Meeting a break-even budget plan is an important objective. For a nonprofit organization to exceed that goal with an excess of revenue over expenses is a success story to be shared because of its ability to reinforce public confidence and trust in the ability of the organization's board and managers. Whether called a "profit" or not, successful fiscal management is a significant accomplishment for any organization.

Quality (TQM and CQI)

Every nonprofit organization wants to claim it is successful in its daily operations, but not all can prove their claims. At the minimum, they must be able to prove that they are delivering their programs and services. Market research studies to interview prior clients alongside those who have not been clients will provide firsthand data about performance, expectations, image, and reputation. Many nonprofit organizations have embraced quality analysis practices, called total quality management (TQM) or continuous quality improvement (CQI). These customer satisfaction criteria are used to measure levels of competence in nearly all areas of direct service and their support systems. Comparative studies will monitor progress as well as to use shared data from similar organizations as benchmarks for achieving desired standards of performance.

Fund development is well suited for quality measurements. Its analysis can begin easily with a review of the procedural steps in gift processing, research, and donor relations. Comparative analysis of actual solicitation activities is more difficult because several of the key factors are outside the organization's control. The results of *each* solicitation activity should be measured against its own prior performance using the nine-point performance index, as presented in this workbook. A further analysis is to compare cost-effectiveness figures after three years of operation with the reasonable cost guidelines based on national experience (see Chapter 19, Exhibit 19.5).

Technology

A proud product of the computer age is access to information about individuals anywhere in the world at the touch of a key. Data searches can comb prospect and donor lists for a match with wealth and influence indicators, valuable material for research purposes. Television has become the most successful of communications channels, but only a few nonprofit organizations can afford to air programs on commercial stations. The advent of cable permits access to much of the general public by even the smallest of nonprofit organizations who can prepare a 15- or 30-second public service announcement at minimal cost and a modest on-air fee. Cable is capable of a greatly expanded use by nonprofit organizations who can tape and edit a 30-minute story about their programs and services using handheld video cameras and other standard technology.

The religious broadcasters and televangelists have pioneered the use of television including cable. The World Wide Web and Internet access by desktop and laptop computers opens access to nearly unlimited information and to correspondence in a variety of forms. The challenge will be to learn how to use this technology, then how to use it effectively and efficiently. The three traditional methods of public solicitation, mail, telephone, and personal contact, have been joined by the fourth dimension, the computer with its multiple capabilities of video and instant voice and text communications.

Telemarketing

The telephone is a powerful and valuable tool for solicitation purposes. It is also a powerful and valuable tool for advertising and marketing purposes and is widely used for commercial purposes. Nonprofit organizations who choose this method to solicit prior donors will enjoy good success with careful application; it is not as effective nor as efficient for recruiting nondonor candidates because of higher costs to call much larger audiences.

Congress is investigating new regulations to curb telemarketing practices, due in part to public complaints about invasion of privacy and fraudulent promotions, some of which are linked to illicit fund-raising use. "The public is tired, unmoved and upset by the ocean of cold-call telephone solicitations. For many institutions, they have already reached the point of less return. The annoyance factor is a real negative. The future doesn't look bright for this type of fund raising."[6] New regulations may limit how nonprofit organizations will have access to this medium for broad-based solicitation purposes.

Underserved People in Need

Despite technology and other advances society enjoys today, there are more people than ever who cannot cope with a more complex world or whose preparation was lacking or absent. The number of people who require extra care and attention continues to grow, adding their need for support programs and professional services to those already being served by nonprofit organizations. As public needs increase, so do the demands on communities and their nonprofit organizations to respond to them. Government resources are not the answer to every need; even those programs with government support suffer from lack of adequate resources and the uncertainty of constant political change in priority and funding levels. The business community, private foundations, civic and service organizations, and the general public are asked to share a portion of their resources to help meet these needs, but their pockets are not deep enough to fund every request.

Competition for funds is not always in the best interest of the solution. There is a growing need for increased coordination and cooperation along with better communications between organizations who are working toward the same solutions to common problems. Coalitions and collaboration may be one of the solutions, which will require everyone joined in such partnerships to master new skills. The final test will be whether the needs of underserved people can be met by nonprofit organizations acting also in their own best interests, either singly or together with others as partners.

Values and Vision

This review of future challenges concludes with a call for a renewed commitment to the values that make nonprofit organizations unique instruments for doing good everywhere in the world. These versatile enterprises are led by volunteers and staffed by employees who are among the most committed of private citizens. They are surrounded by dedicated and generous people who share of themselves and their resources as investors in the cause. Nonprofit organizations conduct their business with demonstrated efficiency, effectiveness, and measurable success. They possess a vision for the future that draws awareness to problems needing solutions, address causes needing attention, and have the energy and dedication to commit to a course of action that holds promise for eventual success.

Each nonprofit organization is a resource of great value; this nation is blessed with a multitude of talent and other resources that must continue to be committed to the highest level of personal and professional conduct toward a better community for all. Everyone can be asked to do something to help just as everyone can give something of themselves to make a difference for others, as these final comments illustrate:

> Collectively we can do what no person can do singly.
>
> *Leland Kaiser*

> I feel that the greatest reward for doing is the opportunity to do more.
>
> *Jonas Salk* (1914–1995)

> It doesn't matter who or where you are, or how successful you become . . . you must care for other people.
>
> *Barbara Bush*

Endnotes

Chapter 1

1. D. Kerry Laycock, "Strategic Planning and Management by Objectives," in *The Nonprofit Management Handbook: Operating Policies and Procedures,* Tracy Daniel Connors, Ed. New York: John Wiley & Sons, 1993, p. 181.

2. The author is grateful to the following firms who shared internal worksheets and report outlines for internal audits: American City Bureau; Bentz, Whaley, Flessner; J. Donovan Associates, Inc.; and Staley/Robeson/Ryan/St. Lawrence, Inc.

3. Wilson C. Levis, "Investing More Money in Fund Raising—Wisely," in *Taking Fund Raising Seriously: Advancing the Profession and Practice of Raising Money,* Dwight F. Burlingame and Lamont J. Hulse, Eds. San Francisco: Jossey-Bass, 1991, pp. 228–229.

4. Wesley E. Lindahl, *Strategic Planning for Fund Raising: How to Bring in More Money Using Strategic Resource Allocation.* San Francisco: Jossey-Bass, 1992, pp. 26–27.

5. James M. Greenfield and John P. Dreves, "Fund-Raising Assessment," in *Nonprofit Management Handbook: Operating Policies and Procedures,* Tracy Daniel Connors, Ed. New York: John Wiley & Sons, 1993, p. 694.

6. Harrington J. Bryce, "Financial and Strategic Management for Nonprofit Organizations" (2nd ed.). Englewood Cliffs, NJ: Prentice-Hall, 1992, pp. 462–463.

Chapter 3

1. Kay Partney Lautman and Henry Goldstein, *Dear Friend: Mastering the Art of Direct Mail Fund Raising* (2nd ed.). Rockville, MD: Fund Raising Institute, 1991, p. 292.

2. For a more complete discussion of testing, acquisition, and renewal mailings, see James M. Greenfield, *Fund-Raising Fundamentals.* New York: John Wiley & Sons, 1994, chapters 2–4.

Chapter 5

1. Thomas E. Broce, *Fund Raising: A Guide to Raising Money from Private Sources*, 2nd ed. (Norman: University of Oklahoma Press, 1986), 91.

Chapter 11

1. American Association of Fund Raising Counsel Trust for Philanthropy. *Giving USA*. New York: AAFRC Trust for Philanthropy, 1995, pp. 76–82.
2. The author's opposition can be found in *Fund Raising: Evaluating and Managing the Fund Development Process*. New York: John Wiley & Sons, 1991, pp. 142–146, 212, 237–239.

Chapter 12

1. American Association of Fund-Raising Counsel, *Giving USA*. New York: AAFRC Trust for Philanthropy, 1995, pp. 62–75.
2. Carol M. Kurzig, *Foundation Fundamentals: A Guide for Grantseekers* (rev. ed.). New York: The Foundation Center, 1981, pp. 65–66.

Chapter 15

1. James M. Greenfield, *Fund-Raising: Evaluating and Managing the Fund Development Process*. New York: John Wiley & Sons, 1991, p. 171.

Chapter 16

Editorial assistance for this chapter was provided by Amanda J. Ferrari, JD, Vice President for Planned Giving, and Gregory Goodrich, Assistant Director of Planned Giving, at Hoag Memorial Hospital Presbyterian. Their contributions are gratefully acknowledged.

1. Thomas E. Broce, *Fund Raising: The Guide to Raising Money from Private Sources* (2nd ed.). Norman: University of Oklahoma Press, 1986, pp. 168–169.
2. American Institute of Certified Public Accountants, "Audits of Providers of Health Care Services," AICPA, 1993, Sec. 10.20-22, p. 72.
3. National Committee on Planned Giving, Directory of Council Members, Summer 1992, p. 4.
4. Linda S. Moerschbaecher and Erik D. Dryburgh, "Planned Giving," in *The Nonprofit Management Handbook: Operating Policies and Procedures*, Tracy Daniel Connors, Ed. New York: John Wiley & Sons, 1993, pp. 539–543.

Chapter 17

1. Council of Better Business Bureaus, *Standards for Charitable Solicitations.* Arlington, VA: CBBB, 1982. National Charities Information Bureau, *Standards in Philanthropy.* New York: NCIB, 1988.

2. Financial Accounting Standards Board, *Statement of Financial Accounting Standards No. 116: Accounting for Contributions Received and Contributions Made,* Norwalk, CT, No. 127-A, June 1993; and Financial Accounting Standards Board, *Financial Statements of Not-for-Profit Organizations,* Norwalk, CT, No. 127-B, June 1993.

Chapter 18

1. Wesley E. Lindahl and Christopher Winship, "Predictive Models for Annual Fundraising and Major Gift Fundraising," *Nonprofit Management and Leadership,* San Francisco: Jossey-Bass, 3(7), Fall 1992, p. 46.

2. Dennis J. Murray, *The Guaranteed Fund-Raising System: A System Approach to Planning and Controlling Fund Raising,* (2nd ed.). Boston: American Institute of Management, 1994, p. 353.

3. Harold J. Seymour, *Designs for Fund-Raising: Principles, Patterns, Techniques.* New York: McGraw Hill, 1966, p. 5. (A second edition of this exemplary text was reissued in 1988 in paperback by The Fund Raising Institute, Ambler, PA.)

Chapter 19

1. Sandra Trice Gray, *A Vision of Evaluation.* Washington, DC: Independent Sector, 1993, p. 47.

2. James M. Greenfield, *Costs and Performance Measurements,* paper presented in Session II: Financial and Management Issues, at the 1995 NSFRE Think Tank on Fund-Raising Research (Center on Philanthropy, Indiana University, Indianapolis), June 1–3, 1995.

Chapter 20

1. Malvern J. Gross, Jr., Richard F. Larkin, Roger S. Bruttomesso, and John J. McNally, *Financial and Accounting Guide for Not-for-Profit Organizations,* (5th ed.). New York: John Wiley & Sons, 1995, pp. 422–423.

2. Bruce R. Hopkins, "A Look Ahead: Fund Raising and Charity," *Fund Raising Management,* 25th Anniversary Issue: Part II, 25(2), April 1994, pp. 14–18.

3. David E. Ormstedt, "Government Regulation of Fundraising: A Struggle for Efficacy," in *Financial Practices for Effective Fundraising*, James M. Greenfield, Ed., in *New Directions for Philanthropic Fundraising*, San Francisco: Jossey-Bass, 3, Spring 1994, p. 131.

4. Jerold Panas, "The Future Isn't What It Used To Be," *Fund Raising Management*, 25th Anniversary Issue: Part II, *25*, April 1994, p. 31.

5. The three cases were *Schaumburg v. Citizens for a Better Environment*, 444 U.S. 618 (1980); *Maryland Secretary of State v. Joseph H. Munson Co.*, 467 U.S. 947 (1984); *Riley v. National Federation of the Blind of North Carolina, Inc.*, 108 S. Ct. 2667 (1988). See also Bruce R. Hopkins, *The Law of Fund Raising*. New York: John Wiley & Sons, 1991, pp. 45–46, 489.

6. Jerold Panas, op. cit.

Glossary of New Accounting Terms Based on FASB Statement of Accounting Standards No. 116 and 117[1]

Conditional Promise to Give: A conditional promise to give, which depends on the occurrence of a specified future and uncertain event to bind the promisor, shall be recognized when the conditions on which they depend are substantially met, that is, when the conditional promise becomes unconditional. A conditional promise to give is considered unconditional if the possibility that the condition will not be met is remote.

Determining whether a promise is conditional or unconditional can be difficult if it contains donor stipulations that do not clearly state whether the right to receive payment or delivery of the promised assets depends on meeting those stipulations. It may be difficult to determine whether those stipulations are conditions or restrictions. In cases of ambiguous donor stipulations, a promise containing stipulations that are not clearly unconditional shall be presumed to be conditional.

Contributed Services: Contributions of services shall be recognized if the services received (a) create or enhance nonfinancial assets or (b) require specialized skills, are provided by individuals possessing those skills, and would typically need to be purchased if not provided by donation. Services

---

[1] Financial Accounting Standards Board, *"Statement of Financial Accounting No. 116: Accounting for Contributions Received and Contributions Made."* Norwalk, CT: June, 1993, No. 127-A; and Financial Accounting Standards Board, *"Statement of Financial Accounting Standards No. 117: Financial Statements of Not-for-Profit Organizations."* Norwalk, CT: June, 1993, No. 127-B.

requiring specialized skills are provided by accountants, architects, carpenters, doctors, electricians, lawyers, nurses, plumbers, teachers, and other professionals and craftspeople. Contributed services and promises to give services that do not meet the above criteria shall not be recognized.

Contribution: An unconditional transfer of cash or other assets to an entity or a settlement or cancellation of its liabilities in a voluntary nonreciprocal transfer by another entity acting other than as an owner.

Donor-Imposed Restriction: A donor stipulation that specifies a future and uncertain event whose occurrence or failure to occur gives the promisor a right of return of the assets it has transferred or releases the promisor from its obligation to transfer its assets.

A donor stipulation that specifies a use for a contributed asset that is more specific than broad limits resulting from the nature or the organization, the environment which it operates, and the purposes specified in its articles of incorporation or bylaws or comparable documents for an unincorporated association. A restriction on an organization's use of the asset contributed may be temporary or permanent.

Endowment Fund: An established fund of cash, securities, or other assets to provide income for the maintenance of a not-for-profit organization. The use of the assets of the fund may be permanently restricted, temporarily restricted, or unrestricted. Endowment funds generally are established by donor-restricted gifts and bequests to provide a permanent endowment, which is to provide a permanent source of income, or a term endowment, which is to provide income for a specified period.

The principal of a permanent endowment must be maintained permanently—not used up, expended, or otherwise exhausted—and is classified as permanently restricted net assets.

The principal of a term endowment must be maintained for a specified term and is classified as temporarily restricted net assets.

An organization's governing board may earmark a portion of its unrestricted net assets as a board-designated endowment (sometimes called funds functioning as endowment or quasi-endowment funds) to be invested to provide income for a long but unspecified period. The principal of a board-designated endowment, which results from an internal designation, is not donor restricted and is classified as unrestricted net assets.

Functional Classification: A method of grouping expenses according to the purpose for which costs were incurred. The primary functional classifications are program services and supporting activities.

Measurements at Fair Value: Quoted market prices, if available, are the best evidence of the fair value of monetary and nonmonetary assets, including services. If quoted market prices are not available, fair value may be estimated based on quoted market prices for similar assets, independent appraisals, or valuation techniques, such as the present value of estimated future cash flows. Contributions of services that create or enhance nonfinancial assets may be measured by referring to either the fair value of the services received or the fair value of the asset or of the asset enhancement resulting from the services. A major uncertainty about the existence of value may indicate that an item received or given should not be recognized.

The present value of estimated future cash flows using a discount rate commensurate with the risks involved is an appropriate measure of fair value of unconditional promises to give cash. Subsequent accruals of the interest element shall be accounted for as contribution income by donees and contribution expenses by donors. Not-for-profit organizations shall report the contribution income as an increase in either temporarily or permanently restricted net assets if the underlying promise to give is donor-restricted.

Unconditional promises to give that are expected to be collected or paid in less than one year may be measured at net realizable value (net settlement value) because that amount, although not equivalent to the present value of estimated future cash flows, results in a reasonable estimate of fair value.

Permanent Restriction: A donor-imposed restriction that stipulates that resources be maintained permanently but permits the organization to use up or expend part or all of the income (or other economic benefits) derived from the donated assets.

Permanently Restricted Net Assets: The part of the net assets of a not-for-profit organization resulting (a) from contributions and other inflows of assets whose use by the organization is limited by donor-imposed stipulations that neither expire by passage of time nor can be fulfilled or otherwise removed by actions of the organization, (b) from other asset enhancements and diminishments subject to the same kinds of stipulations, and (c) from reclassifications from (or to) other classes of net assets as a consequence of donor-imposed stipulations.

Promise to Give: A written or oral agreement to contribute cash or other assets to another entity. A promise to give may be either conditional or unconditional. See also **Conditional Promise to Give.**

Restricted Support: Donor-restricted revenues or gains from contributions that increase either temporarily restricted net assets or permanently restricted net assets. See also **Unrestricted Support.**

Temporarily Restricted Net Assets: The part of the net assets of a not-for-profit organizations resulting (a) from contributions and other inflows of assets whose use by the organization is limited by donor-imposed stipulations that either expire by passage of time or can be fulfilled and removed by actions of the organization pursuant to those stipulations, (b) from other asset enhancements, and (c) from reclassifications to (or from) other classes of net assets as a consequence of donor-imposed stipulations, their expiration by passage of time, or their fulfillment and removal by actions of the organization pursuant to those stipulations.

Temporary Restriction: A donor-imposed restriction that permits the donee organization to use up or expend the donated assets as specified and is satisfied either by the passage of time or by actions of the organization.

Unrestricted Net Assets: The part of net assets of a not-for-profit organization that is neither permanently restricted nor temporarily restricted by donor-imposed stipulations.

Unrestricted Support: Revenues or gains from contributions that are not restricted by donors. See also **Restricted Support.**

National Society of Fund Raising Executives Code of Ethical Principles and Standards of Professional Practice

Statements of Ethical Principles (Adopted November 1991)

The National Society of Fund Raising Executives exists to foster the development and growth of fund-raising professionals and the profession, to preserve and enhance philanthropy and volunteerism, and to promote high ethical standards in the fund-raising profession.

To these ends, this code declares the ethical values and standards of professional practice which NSFRE members embrace and which they strive to uphold in their responsibilities for generating philanthropic support.

Members of the National Society of Fund Raising Executives are motivated by an inner drive to improve the quality of life through the causes they serve. They seek to inspire others through their own sense of dedication and high purpose. They are committed to the improvement of their professional knowledge and skills in order that their performance will better serve others. They recognize their stewardship responsibility to ensure that needed resources are vigorously and ethically sought and that the intent of the donor is honestly fulfilled. Such individuals practice their profession with integrity, honesty, truthfulness, and adherence to the absolute obligation to safeguard the public trust.

FURTHERMORE, NSFRE MEMBERS

- serve the ideal of philanthropy, are committed to the preservation and enhancement of volunteerism, and hold stewardship of these concepts as the overriding principle of professional life;

- put charitable mission above personal gain, accepting compensation by salary or set fee only;
- foster cultural diversity and pluralistic values and treat all people with dignity and respect;
- affirm, through personal giving, a commitment to philanthropy and its role in society;
- adhere to the spirit as well as the letter of all applicable laws and regulations;
- bring credit to the fund-raising profession by their public demeanor;
- recognize their individual boundaries of competence and are forthcoming about their professional qualifications and credentials;
- value the privacy, freedom of choice, and interests of all those affected by their actions;
- disclose all relationships which might constitute, or appear to constitute, conflicts of interest;
- actively encourage all their colleagues to embrace and practice these ethical principles;
- adhere to the following standards of professional practice in their responsibilities for generating philanthropic support.

Standards of Professional Practice (Adopted and incorporated into the NSFRE Code of Ethical Principles November 1992)

1. Members shall act according to the highest standards and visions of their institution, profession, and conscience.
2. Members shall avoid even the appearance of any criminal offense or professional misconduct.
3. Members shall be responsible for advocating, within their own organizations, adherence to all applicable laws and regulations.
4. Members shall work for a salary or fee, not percentage-based compensation or a commission.
5. Members may accept performance-based compensation such as bonuses provided that such bonuses are in accord with prevailing practices within the members' own organizations and are not based on a percentage of philanthropic funds raised.
6. Members shall neither seek nor accept finder's fees and shall, to the best of their ability, discourage their organizations from paying such fees.
7. Members shall effectively disclose all conflicts of interest; such disclosure does not preclude or imply ethical impropriety.
8. Members shall accurately state their professional experience, qualifications, and expertise.

9. Members shall adhere to the principle that all donor and prospect information created by, or on behalf of, an institution is the property of that institution and shall not be transferred or utilized except on behalf of that institution.

10. Members shall, on a scheduled basis, give donors the opportunity to have their names removed from lists which are sold to, rented to, or exchanged with other organizations.

11. Members shall not disclose privileged information to unauthorized parties.

12. Members shall keep constituent information confidential.

13. Members shall take care to ensure that all solicitation materials are accurate and correctly reflect the organization's mission and use of solicited funds.

14. Members shall, to the best of their ability, ensure that contributions are used in accordance with donors' intentions.

15. Members shall ensure, to the best of their ability, proper stewardship of charitable contributions, including timely reporting on the use and management of funds and explicit consent by the donor before altering the conditions of a gift.

16. Members shall ensure, to the best of their ability, that donors receive informed and ethical advice about the value and tax implications of potential gifts.

17. Members' actions shall reflect concern for the interests and well-being of individuals affected by those actions. Members shall not exploit any relationship with a donor, prospect, volunteer, or employee to the benefit of the member or the member's organization.

18. In stating fund-raising results, members shall use accurate and consistent accounting methods that conform to the appropriate guidelines adopted by the American Institute of Certified Public Accountants (AICPA)* for the type of institution involved. (*In countries outside of the United States, comparable authority should be utilized.)

19. All of the above notwithstanding, members shall comply with all applicable local, state, provincial, and federal civil and criminal law.

Amended: March, 1993; October, 1994

Using the Disk

Introduction

Fund-Raising Cost Effectiveness: A Self-Assessment Workbook includes a disk with a set of worksheets for analyzing the financial results of a nonprofit organization's fund-raising activities. These files are designed to help you evaluate the specifics of each fund-raising campaign as well as the overall development program. They can and should be presented to development professionals, executive directors, board members, volunteers, and donors to demonstrate the relationship between fund-raising costs and results.

The disk contains files for many of the exhibits prepared as report forms and measurement tools. Each file on the disk corresponds to an exhibit in the book, with matching format and categories but *without* the data so that users can add their own information to display results from their own organizations. Exhibits that are text-based rather than data-driven (such as sample policy texts or reference tables) are not contained on the disk. There are two types of worksheets:

- Report forms designed as evaluation tools score performance areas in an objective fashion, using 1 for low and 5 for high ratings.
- Spreadsheets designed to measure financial performance use mathematical formulas to analyze the cost effectiveness of development activities.

Each exhibit in the workbook is identified for use as a blank worksheet on the disk by a disk icon—💾. The worksheets are formatted for use with Lotus 1-2-3 Version 2.3 or higher and all have the extension .WK1. Designed to be easily modified and adapted, the files are meant to save you time and to help show results in a consistent manner. The numbers in the filename correspond to the chapter and exhibit number from the workbook. For example, EXH04-01.WK1 refers to Chapter 4, Exhibit 4-1, titled "Nine-Point Performance Measurement Analysis of a Membership Campaign." The Disk Table of Contents, above, is a complete list of all the files on the disk. You may also locate these exhibits and their page numbers in the List of Exhibits at the front of this workbook (See page xxi).

The worksheets in this book are intended to illustrate fund-raising results and provide a clear understanding of fund-raising performance by demonstrating its effectiveness, efficiency, productivity, and profitability. The inclusion of this disk is intended to encourage the use of these worksheets. Uniformity in reporting fund-raising results will benefit every non-profit organization.

Report forms and spreadsheets with financial information require accurate preparation based on a correct understanding of the data used. Consultation with accounting and finance staff is recommended at the outset to agree on data sources, presentation forms, and analysis techniques so that the information reported and presented will be consistent with current accounting and financial summaries of the governing nonprofit organization.

Report forms and worksheets used in any business context should be appropriate to their purpose and therefore must be carefully considered and adapted to each situation. Because no two situations are identical, modifying these forms will be necessary and is encouraged. Although the forms are generally believed to be reliable, they cannot be guaranteed to reflect the peculiarities and nuances of local practice. If accounting, legal, or other expert advice is required, the services of a competent professional should be sought.

Computer Requirements

The enclosed disk requires an IBM PC or compatible computer with the following:

- IBM DOS or MS DOS 3.1 or later.
- A 3½ inch disk drive.
- Lotus 1-2-3 Version 2.3 or higher.

WYSISYG on Lotus 1-2-3 of Lotus for Windows is highly recommended because spreadsheet files are easier to read and more visually pleasing when prepared with WYSIWYG or in Windows. Optional equipment includes a DOS compatible printer and a word processing package like Microsoft Word for Windows. If you have a different spreadsheet software package, consult your user manual for information on using Lotus files in your package. Most popular spreadsheet programs, including Microsoft Excel and Quattro, are capable of reading files formatted for Lotus. Using the index in your software manual, refer to the section on "Converting Lotus Files" or on "Loading Files from Other Programs."

How to Make a Backup Disk

Before you start to use the enclosed disk, we strongly recommend that you make a backup copy of the original. Making a backup copy of your disk allows you to have a clean set of files saved in case you accidentally change or delete a file. Remember, however, that a backup disk is for your own personal use only. Any other use of the backup disk violates copyright law. Please take the time now to make a backup copy, using the instructions below:

If your computer has two floppy disk drives:

1. Insert your DOS disk into drive A of your computer.
2. Insert a blank disk into drive B of your computer.
3. At the **A:>**, type **DISKCOPY A: B:** and press Enter. You will be prompted by DOS to place the Source disk into drive A.
4. Place the disk into Drive A. Follow the directions on screen to complete the copy.
5. When you are through, remove the disk from drive B and label it immediately. Remove the original from drive A and store it in a safe place.

If your computer has one floppy disk drive and a hard drive, you can copy the files from the enclosed disk directly onto your hard disk drive, in lieu of making a backup copy, by following the installation instructions.

Installing the Disk

The enclosed disk contains 77 individual files in a compressed format. In order to use the files, you must run the installation program for the disk. You can install the disk onto your computer by following these steps:

1. Insert the disk into drive A of your computer.
2. Type **A:\INSTALL** and press Enter.
3. You will have the opportunity to name the subdirectory to store the data files. The default subdirectory is WORKBOOK. To accept this name press Return.

The installation program copies the files to your hard disk. When all the copying is complete, you can press any key to exit the installation program. Remove the original disk from drive A and store it in a safe place.

Using the Files

Once you have installed the disk on your hard drive and made a backup copy as instructed, you can begin to add your own data and customize the files. To use the worksheets, load your software program as usual. The files from this disk will be located in the subdirectory WORKBOOK. For example, the file "Three-Year Performance Summary of Annual Giving Solicitation Activities with a Reliable Forecast of Next Year's Results" can be found under C:\WORKBOOK\EXH10-05.WK1. In order to maintain the integrity of the original files, we have used the global protection command. If you would like to make changes to the structure of the worksheets, you may do so by undoing this protection. When you are through using a file, you can save it under a new file name in order to keep the original file intact. For more information about using the worksheets, consult the appropriate software user manuals.

User Assistance and Information

John Wiley & Sons, Inc., is pleased to provide assistance to users of this package. Should you have any questions regarding the use of this package, please call our technical support number (212) 850-6194 weekdays between 9 A.M. and 4 P.M. Eastern Standard Time.

To place additional orders or to request information about other Wiley products, please call (800) 753-0655, extension 4456 or 4457.

Suggested References

American Association of Fund Raising Council. *Giving USA: The Annual Report on Philanthropy for the Year 1994.* New York: American Association of Fund Raising Council. 1995.

Bennis, Warren, and Burt Nanus. *Leaders: The Strategies for Taking Charge.* New York: Harper & Row. 1985.

Berendt, Robert J., and J. Richard Taft. *How to Rate Your Development Department.* Washington, DC: The Taft Group. 1984.

Blazek, Jody. *Tax and Financial Planning for Tax-Exempt Organizations,* 2nd ed. New York: John Wiley & Sons. 1994.

Bradford, David L., and Allan R. Cohen. *Managing for Excellence: The Guide to Developing High Performance in Contemporary Organizations.* New York: John Wiley & Sons. 1984.

Burlingame, Dwight F., and Lamont J. Hulse. *Taking Fund Raising Seriously: Advancing the Profession and Practice of Raising Money.* San Francisco: Jossey-Bass. 1991.

Collier, Arthur S. "Criteria for Audits and Measurements for Demonstrating Fundraising Success," in *Financial Practices for Effective Fundraising,* James M. Greenfield, ed. New Directions for Philanthropic Fundraising, 3, Spring 1994. San Francisco, CA: Jossey-Bass.

Costa, Nick B. *Measuring Progress and Success Fund Raising: How to Use Comparative Statistics to Prove Your Effectiveness.* Falls Church, VA: Association for Healthcare Philanthropy. 1991.

Council of Advancement and Support of Education. *CASE Campaign Standards: Management and Reporting Standards for Educational Fund-Raising Campaigns.* Vance T. Peterson, Chair, Council for Advancement and Support of Education. Washington, DC. 1994.

Council for Advancement and Support of Education and the National Association of College and University Business Officers. *Expenditures in Fund Raising, Alumni Relations, and other Constituent (Public)*

Relations. Washington, DC: Council for Advancement and Support of Education and the National Association of College and University Business Officers. 1990.

Council of Better Business Bureaus. *Standards for Charitable Solicitations.* Arlington, VA: Council of Better Business Bureaus. 1982.

Department of Justice. *Internal Revenue Service Form 990, Schedule A and Instructions.* Washington, DC: Department of Justice. 1994.

Drucker, Peter F. *Managing the Nonprofit Organization: Practices and Principles.* New York: HarperCollins. 1990.

———. *The Drucker Foundation Self-Assessment Tool for Nonprofit Organizations.* San Francisco, CA: Jossey-Bass. 1993.

Fink, Norman S., and Howard C. Metzler. *The Costs and Benefits of Deferred Giving.* New York: Columbia University Press. 1982.

Folpe, Herbert K. "Ratio Analysis in Non-Profit Organizations." *The Philanthropy Monthly*, October 1982.

Grace, Kay Sprinkel. "Managing for Results," in *Achieving Excellent in Fund Raising*, Henry A. Rosso and Associates, Ed. San Francisco, CA: Jossey-Bass. 1991.

Gray, Sandra T. "A Vision for Evaluation." Washington, DC: Independent Sector. 1993.

Greenfield, James M. *Fund-Raising: Evaluating and Managing the Fund Development Program.* New York: John Wiley & Sons, 1991.

———. "Accountability, Program Performance, and Profitability— Part 1: How to Assess Fund-Raising Program Performance." *AHP Journal,* Spring, 1994.

———. Part II: "Comparative Analysis, Profitability, and Forecasting," *AHP Journal* (Fall, 1994).

———. *Fund-Raising Fundamentals: A Guide to Annual Giving for Professionals and Volunteers.* New York: John Wiley & Sons, 1994.

Greenfield, James M., and John P. Dreves. "Fund-Raising Assessment," in *The Nonprofit Management Handbook: Operating Policies and Procedures,* Tracey Daniel Connors, Ed. New York: John Wiley & Sons. 1993.

Gross, Malvern J., Jr., Richard F. Larkin, Robert S. Bruttomesso, and John J. McNally, *Financial and Accounting Guide for Not-for-Profit Organizations,* 5th Ed. New York: John Wiley & Sons. 1994.

Harr, David J., James T. Godfrey, and Robert H. Frank. *Common Costs and Fund-Raising Appeals: A Guide to Joint Cost Allocation in Not-for-Profit Organizations.* Landover, MD: Nonprofit Mailers Federation and Frank & Company. 1991.

_____. "Are Volunteers Worth Their Weight in Gold, But Not in Dollars?" *The Philanthropy Monthly*, September, 1992.

Herman, Robert D., and Associates, *The Jossey-Bass Handbook of Nonprofit Leadership and Management*. San Francisco: CA. Jossey-Bass. 1994.

Hodgkinson, Virginia A., and Associates, *The Nonprofit Almanac 1992–1993: Dimensions of the Independent Sector*. Washington, DC: Independent Sector. 1992.

Hodgkinson, Virginia A., Richard W. Lyman, and Associates. *The Future of the Nonprofit Sector: Challenges, Changes and Policy Considerations*. San Francisco: CA. Jossey-Bass. 1989.

Hodgkinson, Virginia A., and Murray S. Weitzman. *Giving and Volunteering in the United States: Findings from a National Survey*. Washington, DC: Independent Sector. 1992.

Hopkins, Bruce R. "Tax Exempt Status Threatened by Fund Raising." *Fund Raising Management*, October, 1983.

_____. *The Law of Tax Exempt Organizations*, 6th Ed. New York: John Wiley & Sons. 1991.

_____. *A Legal Guide to Starting and Managing a Nonprofit Organization*, 2nd Ed. New York: John Wiley & Sons. 1993.

_____. *The Tax Law of Charitable Giving*. New York: John Wiley & Sons. 1993.

_____. *The Law of Fund Raising*, 2nd Ed. New York: John Wiley & Sons. 1996.

Howe, Fisher. *The Board Members Guide to Fund Raising*. San Francisco, CA: Jossey-Bass. 1991.

Independent Sector. *Giving and Volunteering in the United States: Findings from a National Survey*. Washington, DC: Independent Sector. 1994.

Jacobson, Harvey J. "15 Ways to Measure Fund Raising Program Effectiveness." *Fund Raising Management*, December, 1982.

Jordan, Ronald R., and Katelyn L. Quynn. *Planned Giving: Management, Marketing, and Law*. New York: John Wiley & Sons. 1994.

Lane, Frederick S. "Enhancing the Quality of Public Reporting by Nonprofit Organizations. *The Philanthropy Monthly*, July, 1991.

Larkin, Richard F. "Accounting Issues Relating to Fundraising." *Financial Practices for Effective Fundraising*, James M. Greenfield, ed. New Directions for Philanthropic Fundraising, 3, Spring 1994. San Francisco, CA: Jossey-Bass.

Levis, Wilson C., and Anne New. "The Average Gift Size and Cost per Gift: New Valuation Tools for Grantmakers." *Foundation News*, September/October, 1992.

Lindahl, Wesley E. *Strategic Planning for Fund Raising: How to Bring In More Money Using Strategic Resource Allocation.* San Francisco, CA: Jossey-Bass. 1992.

_____. "Multiyear Evaluation of Fundraising Performance," in *Financial Practices for Effective Fundraising,* James M. Greenfield, ed. New Directions for Philanthropic Fundraising, Number 3, Spring 1994. San Francisco, CA: Jossey-Bass.

Lindahl, Wesley E., and Christopher Winship. "Predictive Models for Annual Fundraising and Major Gift Fundraising," in Dennis R. Young, ed. *Nonprofit Management & Leadership.* Volume 3, Number 1, Fall 1992. San Francisco, CA: Jossey-Bass.

Logan, Timothy D. "Forecasting Fund-Raising Income: Managing the Telemarketing Process." *Fund Raising Management,* April 1995.

Manchester, Jay A. "IRS Form 990: An Analytical Tool for Donors." *The Philanthropy Monthly,* November, 1982.

McLaughlin, Thomas A. *Streetsmart Financial Basics for Nonprofit Managers.* New York: John Wiley & Sons. 1995.

Merlyn, Vaughan, and John Parkinson. *Development Effectiveness: Strategies for IS Organizational Transition.* New York: John Wiley & Sons. 1994.

Mixer, Joseph R. *Principles of Professional Fundraising: Useful Foundations for Successful Practice.* San Francisco, CA: Jossey-Bass. 1993.

Murray, Dennis J. *The Guaranteed Fund-Raising System: A Systems Approach to Planning and Controlling Fund Raising,* 2nd Ed. Poughkeepsie, NY: American Institute of Management. 1994.

_____. *Evaluation of Fund Raising Programs: A Management Audit Approach.* Boston, MA: American Institute of Management. 1983.

Nanus, Burt. *Visionary Leadership: Creating a Compelling Sense of Direction for Your Organization.* San Francisco, CA: Jossey-Bass. 1992.

National Charities Information Bureau. *Grantmakers Guide to a New Tool for Philanthropy—Form 990.* New York: National Charities Information Bureau. 1983.

National Charities Information Bureau. *Standards in Philanthropy.* New York: National Charities Information Bureau. 1988.

New, Anne L., with Wilson C. Levis. *Raise More Money for Your Nonprofit Organization.* New York: The Foundation Center. 1991.

O'Connell, Brian. *Budgeting and Financial Accountability.* Washington, DC: Independent Sector. 1988.

_____. *Evaluating Results.* Washington, DC: Independent Sector. 1988.

Ormstedt, David E. "Government Regulation of Fundraising: A Struggle for Efficacy," in *Financial Practices for Effective Fundraising*, James M. Greenfield, ed. New Directions for Philanthropic Fundraising, Number 3, Spring 1994. San Francisco, CA: Jossey-Bass.

Schmaedick, Gerald L. *Cost-Effectiveness in the Nonprofit Sector.* Westport, CT: Quorum Books. 1993.

Smith, Bucklin & Associates. *The Complete Guide to Nonprofit Management.* New York: John Wiley & Sons. 1994.

Steinberg, Richard. "Economics and Philanthropy: A Marriage of Necessity for Nonprofit Organizations" in *Financial Practices for Effective Fundraising*, James M. Greenfield, ed. New Directions for Philanthropic Fundraising, Number 3, Spring 1994. San Francisco: CA. Jossey-Bass.

Tracy, John A. *How to Read a Financial Report: Wringing Vital Signs out of the Numbers,* 4th Ed. New York: John Wiley & Sons. 1994.

Townsend, Patrick L., and Joan E. Gebhardt. *Quality in Action: 93 Lessons in Leadership, Participation, and Measurement.* New York: John Wiley & Sons. 1992.

United Way. *Accounting and Financial Reporting: A Guide for United Way and Not-for-Profit Human Service Organizations.* 2nd Ed., Alexandria VA. United Way of America. 1989.

Weber, Nathan. "Misusing Charitable Statistics in Evaluating Fundraising Performance" in *Financial Practices for Effective Fundraising*, James M. Greenfield, ed. New Directions for Philanthropic Fundraising, Number 3, Spring 1994. San Francisco, CA: Jossey-Bass.

Weinstein, Stanley. "Time Management and the Development Professional." *NSFRE Journal*, Winter, 1991.

Wholey, Joseph S., Harry P. Hatry, and Kathryn E. Newcomer. Eds. *Handbook of Practice Program Evaluation.* San Francisco, CA: Jossey-Bass. 1994.

INDEX